COLLINS

SPANISH

PHRASE BOOK

KU-568-046

HarperCollins*Publishers*

first published in this edition 1995

© HarperCollins Publishers 1995

first reprint 1996

ISBN 0 00 470869-5

A catalogue record for this book is available from the British Library

All rights reserved

Typeset by Morton Word Processing Ltd, Scarborough
Printed and bound in Great Britain by
Caledonian International Book Manufacturing Ltd, Glasgow, G64

Introduction

Your **Collins Phrase Book** is designed to give you instant access to all the words and phrases you will want while travelling abroad on business or for pleasure.

Unlike other phrase books it is arranged in A-Z order to take you straight to the word you want without having to search through different topics. And its simple, easy-to-use pronunciation guide to every word and phrase will ensure you communicate with confidence.

At the bottom of each page there is a list of ABSOLUTE ESSENTIALS – the key phrases and expressions you will need in any situation. And between the two sides of your **Phrase Book** you will find further explanations of pronunciation, charts showing how to convert from metric to imperial measures and easy reference lists of *Car Parts, Colours, Countries, Drinks, Fish and Seafood, Fruit and Nuts, Meats, Shops*, and *Vegetables*. These pages have a grey border to help you find them easily and to show you where one side of the **Phrase Book** ends and the other begins.

And finally, in the comprehensive glossary at the end of your **Phrase Book** you will find over 4,000 foreign-language words and phrases clearly translated. So in one complete package you have all the benefits of a dictionary with the simplicity of a phrase book. We hope you will enjoy using it.

Abbreviations used in the text

adj	adjective
adv	adverb
cm	centimetre(s)
conj	conjunction
equiv	equivalent
etc	etcetera
f	feminine noun
fpl	feminine plural noun
g	gram(s)
kg	kilogram(s)
km	kilometre(s)
l	litre(s)
m	masculine noun; metre(s)
m/f	masculine or feminine noun
mpl	masculine plural noun
n	noun
pl	plural noun
prep	preposition
®	registered trade mark
sing	singular
vb	verb

Words which we have reason to believe constitute trademarks have been designated as such.
However, neither the presence nor the absence of such designation should be regarded as
affecting the legal status of any trademark.

ENGLISH–SPANISH

a	un	"oon"
	una	**"oona"**
▷ **a man**	un hombre	"oon **om**bre"
▷ **a woman**	una mujer	**"oon**a mu**kher"**
abbey	la abadía	"aba**deea**"
about (*relating to*)	acerca de	"a**ther**ka de"
(*approximately*)	más o menos	"mas o **me**nos"
▷ **at about 4 o'clock**	a eso de las 4	"a **e**so de las **kwa**tro"
above	arriba	"a**rree**ba"
▷ **above the house**	encima de la casa	"en**thee**ma de la **ka**sa"
abseiling	el rappel	"ra**pel**"
▷ **we'd like to go abseiling**	nos gustaría ir a hacer rappel	"nos goosta**ree**a eer a a**ther** ra**pel**"
accident	el accidente	"akthee**den**te"
▷ **I've had an accident**	he tenido un accidente	"e te**nee**do oon akthee**den**te"
▷ **there's been an accident**	ha habido un accidente	"a a**bee**do oon akthee**den**te"
accommodation	el alojamiento	"alokhamee-**en**to"
▷ **I need 3 nights' accommodation**	necesito alojamiento durante 3 noches	"nethe**see**to alokhamee-**en**to doo**ran**te tres **no**ches"
to **ache**	doler	"do**ler**"
▷ **I've got a stomach ache**	me duele el estómago	"me **dwe**le el es**to**mago"
activities	las actividades	"akteebee**da**des"
▷ **do you have activities for children?**	¿qué actividades tienen para los niños?	"ke akteebee**da**des tee-**e**nen **pa**ra los **nee**nyos"
▷ **what indoor/outdoor activities are there?**	¿qué actividades tienen dentro/al aire libre?	"ke akteebee**da**des tee-**e**nen **den**tro/al **a**ere **li**bre"
adaptor (*electrical*)	el enchufe múltiple	"en**choo**fe **mool**teeple"

address	la dirección	"deerektheeon"
▷ **my address is ...**	mi dirección es ...	"mee deerektheeon es"
▷ **take me to this address**	lléveme a esta dirección	"yebeme a esta deerektheeon"
▷ **will you write down the address please?**	¿podría escribirme la dirección, por favor?	"podreea eskribirme la deerektheeon por fabor"
adhesive tape	la cinta adhesiva	"theenta adeseeba"
▷ **I need some adhesive tape**	necesito cinta adhesiva	"netheseeto theenta adeseeba"
admission charge	el precio de entrada	"pretheeo de entrada"
adult	el adulto	"adoolto"
	la adulta	"adoolta"
advance:		
▷ **in advance**	por adelantado	"por adelantado"
	con antelación	"kon antelatheeon"
▷ **do I pay in advance?**	¿le pago por adelantado?	"le pago por adelantado"
▷ **do I need to book in advance?**	¿tengo que hacer las reservas con antelación?	"tengo ke ather las reserbas kon antelatheeon"
aerobics	el aerobic	"aerobik"
after	después	"despwes"
afternoon	la tarde	"tarde"
aftershave	la loción para después del afeitado	"lotheeon para despwes del afayeetado"
again	otra vez	"otra beth"
▷ **can you try again?**	¿puede intentarlo otra vez?	"pwede e285ntentarlo otra beth"
agent	el agente	"akhente"
	la agente	"akhente"
ago:		
▷ **long ago**	hace mucho tiempo	"athe moocho tee-empo"

ABSOLUTE ESSENTIALS		
yes (please)	sí (por favor)	"see (por fabor)"
no (thank you)	no (gracias)	"no (gratheeas)"
hello	hola	"ola"
goodbye	adiós	"adeeos"

▷ **a week ago**	hace una semana	"**a**the **oo**na se**ma**na"
AIDS	el SIDA	"**see**da"
air conditioning	el aire acondicionado	"**a**eere akondeetheeo**na**do"
▷ **the air conditioning is not working**	el aire acondicionado no funciona	"el **a**eere akondeetheeo**na**do no foontheeo**na**"
air hostess	la azafata	"atha**fa**ta"
airline	la linea aérea	"**lee**nea a**e**rea"
air mail	el correo aéreo	"ko**rre**o a**e**reo"
air mattress	el colchón neumático	"kol**chon** neooma**tee**ko"
airport	el aeropuerto	"aero**pwer**to"
▷ **to the airport, please**	al aeropuerto, por favor	"al aero**pwer**to por fa**bor**"
aisle	el pasillo	"pa**see**yo"
▷ **I'd like an aisle seat**	quiero un asiento al lado del pasillo	"kee-**e**ro oon asee-**en**to al **la**do del pa**see**yo"
alarm	la alarma	"a**lar**ma"
alarm call	la llamada despertador	"ya**ma**da desperta**dor**"
▷ **an alarm call at 7 am, please**	llámenme a las 7 de la mañana, por favor	"**ya**menme a las see-**e**te de la man**ya**na por fa**bor**"
alarm clock	el despertador	"desperta**dor**"
alcohol	el alcohol	"al**kol**"
alcoholic	alcohólico	"al**ko**leeko"
	alcohólica	"al**ko**leeka"
all	todo	"**to**do"
	toda	"**to**da"
	todos	"**to**dos"
	todas	"**to**das"

ABSOLUTE ESSENTIALS

I don't understand	no comprendo	"no kom**pren**do"
I don't speak Spanish	no hablo español	"no **a**blo espan**yol**"
do you speak English?	¿habla inglés?	"**a**bla een**gles**"
could you help me?	¿podría ayudarme?	"po**dree**a ayoo**dar**me"

allergic to	alérgico a	"a**ler**kheeko a"
	alérgica a	"a**ler**kheeka a"
▷ **I'm allergic to penicillin**	soy alérgico a la penicilina	"soy a**ler**kheeko a la peneethee**lee**na"
allowance	la cantidad permitida	"kantee**dad** permee**tee**da"
▷ **I have the usual allowances of alcohol/ tobacco**	llevo la cantidad permitida de alcohol/ tabaco	"**ye**bo la kantee**dad** permee**tee**da de al**kol**/ ta**ba**ko"
all right (*agreed*)	de acuerdo	"de a**kwer**do"
▷ **are you all right?**	¿está bien?	"esta bee-**en**"
almond	la almendra	"al**men**dra"
almost	casi	"**ka**see"
also	también	"tambee-**en**"
always	siempre	"see-**em**pre"
am:		
▷ **I am**	soy	"**soee**"
	estoy	"es**toee**"
▷ **I am English**	soy inglés	"**soee** een**gles**"
▷ **I am tired**	estoy cansado	"es**toee** kan**sa**do"
ambulance	la ambulancia	"amboo**lan**theea"
▷ **call an ambulance**	llame a una ambulancia	"**ya**me a oona amboo**lan**theea"
America	América del Norte	"a**me**reeka del **nor**te"
American	norteamericano	"**nor**teamereeka**no**"
	norteamericana	"**nor**teamereeka**na**"
amusement park	el parque de atracciones	"**par**ke de atrak**thee**ones"
anaesthetic	el anestésico	"anes**te**seeko"
anchovy	la anchoa	"an**cho**a"
and	y	"ee"

ABSOLUTE ESSENTIALS		
I would like ...	me gustaría ...	"me goosta**reea**"
I need ...	necesito ...	"nethe**see**to"
where is ...?	¿dónde está ...?	"**don**de esta"
I'm looking for ...	estoy buscando ...	"es**toee** boos**kan**do"

anorak	el anorak	"ano**rak**"
another	otro	"**o**tro"
	otra	"**o**tra"
antibiotic	el antibiótico	"anteebee**o**teeko"
antifreeze	el anticongelante	"anteekonkhe**lant**e"
antihistamine	el antihistamínico	"anteesta**mee**neeko"
antiseptic	el antiséptico	"antee**sep**teeko"
any	alguno	"al**goo**no"
	alguna	"al**goo**na"
▷ **have you any apples?**	¿tiene manzanas?	"tee-**e**ne man**tha**nas"
▷ **I haven't any**	no me quedan	"no me **ke**dan"
apartment	el apartamento	"aparta**men**to"
▷ **we've booked an apartment in the name of ...**	hemos reservado un apartamento a nombre de ...	"**e**mos reser**ba**do oon aparta**men**to a **nom**bre de"
apéritif	el aperitivo	"aperee**tee**bo"
▷ **we'd like an apéritif**	¿nos trae un aperitivo?	"nos **trae** oon aperee**tee**bo"
apple	la manzana	"man**tha**na"
appointment	la cita	"**thee**ta"
▷ **can I please have an appointment?**	¿podría darme cita, por favor?	"po**dree**a **dar**me **thee**ta por fa**bor**"
▷ **I have an appointment with ...**	tengo una cita con ...	"**ten**go **oon**a **thee**ta kon"
▷ **I'd like to make an appointment**	quiero pedir hora	"kee-**e**ro pe**deer o**ra"
apricot	el albaricoque	"albaree**ko**ke"
April	abril (m)	"ab**reel**"
are:		
▷ **are you Spanish?**	¿es español?	"es espa**nyol**"
▷ **how are you?**	¿cómo está?	"**ko**mo es**ta**"

		ABSOLUTE ESSENTIALS
do you have ...?	¿tiene ...?	"tee-**e**ne"
is there ...?	¿hay ...?	"**aee**"
are there ...?	¿hay ...?	"**aee**"
how much is ...?	¿cuánto cuesta ...?	"**kwan**to **kwes**ta"

▷ **you are** (*informal singular*)	eres	"**e**res"
	estás	"est**as**"
(*formal singular*)	es	"es"
	está	"est**a**"
(*plural*)	sois	"**so**ees"
	estáis	"est**a**ees"
▷ **we are**	somos	"**so**mos"
	estamos	"est**a**mos"
▷ **they are**	son	"son"
	están	"est**a**n"
arm	el brazo	"**bra**tho"
armbands (*for swimming*)	los flotadores	"flotad**o**res"
arrival	la llegada	"yeg**a**da"
arrivals (*at airport*)	llegadas	"yeg**a**das"
to **arrive**	llegar	"yeg**a**r"
▷ **what time does the bus/train arrive?**	¿a qué hora llega el autobús/tren?	"a ke **o**ra **ye**ga el owto**boos**/tren"
▷ **we arrived early/late**	llegamos temprano/ tarde	"yeg**a**mos temp**ra**no/**tar**de"
art gallery	la galería de arte	"gale**ree**a de **a**rte"
artichoke	la alcachofa	"alka**cho**fa"
ascent		
when is the last ascent?	¿a qué hora es la última subida?	"a ke **o**ra es la **ool**teema soo**bee**da"
ashore	en tierra	"en tee-**e**rra"
▷ **can we go ashore?**	¿podemos desembarcar?	"po**de**mos desembar**kar**"
ashtray	el cenicero	"thenee**the**ro"
▷ **may I have an ashtray?**	¿me trae un cenicero?	"me **tra**e oon thenee**the**ro"
asparagus	los espárragos	"esp**a**rragos"

ABSOLUTE ESSENTIALS

yes (please)	sí (por favor)	"see (por fa**bor**)"
no (thank you)	no (gracias)	"no (**gra**theeas)"
hello	hola	"**o**la"
goodbye	adiós	"ade**os**"

aspirin	la aspirina	"aspee**ree**na"
asthma	el asma	"**as**ma"
▷ I suffer from asthma	padezco de asma	"pa**deth**ko de **as**ma"
at	a	"a"
▷ at home	en casa	"en **ka**sa"
Athens	Atenas	"a**te**nas"
aubergine	la berenjena	"beren**khe**na"
August	agosto	"a**gos**to"
Australia	Australia	"ows**tra**leea"
Australian	australiano	"owstralee**a**no"
	australiana	"owstralee**a**na"
Austria	Austria	"**ows**treea"
Austrian	austriaco	"owstree**a**ko"
	austriaca	"owstree**a**ka"
automatic	automático	"owto**ma**teeko"
	automática	"owto**ma**teeka"
▷ is it an automatic (car)?	¿es automático?	"es owto**ma**teeko"
autumn	el otoño	"o**to**nyo"
avalanche	la avalancha	"aba**lan**cha"
	el alud	"a**lood**"
▷ is there danger of avalanches?	¿hay peligro de aludes?	"**a**ee pe**lee**gro de a**loo**des"
avocado	el aguacate	"agwa**ka**te"
baby	el bebé	"be**be**"
	la bebé	"be**be**"
baby food	la comida para niños	"ko**mee**da **para nee**nyos"
baby seat (*in car*)	el asiento para el bebé	"asee-**en**to **para** el be**be**"
baby-sitter	la canguro	"kan**goo**ro"

ABSOLUTE ESSENTIALS

I don't understand	no comprendo	"no kom**pren**do"
I don't speak Spanish	no hablo español	"no **a**blo espan**yol**"
do you speak English?	¿habla inglés?	"**a**bla een**gles**"
could you help me?	¿podría ayudarme?	"po**dree**a ayoo**dar**me"

baby-sitting:

▷ **is there a baby-sitting service?** — ¿hay un servicio para cuidar a los niños? — "aee oon ser**bee**theeo para kwee**dar** a los **neen**yos"

back[1] *n* (*of body*) — la espalda — "es**pal**da"

▷ **I've got a bad back** — tengo la espalda mal — "**ten**go la es**pal**da mal"

▷ **I've hurt my back** — me he hecho daño en la espalda — "me e **echo da**nyo en la es**pal**da"

back[2] *adv:*

▷ **we must be back at the hotel before 6 o'clock** — tenemos que volver al hotel antes de las seis — "te**nem**os que bol**ber** al o**tel an**tes de las **say**-ees"

bacon — el beicon — "**bay**-eekon"

bad (*food: rotten*) — podrido — "po**dree**do"

podrida — "po**dree**da"

(*weather, news*) — malo — "**mal**o"

mala — "**mal**a"

badminton — el bádminton — "**bad**meenton"

bag — la bolsa — "**bol**sa"

(*suitcase*) — la maleta — "ma**let**a"

(*handbag*) — el bolso — "**bol**so"

baggage — el equipaje — "ekee**pak**he"

baggage allowance — el límite de equipaje — "**lee**meete de ekee**pak**he"

el equipaje permitido — "ekee**pak**he permee**tee**do"

▷ **what is the baggage allowance?** — ¿cuál es el límite de equipaje? — "kwal es el **lee**meete de ekee**pak**he"

baggage reclaim — la entrega de equipajes — "en**tre**ga de ekee**pak**hes"

bail bond — la garantía de fianza — "garan**tee**a de fee**an**tha"

baker — el panadero — "pana**der**o"

baker's — la panadería — "panade**reea**"

balcony — el balcón — "bal**kon**"

ABSOLUTE ESSENTIALS		
I would like ...	me gustaría ...	"me goosta**reea**"
I need ...	necesito ...	"nethe**seet**o"
where is ...?	¿dónde está ...?	"**don**de esta"
I'm looking for ...	estoy buscando ...	"es**toee** boos**kan**do"

▷ **do you have a room with a balcony?**	¿tienen una habitación con balcón?	"tee-**e**nen oona abeetathee**on** kon bal**kon**"
ball	la pelota	"pel**o**ta"
ball game	el juego de pelota	"**khwe**go de pel**o**ta"
banana	el plátano	"**plat**ano"
band (*musical*) (*rock etc*)	la banda el grupo	"**ban**da" "**groo**po"
bandage	la venda	"**ben**da"
bank	el banco	"**ban**ko"
▷ **is there a bank nearby?**	¿hay un banco por aquí cerca?	"**aee** oon **ban**ko por a**kee ther**ka"
bar	el bar	"bar"
barber	el peluquero	"pelook**e**ro"
barber's	la peluquería de caballeros	"pelooker**ee**a de kaba**ye**ros"
basket	la cesta	"**thes**ta"
bath	el baño	"**ba**nyo"
▷ **to take a bath**	darse un baño	"**dar**se oon **ba**nyo"
bathing cap	el gorro de baño	"**go**rro de **ba**nyo"
bathroom	el cuarto de baño	"**kwar**to de **ba**nyo"
battery (*for appliance*) (*in car*)	la pila la batería	"**pee**la" "bater**ee**a"
to **be**	ser estar	"sayr" "es**tar**"
▷ **I am English**	soy inglés	"**so**ee een**gles**"
▷ **I am tired**	estoy cansado	"es**to**ee kan**sa**do"

ABSOLUTE ESSENTIALS		
do you have ...?	¿tiene ...?	"tee-**e**ne"
is there ...?	¿hay ...?	"**aee**"
are there ...?	¿hay ...?	"**aee**"
how much is ...?	¿cuánto cuesta ...?	"**kwan**to **kwes**ta"

you are (*informal singular*)	eres	"**eres**"
	estás	"es**tas**"
(*formal singular*)	es	"es"
	está	"es**ta**"
(*plural*)	sois	"**so**ees"
	estáis	"estaees"
he/she/it is	es	"es"
	está	"es**ta**"
we are	somos	"**so**mos"
	estamos	"es**ta**mos"
they are	son	"son"
	están	"es**tan**"

beach	la playa	"**pla**ya"
beach ball	el balón de playa	"ba**lon** de **pla**ya"
beach umbrella	la sombrilla	"som**bree**ya"
bean	la judía	"khoo**dee**a"
beautiful	hermoso	"er**mo**so"
	hermosa	"er**mo**sa"
bed	la cama	"**ka**ma"
bedding	la ropa de cama	"**ro**pa de **ka**ma"
▷ **is there any spare bedding?**	¿tiene más ropa de cama?	"tee-**ene** mas **ro**pa de **ka**ma"
bedroom	el dormitorio	"dormee**to**reeo"
beef	la carne de vaca	"**kar**ne de **ba**ka"
beefburger	la hamburguesa	"amboor**ge**sa"
beer	la cerveza	"ther**be**tha"
▷ **a draught beer, please**	una caña, por favor	"**oo**na **ka**nya por fa**bor**"
beetroot	la remolacha	"remo**la**cha"

ABSOLUTE ESSENTIALS		
yes (please)	sí (por favor)	"see (por fa**bor**)"
no (thank you)	no (gracias)	"no (**grath**eeas)"
hello	hola	"**o**la"
goodbye	adiós	"adee**os**"

before (*in time*)	antes de	"**an**tes de"
(*in place*)	delante de	"de**lan**te de"
to **begin**	empezar	"empe**thar**"
behind	detrás	"de**tras**"
▷ **behind the house**	detrás de la casa	"de**tras** de la **ka**sa"
Belgian	belga	"**bel**ga"
Belgium	Bélgica	"**bel**kheeka"
below	abajo	"a**ba**kho"
▷ **below the hotel**	por debajo del hotel	"por de**ba**kho del o**tel**"
belt	el cinturón	"theentoo**ron**"
Berlin	Berlín	"ber**leen**"
beside	al lado de	"al **la**do de"
best	el mejor	"me**khor**"
	la mejor	"me**khor**"
better	mejor	"me**khor**"
between	entre	"**en**tre"
bicycle	la bicicleta	"beethee**kle**ta"
big	grande	"**gran**de"
▷ **it's too big**	es demasiado grande	"es demasee**a**do **gran**de"
bigger	más grande	"mas **gran**de"
▷ **do you have a bigger one?**	¿tiene uno/una más grande?	"tee-**ene oo**no/**oo**na mas **gran**de"
bikini	el bikini	"bee**kee**nee"
bill	la cuenta	"**kwen**ta"
▷ **put it on my bill**	póngalo en mi cuenta	"**pon**galo en mee **kwen**ta"
▷ **the bill, please**	la cuenta, por favor	"la **kwen**ta por fa**bor**"
▷ **can I have an itemized bill?**	¿me da una factura detallada?	"me da **oo**na fak**too**ra deta**ya**da"

ABSOLUTE ESSENTIALS

I don't understand	no comprendo	"no kom**pren**do"
I don't speak Spanish	no hablo español	"no **ab**lo espan**yol**"
do you speak English?	¿habla inglés?	"**ab**la een**gles**"
could you help me?	¿podría ayudarme?	"po**dree**a ayoo**dar**me"

bin	el cubo	"**koo**bo"
binoculars	los prismáticos	"prees**ma**teekos"
bird	el pájaro	"**pa**kharo"
birthday	el cumpleaños	"koompl**ea**nyos"
▷ **Happy Birthday!**	¡feliz cumpleaños!	"fe**leeth** koompl**ea**nyos"
birthday card	la tarjeta de cumpleaños	"tar**khe**ta de koompl**ea**nyos"
bit:		
▷ **a bit of**	un poco de	"oon **po**ko de"
to **bite**	morder	"mor**der**"
(*insect*)	picar	"pee**kar**"
bitten	mordido	"mor**dee**do"
	mordida	"mor**dee**da"
(*by insect, snake*)	picado	"pee**ka**do"
	picada	"pee**ka**da"
bitter	amargo	"a**mar**go"
	amarga	"a**mar**ga"
black	negro	"**ne**gro"
	negra	"**ne**gra"
blackcurrants	los arándanos	"a**ran**danos"
blanket	la manta	"**man**ta"
bleach	la lejía	"le**khee**a"
blister	la ampolla	"am**po**ya"
blocked (*road*)	cerrado	"the**rra**do"
	cerrada	"the**rra**da"
(*pipe*)	obstruido	"obstroo**ee**do"
	obstruida	"obstroo**ee**da"
blood group	el grupo sanguíneo	"**groo**po san**gee**neo"
▷ **my blood group is ...**	mi grupo sanguíneo es ...	"mee **groo**po san**gee**neo es"

ABSOLUTE ESSENTIALS

I would like ...	me gustaría ...	"me goosta**ree**a"
I need ...	necesito ...	"nethe**see**to"
where is ...?	¿dónde está ...?	"**don**de esta"
I'm looking for ...	estoy buscando ...	"es**toy** boos**kan**do"

blouse	la blusa	"**bloo**sa"
blow-dry	el secado a mano	"se**ka**do a **ma**no"
▷ **a cut and blow-dry, please**	corte y secado a mano, por favor	"**kor**te ee se**ka**do a **ma**no por fa**bor**"
blue	azul	"a**thool**"
boarding card	la tarjeta de embarque	"tar**khe**ta de em**bar**ke"
boarding house	la pensión	"pensee**on**"
boat	el barco	"**bar**ko"
boat trip	la excursión en barco	"ekskoorsee**on** en **bar**ko"
▷ **are there any boat trips on the river/lake?**	¿hay excursiones en barco por el río/lago?	"**aee** ekskoorsee**o**nes en **bar**ko por el **ree**o/**la**go"
to **boil**	hervir	"er**beer**"
	cocer	"ko**ther**"
▷ **boiled egg**	el huevo cocido	"**we**bo ko**thee**do"
book¹ *n*	el libro	"**lee**bro"
▷ **book of tickets**	el talonario	"el talo**na**reeo"
to **book**² *vb*	reservar	"reser**bar**"
▷ **the table is booked for 8 o'clock this evening**	la mesa está reservada para esta noche a las 8	"la **me**sa es**ta** reser**ba**da para **es**ta **no**che a las **o**cho"
▷ **can you book me into a hotel?**	¿puede reservarme hotel?	"**pwe**de reser**bar**me o**tel**"
▷ **should I book in advance?**	¿debería hacer la reserva con antelación	"debe**ree**a a**ther** la re**ser**ba kon antelathee**on**"
booking	la reserva	"re**ser**ba"
▷ **I confirmed my booking by letter**	confirmé la reserva por carta	"konfeer**me** la re**ser**ba por **kar**ta"
▷ **can I change my booking?**	¿puedo cambiar el billete?	"**pwe**do kambee**ar** el bee**ye**te"
▷ **is there a booking fee?**	¿cobran un recargo?	"**ko**bran oon re**kar**go"
booking office	el despacho de billetes	"des**pa**cho de bee**ye**tes"

ABSOLUTE ESSENTIALS

do you have ...?	¿tiene ...?	"tee-**e**ne"
is there ...?	¿hay ...?	"**aee**"
are there ...?	¿hay ...?	"**aee**"
how much is ...?	¿cuánto cuesta ...?	"**kwan**to **kwes**ta"

bookshop	la librería	"leebrer**eea**"
boot	la bota	"**bo**ta"
▷ a pair of boots	unas botas	"**oo**nas **bo**tas"
border	la frontera	"fron**te**ra"
botanic gardens	el jardín botánico	"khar**deen** bo**ta**neeko"
both	ambos	"**am**bos"
	ambas	"**am**bas"
bottle	la botella	"bo**te**ya"
▷ a bottle of mineral water, please	una botella de agua mineral, por favor	"**oo**na bo**te**ya de **a**gwa meene**ral** por fa**bor**"
▷ a bottle of gas	una bombona de butano	"**oo**na bom**bo**na de boo**ta**no"
bottle opener	el abrebotellas	"abrebo**te**yas"
box	la caja	"**ka**kha"
box office	la taquilla	"ta**kee**ya"
boy	el chico	"**chee**ko"
boyfriend	el novio	"**no**beeo"
bra	el sujetador	"sookheta**dor**"
bracelet	la pulsera	"pool**se**ra"
brake fluid	el líquido de frenos	"**lee**keedo de **fre**nos"
brakes	el freno	"**fre**no"
brandy	el coñac	"**kon**yak"
▷ I'll have a brandy	tráigame un coñac	"**tra**eegame oon kon**yak**"
bread	el pan	"pan"
▷ could we have some more bread?	¿nos trae más pan?	"nos **tra**e mas pan"
breakable	que se rompe con facilidad	"ke se **rom**pe kon fatheelee**dad**"

ABSOLUTE ESSENTIALS

yes (please)	sí (por favor)	"see (por fa**bor**)"
no (thank you)	no (gracias)	"no (**gra**theeas)"
hello	hola	"**o**la"
goodbye	adiós	"adee**os**"

breakdown	la avería	"abereea"
breakdown van	la grúa	"grooa"
▷ **can you send a breakdown van?**	¿puede mandarme una grúa?	"pwede mandarme oona grooa"
breakfast	el desayuno	"desayoorio"
▷ **what time is breakfast?**	¿a qué hora es el desayuno?	"a ke ora es el desayoono"
▷ **can we have breakfast in our room?**	¿pueden traernos el desayuno a la habitación?	"pweden traernos el desayoono a la abeetatheeon"
breast (*of woman*) (*chest*) (*chicken*)	el pecho el seno la pechuga	"pecho" "seno" "pechooga"
to **breast-feed**	amamantar	"amamantar"
to **breathe**	respirar	"respeerar"
▷ **he can't breathe**	no puede respirar	"no pwede respeerar"
briefcase	la cartera	"kartera"
to **bring**	traer	"traer"
Britain	Gran Bretaña	"gran bretanya"
▷ **have you ever been to Britain?**	¿ha estado alguna vez en Gran Bretaña?	"a estado algoona beth en gran bretanya"
British	británico británica	"breetaneeko" "breetaneeka"
▷ **I'm British**	soy británico/británica	"soee breetaneeko/ breetaneeka"
broccoli	el brécol	"brekol"
brochure	el folleto	"foyeto"
broken	roto rota	"roto" "rota"
▷ **I have broken the window**	he roto la ventana	"e roto la bentana"

ABSOLUTE ESSENTIALS

I don't understand	no comprendo	"no komprendo"
I don't speak Spanish	no hablo español	"no ablo espanyol"
do you speak English?	¿habla inglés?	"abla eengles"
could you help me?	¿podría ayudarme?	"podreea ayoodarme"

▷ **the lock is broken**	la cerradura está rota	"la therra**doo**ra esta **ro**ta"
broken down (*machine, car*)	averiado averiada	"abereea**do**" "abereea**da**"
▷ **my car has broken down**	se me ha averiado el coche	"se me a abereea**do** el **ko**che"
broken into:		
▷ **my car has been broken into**	me han forzado la cerradura del coche	"me an for**tha**do la therra**doo**ra del **ko**che"
brooch	el broche	"**bro**che"
broom	la escoba	"es**ko**ba"
brother	el hermano	"er**ma**no"
brown	marrón	"ma**rron**"
brush	el cepillo	"the**pee**yo"
Brussels sprouts	las coles de Bruselas	"**ko**les de broo**se**las"
bucket	el cubo	"**koo**bo"
buffet	la cafetería	"kafete**ree**a"
buffet car	el coche-comedor	"**ko**chekome**dor**"
bulb (*electric*)	la bombilla	"bom**bee**ya"
bum bag	la riñonera	"reenyo**ne**ra"
bun	el bollo	"**bo**yo"
bureau de change	el cambio	"**kam**beeo"
burst:		
▷ **a burst tyre**	un neumático pinchado	"oon neoo**ma**teeko peen**cha**do"
bus	el autobús	"owto**boos**"
▷ **where do I get the bus to town?**	¿dónde se coge el autobús para el centro?	"**don**de se **ko**khe el owto**boos** **pa**ra el **then**tro"
▷ **does this bus go to ...?**	¿este autobús va a ...?	"**es**te owto**boos** ba a"

ABSOLUTE ESSENTIALS

I would like ...	me gustaría ...	"me goosta**ree**a"
I need ...	necesito ...	"nethe**see**to"
where is ...?	¿dónde está ...?	"**don**de esta"
I'm looking for ...	estoy buscando ...	"es**toee** boos**kan**do"

▷ **where do I get a bus for the cathedral?**	¿dónde se coge el autobús para la catedral?	"**don**de se **ko**khe el owto**boos pa**ra la kate**dral**"
▷ **which bus do I take for the museum?**	¿qué autobús tengo que coger para ir al museo?	"ke owto**boos ten**go ke ko**kher pa**ra eer al moo**se**o"
▷ **how frequent are the buses to town?**	¿con qué frecuencia pasan los autobuses para el centro?	"kon ke frek**wen**theea **pa**san los owto**boo**ses **pa**ra el **then**tro"
▷ **what time is the last bus?**	¿a qué hora sale el último autobús?	"a ke **o**ra **sa**le el **ool**teemo owto**boos**"
▷ **what time does the bus leave?**	¿a qué hora sale el autobús?	"a ke **o**ra **sa**le el owto**boos**"
▷ **what time does the bus arrive?**	¿a qué hora llega el autobús?	"a ke **o**ra **ye**ga el owto**boos**"
business	los negocios	"ne**go**theeos"
▷ **I am here on business**	he venido de negocios	"e be**nee**do de ne**go**theeos"
▷ **a business trip**	un viaje de negocios	"oon bee**akhe** de ne**go**theeos"
bus station	la terminal de autobuses	"termee**nal** de owto**boo**ses"
bus stop	la parada de autobús	"pa**ra**da de owto**boos**"
bus tour	la excursión en autobús	"ekskoorsee**on** en owto**boos**"
busy	ocupado ocupada	"okoo**pa**do" "okoo**pa**da"
▷ **the line is busy**	la línea está ocupada	"la **lee**nea es**ta** okoo**pa**da"
but	pero	"**pe**ro"
butcher	el carnicero	"karnee**the**ro"
butcher's	la carnicería	"karneethe**ree**a"
butter	la mantequilla	"mante**kee**ya"
button	el botón	"bo**ton**"

ABSOLUTE ESSENTIALS		
do you have ...?	¿tiene ...?	"tee-**e**ne"
is there ...?	¿hay ...?	"**aee**"
are there ...?	¿hay ...?	"**aee**"
how much is ...?	¿cuánto cuesta ...?	"**kwan**to **kwes**ta"

to **buy**	comprar	"kom**prar**"
▷ **where can I buy some postcards?**	¿dónde se pueden comprar postales?	"**don**de se **pwe**den kom**prar** postales"
▷ **where do we buy our tickets?**	¿dónde podemos sacar los billetes?	"**don**de po**de**mos sa**kar** los bee**ye**tes"
by (*via*)	por	"por"
(*beside*)	al lado de	"al **la**do de"
bypass	la carretera de circunvalación	"karre**te**ra de theerkoonbalathee**on**"
cabaret	el cabaret	"kaba**re**"
▷ **where can we go to see a cabaret?**	¿dónde podemos ir a ver un cabaret?	"**don**de po**de**mos eer a ber oon kaba**re**"
cabbage	la col	"kol"
cabin (*hut*)	la cabaña	"ka**ba**nya"
(*on ship*)	el camarote	"kama**ro**te"
▷ **a first/second class cabin**	un camarote de primera/segunda clase	"oon kama**ro**te de pree**me**ra/se**goon**da **kla**se"
cable car	el teleférico	"tele**fe**reeko"
cactus	el cáctus	"**kak**toos"
café	el café	"ka**fe**"
cagoule	el anorak	"ano**rak**"
cake	el pastel	"pas**tel**"
calculator	la calculadora	"kalkoola**do**ra"
call[1] *n* (*on telephone*)	la llamada	"ya**ma**da"
▷ **I'd like to make a call**	quiero hacer una llamada	"kee-**e**ro a**ther oo**na ya**ma**da"
▷ **a long distance call**	una llamada interurbana	"**oo**na ya**ma**da eenteroor**ba**na"
▷ **an international call**	una llamada internacional	"**oo**na ya**ma**da eenternathee**o**nal"

ABSOLUTE ESSENTIALS		
yes (please)	sí (por favor)	"see (por fa**bor**)"
no (thank you)	no (gracias)	"no (**grath**eeas)"
hello	hola	"**o**la"
goodbye	adiós	"adee**os**"

to **call**² vb (shout)	llamar	"ya**mar**"
(on telephone)	llamar por teléfono	"ya**mar** por te**le**fono"
▷ **may I call you tomorrow?**	¿puedo llamarle mañana?	"**pwe**do ya**mar**le man**ya**na"
▷ **please call me back**	por favor, llámeme más tarde	"por fa**bor** ya**me**me mas **tar**de"
call box	la cabina telefónica	"ka**bee**na tele**fo**neeka"
calm	tranquilo	"tran**kee**lo"
	tranquila	"tran**kee**la"
▷ **keep calm!**	¡calma!	"**kal**ma"
camcorder	la cámara de vídeo	"**ka**mara de **bee**deo"
camera	la cámara	"**ka**mara"
to **camp**	acampar	"akam**par**"
▷ **may we camp here?**	¿podemos acampar aquí?	"po**de**mos akam**par** a**kee**"
camp bed	la cama plegable	"**ka**ma ple**ga**ble"
camp site	el camping	"**kam**peen"
▷ **we're looking for a camp site**	estamos buscando un camping	"es**ta**mos boos**kan**do oon **kam**peen"
can¹ n	el bote	"**bo**te"
can² vb (be able)	poder	"po**der**"

I can	puedo	"**pwe**do"
you can (informal singular)	puedes	"**pwe**des"
(formal singular)	puede	"**pwe**de"
(plural)	podéis	"po**de**-es"
he/she/it can	puede	"**pwe**de"
we can	podemos	"po**de**mos"
they can	pueden	"**pwe**den"

▷ **we can't come**	no podemos venir	"no po**de**mos be**neer**"

ABSOLUTE ESSENTIALS

I don't understand	no comprendo	"no kom**pren**do"
I don't speak Spanish	no hablo español	"no **ab**lo espan**yol**"
do you speak English?	¿habla inglés?	"**ab**la een**gles**"
could you help me?	¿podría ayudarme?	"po**dree**a ayoo**dar**me"

▷ **can I ...?**	¿puedo ...?	"**pwe**do"
Canada	Canadá	"kana**da**"
Canadian	canadiense	"kanadee-**en**se"
canal	el canal	"ka**nal**"
to cancel	cancelar	"kanthe**lar**"
▷ **I want to cancel my booking**	quiero cancelar la reserva	"kee-**e**ro kanthe**lar** la re**ser**ba"
cancellation:		
▷ **are there any cancellations?**	¿hay cancelaciones?	"**a**ee kanthelathee**o**nes"
canoe	la canoa	"ka**no**a"
canoeing	el piragüismo	"peera**gwees**mo"
▷ **where can we go canoeing?**	¿dónde podemos ir a hacer piragüismo?	"**don**de po**de**mos eer a a**ther** peera**gwees**mo"
can-opener	el abrelatas	"abre**la**tas"
car	el coche	"**ko**che"
▷ **I want to hire a car**	quiero alquilar un coche	"kee-**e**ro alkee**lar** oon **ko**che"
▷ **my car has been broken into**	me han forzado la cerradura del coche	"me an for**tha**do la therra**doo**ra del **ko**che"
▷ **my car has broken down**	se me ha averiado el coche	"se me a abere**a**do el **ko**che"
carafe	la garrafa	"ga**rra**fa"
▷ **a carafe of house wine please**	una garrafa de vino de la casa, por favor	"**oo**na ga**rra**fa de **bee**no de la **ka**sa por fa**bor**"
caramel	el caramelo	"kara**me**lo"
caravan	la caravana	"kara**ba**na"
	la roulotte	"roo**lot**"
▷ **can we park our caravan here?**	¿podemos aparcar la caravana/roulotte aquí?	"po**de**mos apar**kar** la kara**ba**na/roo**lot** a**kee**"

ABSOLUTE ESSENTIALS

I would like ...	me gustaría ...	"me goosta**ree**a"
I need ...	necesito ...	"nethe**see**to"
where is ...?	¿dónde está ...?	"**don**de es**ta**"
I'm looking for ...	estoy buscando ...	"es**toee** boos**kan**do"

caravan site	el camping para caravanas/roulottes	"**kam**peen para kara**ba**nas/roo**lots**"
carburettor	el carburador	"karboora**dor**"
card (*greetings*)	la tarjeta	"tar**khe**ta"
(*playing*)	la carta	"**kar**ta"
▷ **playing cards**	las cartas	"las **kar**tas"
▷ **birthday card**	la tarjeta de cumpleaños	"tar**khe**ta de koomplea**nyos**"
cardigan	la rebeca	"re**be**ka"
careful	cuidadoso	"kweeda**do**so"
	cuidadosa	"kweeda**do**sa"
▷ **be careful!**	¡tenga cuidado!	"**ten**ga kwee**da**do"
car ferry	el transbordador	"transborda**dor**"
car number	la matrícula	"ma**tree**koola"
car park	el aparcamiento	"aparkamee-**en**to"
▷ **is there a car park near here?**	¿hay aparcamiento por aquí cerca?	"**aee** aparkamee-**en**to por a**kee ther**ka"
carpet (*fitted*)	la moqueta	"mo**ke**ta"
(*rug*)	la alfombra	"al**fom**bra"
carriage (*railway*)	el vagón	"ba**gon**"
carrier bag	la bolsa	"**bol**sa"
▷ **can I have a carrier bag please?**	¿me da una bolsa, por favor?	"me da oona **bol**sa por fa**bor**"
carrot	la zanahoria	"thana**o**reea"
to **carry**	llevar	"ye**bar**"
car wash	el lavado automático	"la**ba**do owto**ma**teeko"
▷ **how do I use the car wash?**	¿cómo funciona el lavado automático?	"**ko**mo foonthee**o**na el la**ba**do owto**ma**teeko"
case (*suitcase*)	la maleta	"ma**le**ta"

ABSOLUTE ESSENTIALS

do you have ...?	¿tiene ...?	"tee-**e**ne"
is there ...?	¿hay ...?	"**aee**"
are there ...?	¿hay ...?	"**aee**"
how much is ...?	¿cuánto cuesta ...?	"**kwan**to **kwes**ta"

cash[1] *n*	el dinero en efectivo	"dee**ne**ro en efek**tee**bo"
▷ **I haven't any cash**	no tengo dinero en efectivo	"no **ten**go dee**ne**ro en efek**tee**bo"
▷ **can I get cash with my credit card?**	¿puedo sacar dinero con mi tarjeta de crédito?	"**pwe**do sa**kar** dee**ne**ro kon mee tar**khe**ta de **kre**deeto"
to **cash**[2] *vb (cheque)*	cobrar	"ko**brar**"
▷ **can I cash a cheque?**	¿puedo cobrar un cheque?	"**pwe**do ko**brar** oon **che**ke"
cash desk	la caja	"**ka**ha"
cash dispenser	el cajero automático	"ka**he**ro owto**ma**teeko"
cashier	el cajero	"ka**he**ro"
	la cajera	"ka**he**ra"
casino	el casino	"ka**see**no"
cassette	la cassette	"ka**set**"
cassette player	el cassette	"ka**set**"
castle	el castillo	"kas**tee**yo"
▷ **is the castle open to the public?**	¿está abierto al público el castillo?	"es**ta** abee**er**to al **poo**bleeko el kas**tee**yo"
to **catch**	coger	"ko**kher**"
▷ **where do we catch the ferry to ...?**	¿dónde se coge el transbordador para ...?	"**don**de se **ko**khe el transborda**dor** **pa**ra"
cathedral	la catedral	"kate**dral**"
▷ **excuse me, how do I get to the cathedral?**	por favor, ¿por dónde se va a la catedral?	"por fa**bor** por **don**de se ba a la kate**dral**"
Catholic	católico	"ka**to**leeko"
	católica	"ka**to**leeka"
cauliflower	la coliflor	"kolee**flor**"
cave	la cueva	"**kwe**ba"
caviar	el caviar	"kabee**ar**"

ABSOLUTE ESSENTIALS		
yes (please)	sí (por favor)	"see (por fa**bor**)"
no (thank you)	no (gracias)	"no (**gra**theeas)"
hello	hola	"**o**la"
goodbye	adiós	"adee**os**"

CD	el compact	"**kom**pak"
celery	el apio	"**a**peeo"
cemetery	el cementerio	"themen**te**reeo"
centimetre	el centímetro	"then**tee**metro"
central	central	"then**tral**"
central station	la estación central	"estathee**on** then**tral**"
▷ **where is the central station?**	¿dónde está la estación central?	"**don**de esta la estathee**on** then**tral**"
centre	el centro	"**then**tro"
▷ **how far are we from the town centre?**	¿a qué distancia estamos del centro?	"a ke dees**tan**theea estamos del **then**tro"
cereal (*for breakfast*)	los cereales	"the**re**ales"
certain (*sure*)	seguro	"se**goo**ro"
	segura	"se**goo**ra"
certificate	el certificado	"therteefee**ka**do"
▷ **an insurance certificate**	una póliza de seguros	"**oo**na **po**leetha de se**goo**ros"
chain	la cadena	"ka**de**na"
▷ **do I need snow chains?**	¿hacen falta cadenas?	"**a**then **fal**ta ka**de**nas"
chair	la silla	"**see**ya"
chairlift	el telesilla	"tele**see**ya"
chalet	el chalet	"cha**le**"
champagne	el champán	"cham**pan**"
change[1] *n*	el cambio	"**kam**beeo"
(*small coins*)	el suelto	"**swel**to"
(*money returned*)	la vuelta	"**bwel**ta"
▷ **do you have change?**	¿tiene cambio?	"tee-**ene kam**beeo"

ABSOLUTE ESSENTIALS

I don't understand	no comprendo	"no kom**pren**do"
I don't speak Spanish	no hablo español	"no **ab**lo espan**yol**"
do you speak English?	¿habla inglés?	"**ab**la een**gles**"
could you help me?	¿podría ayudarme?	"po**dree**a ayoo**dar**me"

▷ could you give me change of 1,000 pesetas?	¿me cambia 1.000 pesetas?	"me **kam**beea meel pe**se**tas"
▷ sorry, I don't have any change	lo siento, no tengo cambio	"lo see-**en**to no **ten**go **kam**beeo"
▷ keep the change	quédese con la vuelta	"**ke**dese kon la **bwel**ta"

to change² *vb*	cambiar	"kambee**ar**"
▷ where can I change some money?	¿dónde se puede cambiar dinero?	"**don**de se **pwe**de kambee**ar** dee**ne**ro"
▷ I'd like to change these traveller's cheques	quiero cambiar estos cheques de viaje	"kee-**e**ro kambee**ar es**tos **che**kes de bee**akhe**"
▷ I want to change some pounds into pesetas	quiero cambiar libras en pesetas	"kee-**e**ro kambee**ar lee**bras en pe**se**tas"
▷ where can I change the baby?	¿dónde puedo cambiar el niño?	"**don**de **pwe**do kambee**ar** el **nee**nyo"
▷ where do we change? (clothes)	¿dónde nos cambiamos?	"**don**de nos kambee**a**mos"
▷ where do I change? (bus etc)	¿dónde tengo que cambiar?	"**don**de **ten**go ke kambee**ar**"
▷ is the weather going to change?	¿va a cambiar el tiempo?	"ba a kambee**ar** el tee-**em**po"
▷ can I change my booking?	¿puedo cambiar el billete?	"**pwe**do kambee**ar** el bee**ye**te"

changing room	el probador	"proba**dor**"
Channel tunnel	el Eurotúnel	"ewro**too**nel"
chapel	la capilla	"ka**pee**ya"
charge	el precio	"**pre**theeo"
▷ is there a charge per kilometre?	¿hay una tasa por kilómetro?	"aee **oo**na **ta**sa por kee**lo**metro"
▷ I want to reverse the charges	quiero llamar a cobro revertido	"kee-**e**ro ya**mar** a **ko**bro reber**tee**do"
▷ how much do you charge?	¿cuánto cobran?	"**kwan**to **ko**bran"
▷ is there a charge for the service?	¿cobran por el servicio?	"**ko**bran por el serbee**thee**o"

ABSOLUTE ESSENTIALS

I would like ...	me gustaría ...	"me goosta**ree**a"
I need ...	necesito ...	"nethe**see**to"
where is ...?	¿dónde está ...?	"**don**de esta"
I'm looking for ...	estoy buscando ...	"es**toee** boos**kan**do"

▷ **please charge it to my room**	cárguelo a la cuenta de la habitación	"**kar**gelo a la **kwen**ta de la abeetathee**on**"
cheap	barato	"ba**ra**to"
	barata	"ba**ra**ta"
cheaper	más barato	"mas ba**ra**to"
	más barata	"mas ba**ra**ta"
▷ **have you anything cheaper?**	¿tiene algo más barato?	"tee-**e**ne **al**go mas ba**ra**to"
to **check**	controlar	"kontro**lar**"
to **check in** (*at airport*)	facturar	"faktoo**rar**"
(*at hotel*)	registrarse	"rekhees**trar**se"
▷ **I'd like to check in, please**	quiero registrarme/ facturar, por favor	"kee-**e**ro rekhees**trar**me/ faktoo**rar** por fa**bor**"
▷ **where do I check in for the flight to ...?**	¿dónde tengo que facturar para el vuelo a ...?	"**don**de **ten**go ke faktoo**rar** para el **bwe**lo a"
▷ **where do I check in my luggage?**	¿dónde tengo que facturar el equipaje?	"**don**de **ten**go ke faktoo**rar** el ekee**pakhe**"
▷ **when do I have to check in?**	¿cuándo tengo que facturar?	"**kwan**do **ten**go ke faktoo**rar**"
check-in desk	el mostrador de facturación	"mostra**dor** de faktoorathee**on**"
cheerio	¡hasta luego!	"**a**sta l**we**go"
cheers!	¡salud!	"sa**lood**"
cheese	el queso	"**ke**so"
cheeseburger	la hamburguesa con queso	"amboor**ge**sa kon **ke**so"
cheesecake	la tarta de queso	"**tar**ta de **ke**so"
chemist's	la farmacia	"far**ma**theea"
cheque	el cheque	"**che**ke"
▷ **can I pay by cheque?**	¿puedo pagar con un cheque?	"**pwe**do pa**gar** con oon **che**ke"

ABSOLUTE ESSENTIALS

do you have ...?	¿tiene ...?	"tee-**e**ne"
is there ...?	¿hay ...?	"**aee**"
are there ...?	¿hay ...?	"**aee**"
how much is ...?	¿cuánto cuesta ...?	"**kwan**to **kwes**ta"

▷ I want to cash a cheque, please	quiero cobrar un cheque, por favor	"kee-**e**ro ko**brar** oon **che**ke por fa**bor**"
cheque book	el talonario de cheques	"talo**na**reeo de **che**kes"
▷ I've lost my cheque book	he perdido el talonario de cheques	"e per**dee**do el talo**na**reeo de **che**kes"
cheque card	la tarjeta de identidad bancaria	"tar**khe**ta de eedentee**dad** ban**ka**reea"
cherry	la cereza	"the**re**tha"
chess	el ajedrez	"akhe**dreth**"
▷ to play chess	jugar al ajedrez	"khoo**gar** al akhe**dreth**"
chest	el pecho	"**pe**cho"
▷ I have a pain in my chest	tengo un dolor en el pecho	"**ten**go oon do**lor** en el **pe**cho"
chestnut	la castaña	"kas**ta**nya"
chewing gum	el chicle	"**chee**kle"
chicken	el pollo	"**po**yo"
chickenpox	la varicela	"baree**the**la"
chicken soup	la sopa de pollo	"**so**pa de **po**yo"
child	el niño la niña	"**nee**nyo" "**nee**nya"
child minder	la niñera	"nin**ye**ra"
children (*infants*)	los niños	"**nee**nyos"
▷ is there a children's pool?	¿hay piscina para los niños?	"**a**ee pees**thee**na **pa**ra los **nee**nyos"
▷ is there a paddling pool for the children?	¿hay estanque de juegos para los niños?	"**a**ee es**tan**ke de **khwe**gos **pa**ra los **nee**nyos"
chilli	el chile	"**chee**le"
chips	las patatas fritas	"pa**ta**tas **free**tas"
chives	los cebollinos	"thebo**yee**nos"

ABSOLUTE ESSENTIALS		
yes (please)	sí (por favor)	"see (por fa**bor**)"
no (thank you)	no (gracias)	"no (**gra**theeas)"
hello	hola	"**o**la"
goodbye	adiós	"adee**os**"

chocolate	el chocolate	"choko**la**te"
▷ **I'd like a bar of chocolate, please**	una tableta de chocolate, por favor	"**oo**na ta**ble**ta de choko**la**te por fa**bor**"
chocolates	los bombones	"bom**bo**nes"
chop	la chuleta	"choo**le**ta"
▷ **a pork/lamb chop**	una chuleta de cerdo/ cordero	"**oo**na choo**le**ta de **ther**do/kor**de**ro"
Christmas	la Navidad	"nabee**dad**"
▷ **Merry Christmas!**	¡feliz Navidad!	"fe**leeth** nabee**dad**"
church	la iglesia	"ee**gle**seea"
▷ **where is the nearest church?**	¿dónde queda la iglesia más próxima?	"**don**de **ke**da la ee**gle**seea mas **prok**seema"
▷ **where is there a Protestant/Catholic church?**	¿dónde hay una iglesia protestante/católica?	"**don**de aee **oo**na ee**gle**seea protes**tan**te/ ka**to**leeka"
cider	la sidra	"**see**dra"
cigar	el puro	"**poo**ro"
cigarette	el cigarrillo el cigarro	"theega**rree**yo" "thee**ga**rro"
▷ **a packet of cigarettes, please**	un paquete de cigarrillos, por favor	"oon pa**ke**te de theega**rree**yos por fa**bor**"
cigarette papers	los papeles de fumar	"pa**pe**les de foo**mar**"
cinema	el cine	"**thee**ne"
▷ **what's on at the cinema?**	¿qué ponen en el cine?	"ke **po**nen en el **thee**ne"
circus	el circo	"**theer**ko"
city	la ciudad	"theeoo**dad**"
clean¹ *adj*	limpio limpia	"**leem**peeo" "**leem**peea"

ABSOLUTE ESSENTIALS

I don't understand	no comprendo	"no kom**pren**do"
I don't speak Spanish	no hablo español	"no **ablo** espan**yol**"
do you speak English?	¿habla inglés?	"**abla** een**gles**"
could you help me?	¿podría ayudarme?	"po**dree**a ayoo**dar**me"

▷ **the room isn't clean**	la habitación no está limpia	"la abeetathee**on** no es**ta leem**peea"
▷ **could I have a clean spoon please?**	¿podría darme una cuchara limpia, por favor?	"po**dree**a **dar**me oona koo**cha**ra **leem**peea por fa**bor**"
to **clean**[2] *vb*	limpiar	"leempee**ar**"
▷ **where can I get this skirt cleaned?**	¿dónde me podrían limpiar esta falda?	"**don**de me po**dree**an leempee**ar es**ta **fal**da"
cleaner	la limpiadora	"leempeea**do**ra"
	la mujer de la limpieza	"moo**kher** de la leempee-**e**tha"
▷ **which day does the cleaner come?**	¿qué día vienen a limpiar?	"ke **dee**a bee-**e**nen a leempee**ar**"
cleansing cream	la crema limpiadora	"**kre**ma leempeea**do**ra"
cleansing solution (*for contact lenses*)	la solución limpiadora	"soloothee**on** leempeea**do**ra"
client	el cliente	"klee**en**te"
	la cliente	"klee**en**te"
cliff	el acantilado	"akantee**la**do"
climbing	el alpinismo	"alpee**nees**mo"
climbing boots	las botas de montañero	"**bo**tas de mon**tan**yero"
cloakroom	el guardarropa	"gwarda**rro**pa"
clock	el reloj	"re**lo**"
close[1] *adj* (*near*)	cercano	"ther**ka**no"
	cercana	"ther**ka**na"
to **close**[2] *vb*	cerrar	"the**rrar**"
▷ **what time do you close?**	¿a qué hora cierran?	"a ke **o**ra thee-**e**rran"
▷ **the door will not close**	la puerta no se cierra	"la **pwer**ta no se thee-**e**rra"
closed	cerrado	"the**rra**do"
	cerrada	"the**rra**da"

ABSOLUTE ESSENTIALS

I would like ...	me gustaría ...	"me goosta**ree**a"
I need ...	necesito ...	"nethe**see**to"
where is ...?	¿dónde está ...?	"**don**de es**ta**"
I'm looking for ...	estoy buscando ...	"es**toee** boos**kan**do"

cloth	el trapo	"**tra**po"
clothes	la ropa	"**ro**pa"
clothes peg	la pinza	"**peen**tha"
cloudy	nublado	"noo**bla**do"
	nublada	"noo**bla**da"
▷ **it's cloudy**	está nublado	"esta noo**bla**do"
clove	el clavo	"**kla**bo"
club	el club	"**kloob**"
▷ **a night club**	un club nocturno	"oon kloob nok**toor**no"
▷ **a set of golf clubs**	un juego de palos de golf	"oon **khwe**go de **pa**los de golf"
coach (*bus*)	el autocar	"owto**kar**"
(*train*)	el vagón	"ba**gon**"
▷ **when does the coach leave in the morning?**	¿a qué hora sale el autocar por la mañana?	"a ke **ora sa**le el owto**kar** por la man**ya**na"
coach station	la estación de autobuses	"estathee**on** de owto**boo**ses"
coach trip	la excursión en autocar	"ekskoorsee**on** en owto**kar**"
coast	la costa	"**kos**ta"
coastguard	el guardacostas	"gwarda**kos**tas"
coat	el abrigo	"a**bree**go"
coat hanger	la percha	"**per**cha"
cockroaches	las cucarachas	"kooka**ra**chas"
cocktail	el cóctel	"**kok**tel"
cocoa	el cacao	"ka**ka**o"
coconut	el coco	"**ko**ko"
cod	el bacalao	"baka**la**o"

ABSOLUTE ESSENTIALS

do you have ...?	¿tiene ...?	"tee-**e**ne"
is there ...?	¿hay ...?	"**aee**"
are there ...?	¿hay ...?	"**aee**"
how much is ...?	¿cuánto cuesta ...?	"**kwan**to **kwes**ta"

coffee	el café	"kafe"
▷ **white coffee**	el café con leche	"kafe kon leche"
▷ **black coffee**	el café solo	"kafe solo"
coin	la moneda	"moneda"
▷ **what coins do I need?**	¿qué monedas me hacen falta?	"ke monedas me athen falta"
Coke®	la coca cola	"kokakola"
colander	el colador	"kolador"
cold¹ n	el resfriado	"resfreeado"
▷ **I have a cold**	tengo un resfriado	"tengo oon resfreeado"
cold² adj	frío	"freeo"
	fría	"freea"
▷ **I'm cold**	tengo frío	"tengo freeo"
▷ **will it be cold tonight?**	¿hará frío esta noche?	"ara freeo esta noche"
cold meat	las fiambres	"feeambres"
cologne	la colonia	"koloneea"
▷ **(eau de) Cologne**	(agua de) colonia	"(agwa de) koloneea"
colour	el color	"kolor"
▷ **I don't like the colour**	no me gusta el color	"no me goosta el kolor"
▷ **I need a colour film for this camera**	necesito un carrete en color para esta cámara	"netheseeto oon karrete en kolor para esta kamara"
▷ **do you have it in another colour?**	¿lo tiene en otro color?	"lo tee-ene en otro kolor"
▷ **a colour TV**	una televisión en color	"oona telebeeseeon en kolor"
comb	el peine	"pay-eene"
to come	venir	"beneer"
(arrive)	llegar	"yegar"
▷ **how much does that come to?**	¿cuánto hace eso?	"kwanto athe eso"

ABSOLUTE ESSENTIALS

yes (please)	sí (por favor)	"see (por fabor)"
no (thank you)	no (gracias)	"no (gratheeas)"
hello	hola	"ola"
goodbye	adiós	"adeeos"

to **come back**	volver	"bol**ber**"
to **come in**	entrar	"en**trar**"
▷ **come in!**	¡pase!	"**pase**"
comfortable	cómodo	"**ko**modo"
	cómoda	"**ko**moda"
commission	la comisión	"komeesee**on**"
▷ **how much commission do you charge?**	¿cuánto se llevan de comisión?	"**kwan**to se **lle**ban de komeesee**on**"
communion	la comunión	"komoonee**on**"
compact disc	el compact disc	"**kom**pak deesk"
compact disc player	el (reproductor de) compact	"(reprodook**tor** de) **kom**pak"
company	la empresa	"em**pre**sa"
	la compañía	"kompan**yee**a"
compartment	el compartimento	"kompartee**men**to"
▷ **I would like a seat in a non-smoking compartment**	quiero un asiento de no-fumadores	"kee-**ero** oon asee-**en**to de nofooma**do**res"
to **complain**	quejarse	"ke**khar**se"
▷ **I want to complain about the service** (*in shop etc*)	quiero poner una queja por el servicio	"kee-**ero** po**ner** **oo**na **ke**kha por el ser**bee**theeo"
comprehensive insurance cover	el seguro a todo riesgo	"se**goo**ro a **to**do ree-**es**go"
▷ **how much extra is comprehensive insurance cover?**	¿cuánto más cuesta el seguro a todo riesgo?	"**kwan**to mas **kwes**ta el se**goo**ro a **to**do ree-**es**go"
compulsory	obligatorio	"obleega**to**reeo"
	obligatoria	"obleega**to**reea"
computer	el ordenador	"ordena**dor**"

ABSOLUTE ESSENTIALS

I don't understand	no comprendo	"no kom**pren**do"
I don't speak Spanish	no hablo español	"no **ab**lo espan**yol**"
do you speak English?	¿habla inglés?	"**ab**la een**gles**"
could you help me?	¿podría ayudarme?	"po**dree**a ayoo**dar**me"

concert	el concierto	"konthee-**er**to"
condensed milk	la leche condensada	"**le**che konden**sa**da"
conditioner	el suavizante	"swabee**than**te"
condom	el condón	"kon**don**"
▷ **a packet of condoms**	un paquete de condones	"oon pa**ke**te de kon**do**nes"
conductor (on bus) (on train)	el cobrador el revisor	"kobra**dor**" "rebee**sor**"
conference	la conferencia	"konfe**ren**theea"
confession	la confesión	"konfesee**on**"
▷ **I want to go to confession**	quiero confesarme	"kee-**e**ro konfe**sar**me"
to **confirm**	confirmar	"konfeer**mar**"
congratulations!	¡felicidades! ¡enhorabuena!	"feleethe**da**des" "enora**bwe**na"
to **connect**	conectar	"konek**tar**"
connection (for train, plane etc)	el enlace la combinación	"en**la**the" "kombeenathee**on**"
▷ **I missed my connection**	perdí la combinación	"per**dee** la kombeenathee**on**"
constipated	estreñido estreñida	"estreny**ee**do" "estreny**ee**da"
constipation	el estreñimiento	"estrenyeemee-**en**to"
consulate	el consulado	"konsoo**la**do"
▷ **where is the British consulate?**	¿dónde está el Consulado británico?	"**don**de esta el konsoo**la**do breeta**nee**ko"
to **contact**	ponerse en contacto con	"po**ner**se en kon**tak**to kon"
▷ **where can I contact you?**	¿dónde puedo ponerme en contacto contigo?	"**don**de pwedo po**ner**me en kon**tak**to con**tee**go"

ABSOLUTE ESSENTIALS		
I would like ...	me gustaría ...	"me goosta**ree**a"
I need ...	necesito ...	"nethe**see**to"
where is ...?	¿dónde está ...?	"**don**de esta"
I'm looking for ...	estoy buscando ...	"estoee boos**kan**do"

contact lenses	las lentes de contacto	"**len**tes de kon**tak**to"
▷ **contact lens cleaner**	la solución limpiadora para lentes de contacto	"la solooth**eon** leempeea**do**ra para **len**tes de kon**tak**to"
▷ **hard contact lenses**	las lentes de contacto duras	"las **len**tes de kon**tak**to **doo**ras"
▷ **soft contact lenses**	las lentes de contacto blandas	"las **len**tes de kon**tak**to **blan**das"
continental breakfast	el desayuno continental	"desa**yoo**no konteenen**tal**"
contraceptive	el anticonceptivo	"anteekonthep**tee**bo"
controls	los mandos	"**man**dos"
▷ **how do I operate the controls?**	¿cómo funcionan los mandos?	"**ko**mo foonthee**o**nan los **man**dos"
to **cook**	cocinar	"kothee**nar**"
cooker	la cocina	"kot**hee**na"
▷ **how does the cooker work?**	¿cómo funciona la cocina?	"**ko**mo foonthee**o**na la kot**hee**na"
cool	fresco	"**fres**ko"
	fresca	"**fres**ka"
copy¹ *n*	la copia	"**ko**peea"
▷ **4 copies please**	4 copias, por favor	"**kwa**tro **ko**peeas por fa**bor**"
to **copy**² *vb*	copiar	"kopee**ar**"
	hacer una copia	"a**ther oo**na **ko**peea"
▷ **I want to copy this document**	quiero hacer una copia de este documento	"kee-**e**ro a**ther oo**na **ko**peea de **es**te doko**omen**to"
corkscrew	el sacacorchos	"saka**kor**chos"
corner	la esquina	"es**kee**na"

ABSOLUTE ESSENTIALS

do you have ...?	¿tiene ...?	"tee-**e**ne"
is there ...?	¿hay ...?	"**aee**"
are there ...?	¿hay ...?	"**aee**"
how much is ...?	¿cuánto cuesta ...?	"**kwan**to **kwes**ta"

▷ **it's round the corner**	está doblando la esquina	"esta do**blan**do la es**kee**na"
cornflakes	los copos de maíz	"**ko**pos de ma**eeth**"
cortisone	la cortisona	"kortee**so**na"
cosmetics	los cosméticos	"kos**me**teekos"
to **cost**	costar	"kos**tar**"
▷ **how much does it cost to get in?**	¿cuánto cuesta la entrada?	"**kwan**to **kwes**ta la en**tra**da"
▷ **how much does that cost?**	¿cuánto cuesta?	"**kwan**to **kwes**ta"
cot	la cuna	"**koo**na"
▷ **do you have a cot for the baby?**	¿tienen una cuna para el niño?	"tee-**enen oo**na **koo**na **pa**ra el **nee**nyo"
cotton	el algodón	"algo**don**"
cotton wool	el algodón hidrófilo	"algo**don** ee**dro**feelo"
couchette	la litera	"lee**te**ra"
▷ **I want to reserve a couchette**	quiero reservar una litera	"kee-**ero** reser**bar oo**na lee**te**ra"
cough	la tos	"tos"
▷ **I have a cough**	tengo tos	"**ten**go tos"
▷ **do you have any cough mixture?**	¿tienen jarabe para la tos?	"tee-**enen** kha**ra**be **pa**ra la tos"

could:

I/he/she could	podría	"po**dree**a"
you could (*informal singular*)	podrías	"po**dree**as"
(*formal singular*)	podría	"po**dree**a"
(*plural*)	podríais	"po**dree**a-ees"
we could	podríamos	"po**dree**a-mos"
they could	podrían	"po**dree**an"

ABSOLUTE ESSENTIALS		
yes (please)	sí (por favor)	"see (por fa**bor**)"
no (thank you)	no (gracias)	"no (**grat**heeas)"
hello	hola	"**o**la"
goodbye	adiós	"adee**os**"

country (*not town*)	el campo	"**kam**po"
(*nation*)	el país	"pa**ees**"
couple (*2 people*)	la pareja	"pa**re**kha"
courgettes	los calabacines	"kalaba**thee**nes"
courier	el mensajero	"mensa**khe**ro"
	la mensajera	"mensa**khe**ra"
▷ **I want to send this by courier**	quiero enviar esto con un mensajero	"kee-**e**ro embee**ar es**to kon oon mensa**khe**ro"
course (*of meal*)	el plato	"**pla**to"
cover charge	el precio del cubierto	"**pre**theeo del koobee-**er**to"
crab	el cangrejo	"kan**gre**kho"
cramp (*in leg*)	el calambre	"ka**lam**bre"
(*in stomach*)	el retortijón	"retortee**khon**"
▷ **I've got cramp (in my leg)**	me ha dado un calambre (en la pierna)	"me a **da**do oon ka**lam**bre (en la pee-**er**na)"
crash¹ *n*:		
▷ **there's been a crash**	ha habido un accidente	"a a**bee**do oon akthee**den**te"
to **crash²** *vb* (*2 cars etc*)	colisionar	"koleeseeo**nar**"
▷ **I've crashed my car**	he chocado con el coche	"e cho**ka**do kon el **ko**che"
crash helmet	el casco protector	"**kas**ko protek**tor**"
cream (*lotion*)	la crema	"**kre**ma"
(*on milk*)	la nata	"**na**ta"
cream cheese	el requesón	"reke**son**"
	el queso en crema	"**ke**so en **kre**ma"
credit card	la tarjeta de crédito	"tar**khe**ta de **kre**deeto"

ABSOLUTE ESSENTIALS

I don't understand	no comprendo	"no kom**pren**do"
I don't speak Spanish	no hablo español	"no **a**blo espan**yol**"
do you speak English?	¿habla inglés?	"**a**bla een**gles**"
could you help me?	¿podría ayudarme?	"po**dree**a ayoo**dar**me"

▷ **can I pay by credit card?**	¿puedo pagar con tarjeta de crédito?	"**pwe**do pa**gar** con tar**khe**ta de **kre**deeto"
▷ **I've lost my credit card**	he perdido la tarjeta de crédito	"e per**dee**do la tar**khe**ta de **kre**deeto"
crisps	las patatas fritas de bolsa	"pa**ta**tas **free**tas de **bol**sa"
▷ **a bag of crisps**	una bolsa de patatas fritas	"**oo**na **bol**sa de pa**ta**tas **free**tas"
croissant	el croissant	"krwa**san**"
croquette	la croqueta	"kro**ke**ta"
to **cross** (*road*)	atravesar	"atrabe**sar**"
	cruzar	"kroo**thar**"
cross-country skiing:		
▷ **is it possible to go cross-country skiing?**	¿se puede hacer esquí de fondo?	"se **pwe**de a**ther** es**kee** de **fon**do"
crossed line	el cruce de línea	"**kroo**the de **lee**nea"
crossing (*by boat*)	la travesía	"trabe**see**a"
▷ **how long does the crossing take?**	¿cuánto dura la travesía?	"**kwan**to **doo**ra la trabe**see**a"
crossroads	el cruce	"**kroo**the"
crowded	atestado	"ates**ta**do"
	atestada	"ates**ta**da"
cruise	el crucero	"kroo**the**ro"
cucumber	el pepino	"pe**pee**no"
cup	la taza	"**ta**tha"
▷ **could we have another cup of tea/coffee, please**	otra taza de té/café, por favor	"otra **ta**tha de te/ka**fe** por fa**bor**"
cupboard	el armario	"ar**ma**reeo"

ABSOLUTE ESSENTIALS		
I would like ...	me gustaría ...	"me goosta**ree**a"
I need ...	necesito ...	"nethe**see**to"
where is ...?	¿dónde está ...?	"**don**de esta"
I'm looking for ...	estoy buscando ...	"es**toe**e boos**kan**do"

curlers	los rulos	"**roo**los"
currant	la pasa de Corinto	"**pa**sa de ko**reen**to"
current	la corriente	"korree-**ente**"
▷ **are there strong currents?**	¿hay corrientes fuertes?	"aee korree-**en**tes **fwer**tes"
cushion	el cojín	"ko**kheen**"
custard	las natillas	"na**tee**yas"
customs	la aduana	"a**dwa**na"
cut¹ *n*	el corte	"**kor**te"
▷ **a cut and blow-dry, please**	corte y secado a mano, por favor	"**kor**te ee se**ka**do a **ma**no por fa**bor**"
to **cut**² *vb*	cortar	"kor**tar**"
▷ **he has cut himself**	se ha cortado	"se a kor**ta**do"
▷ **I've been cut off**	me han cortado	"me an kor**ta**do"
cutlery	los cubiertos	"koobee-**er**tos"
cycle	la bicicleta	"beethee**kle**ta"
cycle path	el carril para bicicletas	"ka**reel pa**ra beethee**kle**tas"
cycle helmet	el casco protector para ciclistas	"**kas**ko protek**tor pa**ra thee**klees**tas"
cycling	el ciclismo	"thee**klees**mo"
▷ **we would like to go cycling**	nos gustaría pasear en bicicleta	"nos goosta**ree**a pa**sear** en beethee**kle**ta"
daily (*each day*)	cada día diariamente	"**ka**da **dee**a" "deearee**a**mente"
dairy products	los productos lácteos	"pro**dook**tos **lak**teos"
damage	los desperfectos	"desper**fek**tos"
damp	húmedo húmeda	"**oo**medo" "**oo**meda"

ABSOLUTE ESSENTIALS		
do you have ...?	¿tiene ...?	"tee-**ene**"
is there ...?	¿hay ...?	"aee"
are there ...?	¿hay ...?	"aee"
how much is ...?	¿cuánto cuesta ...?	"**kwan**to **kwes**ta"

▷ **my clothes are damp**	tengo la ropa húmeda	"**ten**go la **ro**pa **oo**meda"
dance¹ *n*	el baile	"**ba**eele"
to **dance**² *vb*	bailar	"baee**lar**"
dangerous	peligroso	"pelee**gro**so"
	peligrosa	"pelee**gro**sa"
dark	oscuro	"os**koo**ro"
	oscura	"os**koo**ra"
date	la fecha	"**fe**cha"
▷ **what is the date today?**	¿a qué día estamos?	"a ke **dee**a es**ta**mos"
date of birth	la fecha de nacimiento	"**fe**cha de natheemee-**en**to"
daughter	la hija	"**ee**kha"
day	el día	"**dee**a"
day trip	la excursión	"ekskoorsee**on**"
dear	querido	"ke**ree**do"
	querida	"ke**ree**da"
(*expensive*)	caro	"**ka**ro"
	cara	"**ka**ra"
decaffeinated coffee	el café descafeinado	"**ka**fe deskafay-ee**na**do"
December	diciembre	"deethee-**em**bre"
deck	la cubierta	"koobee-**er**ta"
▷ **can we go out on deck?**	¿podemos salir a cubierta?	"po**de**mos sa**leer** a koobee-**er**ta"
deck chair	la tumbona	"toom**bo**na"
to **declare**	declarar	"dekla**rar**"
▷ **I have nothing to declare**	no tengo nada que declarar	"no **ten**go **na**da ke dekla**rar**"
▷ **I have a bottle of spirits to declare**	tengo una botella de licor que declarar	"**ten**go **oo**na bo**te**ya de lee**kor** ke dekla**rar**"

ABSOLUTE ESSENTIALS

yes (please)	sí (por favor)	"see (por fa**bor**)"
no (thank you)	no (gracias)	"no (**gra**theeas)"
hello	hola	"**o**la"
goodbye	adiós	"adee**os**"

deep	profundo profunda	"pro**foon**do" "pro**foon**da"
▷ **how deep is the water?**	¿qué profundidad tiene el agua?	"ke profoondee**dad** tee-**e**ne el **a**gwa"
deep freeze	el congelador	"konkhela**dor**"
to **defrost**	descongelar	"deskonkhe**lar**"
to **de-ice**	deshelar	"dese**lar**"
delay	el retraso	"re**tra**so"
▷ **the flight has been delayed (by 6 hours)**	el vuelo se ha retrasado (6 horas)	"el **bwe**lo se a retra**sa**do (**say**-ees **o**ras)"
delicious	delicioso deliciosa	"deleethee**o**so" "deleethee**o**sa"
dentist	el/la dentista	"den**tees**ta"
▷ **I need to see a dentist (urgently)**	necesito ver (urgentemente) al dentista	"nethe**see**to ber (oorkhente**men**te) al den**tees**ta"
dentures	la dentadura postiza	"denta**doo**ra pos**tee**tha"
▷ **my dentures need repairing**	necesito que me arreglen la dentadura postiza	"nethe**see**to ke me a**rre**glen la denta**doo**ra pos**tee**tha"
deodorant	el desodorante	"desodo**ran**te"
department stores	los grandes almacenes	"**gran**des alma**the**nes"
departure	la salida	"sa**lee**da"
departure lounge	la sala de embarque	"**sa**la de em**bar**ke"
departures	salidas	"sa**lee**das"
deposit	la señal	"se**nyal**"
▷ **what is the deposit?**	¿cuánto es la señal?	"**kwan**to es la se**nyal**"
dessert	el postre	"**pos**tre"
▷ **we'd like a dessert**	queremos postre	"ke**re**mos **pos**tre"

ABSOLUTE ESSENTIALS

I don't understand	no comprendo	"no kom**pren**do"
I don't speak Spanish	no hablo español	"no **a**blo espan**yol**"
do you speak English?	¿habla inglés?	"**a**bla een**gles**"
could you help me?	¿podría ayudarme?	"po**dree**a ayoo**dar**me"

▷ **the dessert menu, please**	la carta de los postres, por favor	"la **kar**ta de los **pos**tres por fa**bor**"
details	los detalles	"de**ta**yes"
detergent	el detergente	"deter**khen**te"
detour	la desviación	"desbeeathee**on**"
to **develop**	desarrollar	"desarro**yar**"
diabetic	diabético	"deea**be**teeko"
	diabética	"deea**be**teeka"
▷ **I am diabetic**	soy diabético	"**so**ee deea**be**teeko"
dialling code	el prefijo	"pre**fee**kho"
▷ **what is the dialling code for the UK?**	¿cuál es el prefijo del Reino Unido?	"kwal es el pre**fee**kho del **re**-eeno oo**nee**do"
diamond	el diamante	"deea**man**te"
diarrhoea	la diarrea	"deea**rre**a"
▷ **I need something for diarrhoea**	necesito algo para cortar la diarrea	"nethe**see**to **al**go **pa**ra kor**tar** la deea**rre**a"
diary	la agenda	"a**khen**da"
dictionary	el diccionario	"deekthee**ona**reeo"
diesel	el gasoil	"ga**so**eel"
diet	el régimen	"**re**kheemen"
▷ **I'm on a diet**	estoy a régimen	"**es**toee a **re**kheemen"
different	distinto	"dees**teen**to"
	distinta	"dees**teen**ta"
▷ **I would like something different**	quiero algo distinto	"kee-**e**ro **al**go dis**tin**to"
difficult	difícil	"dee**fee**theel"
dinghy	el bote (neumático)	"**bo**te ne-oo**ma**teeko"
dining car	el vagón restaurante	"ba**gon** restow**ran**te"

ABSOLUTE ESSENTIALS

I would like ...	me gustaría ...	"me goosta**ree**a"
I need ...	necesito ...	"nethe**see**to"
where is ...?	¿dónde está ...?	"**don**de esta"
I'm looking for ...	estoy buscando ...	"**es**toee boos**kan**do"

dining room	el comedor	"kome**dor**"
dinner	la cena	"**the**na"
▷ **to have dinner**	cenar	"the**nar**"
direct (*train etc*)	directo	"dee**rek**to"
	directa	"dee**rek**ta"
directory	la guía telefónica	"**gee**a tele**fo**neeka"

directory enquiries:

▷ **what is the number for directory enquiries?**	¿cuál es el número del servicio de información telefónica?	"kwal es el **noo**mero del ser**bee**theeo de eenforma**thee**on tele**fo**neeka"
dirty	sucio	"**soo**theeo"
	sucia	"**soo**theea"
▷ **the washbasin is dirty**	el lavabo está sucio	"el la**ba**bo es**ta soo**theeo"
disabled	minusválido	"meenoos**ba**leedo"
	minusválida	"meenoos**ba**leeda"
▷ **is there a toilet for the disabled?**	¿hay wáter especial para minusválidos?	"**aee ba**ter espe**thee**al **pa**ra meenoos**ba**leedos"
▷ **do you have facilities for the disabled?**	¿tienen ustedes instalaciones especiales para los minusválidos?	"tee-**e**nen oos**te**des eenstalathee**o**nes espe**thee**ales **pa**ra los meenoos**ba**leedos"
▷ **do you provide access for the disabled?**	¿disponen de rampas de acceso para los minusválidos?	"dees**po**nen de **ram**pas de ak**the**so **pa**ra los meenoos**ba**leedos"
disco	la discoteca	"deesko**te**ka"
discount	el descuento	"des**kwen**to"
▷ **do you offer a discount for cash?**	¿ofrecen descuento si se paga en efectivo?	"o**fre**then des**kwen**to see se **pa**ga en efek**tee**bo"
▷ **are there discounts for students?**	¿hay descuento para los estudiantes?	"**aee** des**kwen**to **pa**ra los estoodee**an**tes"
dish	el plato	"**pla**to"

ABSOLUTE ESSENTIALS

do you have ...?	¿tiene ...?	"tee-**e**ne"
is there ...?	¿hay ...?	"**aee**"
are there ...?	¿hay ...?	"**aee**"
how much is ...?	¿cuánto cuesta ...?	"**kwan**to **kwes**ta"

▷ how is this dish cooked?	¿cómo se cocina este plato?	"**ko**mo se ko**thee**na **es**te **pla**to"
▷ what is in this dish?	¿qué tiene este plato?	"ke tee-**e**ne **es**te **pla**to"
dishtowel	el trapo de secar	"**tra**po de se**kar**"
dishwasher	el lavavajillas	"lababa**khee**yas"
disinfectant	el desinfectante	"deseenfek**tan**te"
distilled water	el agua destilada	"**a**gwa destee**la**da"
to **dive**	sumergirse	"soomer**kheer**se"
	bucear	"boo**thear**"
▷ where is the best place to dive?	¿dónde está el mejor sitio para hacer submarinismo?	"**don**de esta el me**khor see**teeo **pa**ra a**ther** soobmaree**nees**mo"
diversion	el desvío	"des**bee**o"
▷ is there a diversion?	¿hay algun desvío?	"**aee** al**goon** des**bee**o"
diving:		
▷ I'd like to go diving	me gustaría practicar submarinismo	"me goosta**ree**a praktee**kar** soobmaree**nees**mo"
divorced	divorciado/a	"deebor**thee**ado/a"
dizzy	mareado/a	"ma**rea**do/a"
▷ I feel dizzy	me siento mareado	"me see-**en**to ma**rea**do"
to **do**	hacer	"a**ther**"

I do	hago	"**a**go"
you do (*informal singular*)	(tú) haces	"(too) **a**thes"
(*formal singular*)	hace	"**a**the"
(*plural*)	hacéis	"**a**the-ees"
he/she/it does	hace	"**a**the"
we do	hacemos	"a**the**mos"
they do	hacen	"**a**then"

ABSOLUTE ESSENTIALS

yes (please)	sí (por favor)	"see (por fa**bor**)"
no (thank you)	no (gracias)	"no (**gra**theeas)"
hello	hola	"**o**la"
goodbye	adiós	"a**dee**os"

dock (*wharf*)	el muelle	"**mw**eye"
doctor	el médico	"**me**deeko"
	la médica	"**me**deeka"
▷ **can I have an appointment with the doctor?**	¿puede darme hora para el médico?	"**pwe**de **dar**me **o**ra para el **me**deeko"
▷ **I need a doctor**	necesito un médico	"nethe**see**to oon **me**deeko"
▷ **call a doctor!**	¡llame a un médico!	"**ya**me a oon **me**deeko"
documents	los documentos	"doko**o**mentos"
dog	el perro	"**pe**rro"
doll	la muñeca	"moo**nye**ka"
dollar	el dólar	"**do**lar"
door	la puerta	"**pwer**ta"
double	doble	"**do**ble"
double bed	la cama de matrimonio	"**ka**ma de matree**mo**neeo"
double room	la habitación doble	"abeetathee**on do**ble"
▷ **I want to reserve a double room**	quiero reservar una habitación doble	"kee-**e**ro reser**bar** oona abeetathee**on do**ble"
doughnut	el dónut	"**do**noot"
	la rosquilla	"ros**kee**ya"
down	abajo	"a**ba**kho"
downstairs	abajo	"a**ba**kho"
▷ **they live downstairs**	viven abajo	"**bee**ben a**ba**kho"
drain:		
▷ **the drain is blocked**	el desagüe está atascado	"el de**sa**gwe es**ta** atas**ka**do"

ABSOLUTE ESSENTIALS

I don't understand	no comprendo	"no kom**pren**do"
I don't speak Spanish	no hablo español	"no **a**blo espan**yol**"
do you speak English?	¿habla inglés?	"**a**bla een**gles**"
could you help me?	¿podría ayudarme?	"po**dree**a ayoo**dar**me"

draught	la corriente	"korree-**ente**"
draught beer	la cerveza de barril	"therbetha de ba**rreel**"
▷ **a draught beer, please**	una caña, por favor	"oona **ka**nya por fa**bor**"
dress[1] *n*	el vestido	"bes**tee**do"
to dress[2] *vb*:		
▷ **to get dressed**	vestirse	"bes**teer**se"
dressing (*for food*)	el aliño	"a**lee**nyo"
drink[1] *n*	la bebida	"be**bee**da"
▷ **would you like a drink?**	¿quiere beber algo?	"kee-**ere** beber **al**go"
▷ **a cold/hot drink**	una bebida fría/caliente	"oona be**bee**da **free**a/ kalee-**ent**e"
to drink[2] *vb*	beber	"be**ber**"
▷ **what would you like to drink?**	¿qué quiere de beber?	"ke kee-**ere** de be**ber**"
drinking chocolate	el chocolate en polvo	"cho**kolat**e en **pol**vo"
drinking water	el agua potable	"**a**gwa po**table**"
to drive	conducir	"kondoo**theer**"
▷ **he was driving too fast**	conducía demasiado deprisa	"kodoo**thee**a demasee**a**do de**pree**sa"
driver (*of car*)	el conductor la conductora	"kondook**tor**" "kondook**tora**"
driving licence	el carné de conducir	"kar**ne** de kondoo**theer**"
▷ **my driving licence number is ...**	el número de mi carné de conducir es ...	"el **noo**mero de mee kar**ne** de kondoo**theer** es"
▷ **I don't have my driving licence on me**	no llevo mi carné de conducir	"no **ye**bo mee kar**ne** de kondoo**theer**"
to drown	ahogarse	"ao**garse**"

ABSOLUTE ESSENTIALS

I would like ...	me gustaría ...	"me goosta**ree**a"
I need ...	necesito ...	"nethe**see**to"
where is ...?	¿dónde está ...?	"**don**de esta"
I'm looking for ...	estoy buscando ...	"es**toe**e boos**kando**"

▷ **someone is drowning!**	¡alguien se está ahogando!	"algee-**en** se es**ta** ao**gan**do"
drunk	borracho	"bo**rra**cho"
	borracha	"bo**rra**cha"
dry¹ *adj*	seco	"**se**ko"
	seca	"**se**ka"
to **dry**² *vb*	secar	"se**kar**"
▷ **where can I dry my clothes?**	¿dónde puedo poner la ropa a secar?	"**don**de **pwe**do po**ner** la **ro**pa a se**kar**"
to **dry-clean**:		
▷ **I need this dry-cleaned**	necesito que me limpien esto en seco	"nethe**see**to ke me **leem**pee-en **es**to en **se**ko"
dry-cleaner's	la tintorería	"teentore**ree**a"
duck	el pato	"**pa**to"
due:		
▷ **when is the train due?**	¿cuándo está previsto que llegue el tren?	"**kwan**do esta pre**bees**to ke **ye**ge el tren"
dummy	el chupete	"choo**pe**te"
dune	la duna	"**doo**na"
during	durante	"doo**ran**te"
duty-free	libre de derechos de aduana	"**lee**bre de de**re**chos de ad**wa**na"
duty-free shop	la tienda "duty free"	"tee-**en**da dootee**free**"
duvet	el edredón	"edre**don**"
dynamo	la dínamo	"**dee**namo"
each	cada	"**ka**da"
ear	la oreja	"o**re**kha"
	el oído	"o**ee**do"

ABSOLUTE ESSENTIALS

do you have ...?	¿tiene ...?	"tee-**en**e"
is there ...?	¿hay ...?	"**aee**"
are there ...?	¿hay ...?	"**aee**"
how much is ...?	¿cuánto cuesta ...?	"**kwan**to **kwes**ta"

earache	el dolor de oídos	"do**lor** de o**ee**dos"
▷ **I have earache**	me duelen los oídos	"me **dwe**len los o**ee**dos"
earlier	antes	"**an**tes"
▷ **I would prefer an earlier flight**	preferiría un vuelo que saliera antes	"preferee**ree**a oon **bwe**lo ke salee-**e**ra **an**tes"
early	temprano	"tem**pra**no"
earrings	los pendientes	"pendee-**en**tes"
east	el este	"**es**te"
Easter	la Pascua	"**pas**kwa"
easy	fácil	"**fa**theel"
to eat	comer	"ko**mer**"
▷ **I don't eat meat**	no como carne	"no **ko**mo **kar**ne"
▷ **would you like something to eat?**	¿quiere algo de comer?	"kee-**e**re **al**go de ko**mer**"
▷ **have you eaten?**	¿ha comido?	"a ko**mee**do"
EC	la Comunidad Europea	"komoonee**dad** eooro**pe**a"
eel	la anguila	"an**gee**la"
egg	el huevo	"**we**bo"
▷ **eggs**	los huevos	"los **we**bos"
▷ **fried egg**	el huevo frito	"el **we**bo **free**to"
▷ **hard-boiled egg**	el huevo cocido/duro	"el **we**bo ko**thee**do/**doo**ro"
▷ **scrambled eggs**	los huevos revueltos	"los **we**bos re**bwel**tos"
eight	ocho	"**o**cho"
eighteen	dieciocho	"dee-ethee**o**cho"
eighty	ochenta	"o**chen**ta"
either:		
▷ **either one**	cualquiera de los dos	"kwalkee-**e**ra de los dos"
▷ **I don't like it either**	a mí tampoco me gusta	"a mee tam**po**ko me **goos**ta"

ABSOLUTE ESSENTIALS		
yes (please)	sí (por favor)	"see (por fa**bor**)"
no (thank you)	no (gracias)	"no (**grath**eeas)"
hello	hola	"**o**la"
goodbye	adiós	"adee**os**"

elastic	el elástico	"el**as**teeko"
elastic band	la goma	"**go**ma"
electric	eléctrico	"e**lek**treeko"
	eléctrica	"e**lek**treeka"
electrician	el electricista	"elektree**thees**ta"
electricity	la electricidad	"elektreethee**dad**"
▷ **is the cost of electricity included in the rental?**	¿va el coste de la electricidad incluido en el alquiler?	"ba el **kos**te de la elektreethee**dad** eenkloo**ee**do en el alkee**ler**"
electricity meter	el contador de la luz	"konta**dor** de la looth"
electric razor	la máquina de afeitar eléctrica	"la **ma**keena de afay-ee**tar** e**lek**treeka"
eleven	once	"**on**the"
to **embark**	embarcar	"embar**kar**"
▷ **when do we embark?**	¿cuándo embarcamos?	"**kwan**do embar**ka**mos"
embassy	la embajada	"emba**kha**da"
emergency	la emergencia	"emer**khen**theea"
empty	vacío	"ba**thee**o"
	vacía	"ba**thee**a"
end	el fin	"feen"
engaged (*to be married*)	prometido	"prome**tee**do"
	prometida	"prome**tee**da"
(*toilet*)	ocupado	"okoo**pa**do"
	ocupada	"okoo**pa**da"
▷ **the line's engaged**	está comunicando	"es**ta** komoonee**kan**do"
engine	el motor	"mo**tor**"
England	Inglaterra	"eengla**te**rra"
English	inglés	"een**gles**"
	inglesa	"een**gle**sa"

ABSOLUTE ESSENTIALS

I don't understand	no comprendo	"no kom**pren**do"
I don't speak Spanish	no hablo español	"no **a**blo espan**yol**"
do you speak English?	¿habla inglés?	"**a**bla een**gles**"
could you help me?	¿podría ayudarme?	"po**dree**a ayoo**dar**me"

▷ do you speak English?	¿habla usted inglés?	"abla oosted eengles"
▷ I'm English	soy inglés/inglesa	"soee eengles/eenglesa"
▷ do you have any English books/ newspapers?	¿tienen libros/ periódicos ingleses?	"tee-enen leebros/ pereeodeekos eengleses"
to enjoy	disfrutar	"deesfrootar"
▷ I enjoyed the tour	me gustó la visita	"me goosto la beeseeta"
▷ I enjoy swimming	me gusta nadar	"me goosta nadar"
▷ enjoy your meal!	¡que aproveche!	"ke aprobeche"
enough	bastante	"bastante"
enquiry desk	el mostrador de informacíon	"mostrador de eenformatheeon"
entertainment:		
▷ what entertainment is there?	¿qué diversiones hay?	"ke diberseeones aee"
entertainments	las diversiones	"deeberseeones"
entrance	la entrada	"entrada"
entrance fee	la entrada	"entrada"
entry visa	el visado de entrada	"beesado de entrada"
▷ I have an entry visa	tengo un visado de entrada	"tengo oon beesado de entrada"
envelope	el sobre	"sobre"
epileptic	epiléptico epiléptica	"epeelepteeko" "epeelepteeka"
equipment	el equipo	"ekeepo"
▷ can we rent the equipment?	¿podemos alquilar el equipo?	"podemos alkeelar el ekeepo"
escalator	la escalera mecánica	"eskalera mekaneeka"
especially	especialmente	"espetheealmente"
essential	imprescindible	"eemprestheendeeble"

ABSOLUTE ESSENTIALS

I would like ...	me gustaría ...	"me goostareea"
I need ...	necesito ...	"netheseeto"
where is ...?	¿dónde está ...?	"donde esta"
I'm looking for ...	estoy buscando ...	"estoee booskando"

Eurocheque	el Eurocheque	"eooro**che**ke"
▷ **do you take Eurocheques?**	¿aceptan Eurocheques?	"a**thep**tan eooro**che**kes"
Europe	Europa	"eoo**ro**pa"
European	europeo	"eooro**pe**o"
	europea	"eooro**pe**a"
European Community	la Comunidad Europea	"komoonee**dad** eooro**pe**a"
evening	la tarde	"**tar**de"
▷ **in the evening**	por la tarde	"por la **tar**de"
▷ **what is there to do in the evenings?**	¿qué se puede hacer por las noches?	"ke se **pwe**de a**ther** por las **no**ches"
▷ **what are you doing this evening?**	¿qué haces esta noche?	"ke a**thes es**ta **no**che"
▷ **an evening meal**	una cena	"**oo**na **the**na"
evening meal	la cena	"**the**na"
every	cada	"**ka**da"
everyone	todo el mundo	"**to**do el **moon**do"
everything	todo	"**to**do"
excellent	excelente	"eksthe**len**te"
▷ **the meal was excellent**	la comida estaba riquísima	"la ko**mee**da es**ta**ba ree**kee**seema"
except	salvo	"**sal**bo"
	excepto	"eks**thep**to"
excess luggage	el exceso de equipaje	"eks**the**so de ekee**pa**khe"
exchange[1] *n*	el cambio	"**kam**beeo"
to **exchange**[2] *vb*	cambiar	"kambee**ar**"
▷ **could I exchange this please?**	por favor, ¿podría cambiar esto?	"por fa**bor** po**dree**a kambee**ar es**to"

ABSOLUTE ESSENTIALS

do you have ...?	¿tiene ...?	"tee-**e**ne"
is there ...?	¿hay ...?	"**aee**"
are there ...?	¿hay ...?	"**aee**"
how much is ...?	¿cuánto cuesta ...?	"**kwan**to **kwes**ta"

exchange rate	el tipo de cambio	"**tee**po de **kam**beeo"
▷ **what is the exchange rate?**	¿cuál es el tipo de cambio?	"kwal es el **tee**po de **kam**beeo"
excursion	la excursión	"ekskoorsee**on**"
▷ **what excursions are there?**	¿qué excursiones hay?	"ke ekskoorsee**o**nes **a**ee"
to excuse	perdonar	"perdo**nar**"
▷ **excuse me!** (sorry)	¡perdón!	"per**don**"
(when passing)	¡disculpe!	"dees**kool**pe"
exhaust pipe	el tubo de escape	"**too**bo de es**ka**pe"
exhibition	la exposición	"eksposeethee**on**"
exit	la salida	"sa**lee**da"
▷ **where is the exit?**	¿dónde está la salida?	"**don**de es**ta** la sa**lee**da"
▷ **which exit for ...?**	¿cuál es la salida para ...?	"kwal es la sa**lee**da **pa**ra"
expensive	caro	"**ka**ro"
	cara	"**ka**ra"
▷ **I want something more expensive**	quiero algo más caro	"kee-**e**ro **al**go mas **ka**ro"
▷ **it's too expensive**	es demasiado caro	"es demasee**a**do **ka**ro"
expert	el experto	"eks**per**to"
	la experta	"eks**per**ta"
to expire (ticket, passport)	caducar	"kadoo**kar**"
express¹ n (train)	el rápido	"**ra**peedo"
express² adj:		
▷ **to send a letter express**	enviar una carta por correo urgente	"embee**ar** **oo**na **kar**ta por kor**re**o oor**khen**te"
extra (spare)	de sobra	"de **so**bra"
(more)	adicional	"adeethee**o**nal"
eye	el ojo	"**o**kho"

ABSOLUTE ESSENTIALS		
yes (please)	sí (por favor)	"see (por fa**bor**)"
no (thank you)	no (gracias)	"no (**gra**theeas)"
hello	hola	"**o**la"
goodbye	adiós	"adee**os**"

▷ I have something in my eye	tengo algo en el ojo	"**ten**go **al**go en el **o**kho"
eye liner	el rímel	"**ree**mel"
eye shadow	la sombra de ojos	"**som**bra de **o**khos"
face	la cara	"**ka**ra"
face cream	la crema facial	"**kre**ma fath**ee**al"
facilities	las instalaciones	"eenstalath**ee**ones"
▷ do you have any facilities for the disabled?	¿tienen ustedes instalaciones especiales para los minusválidos?	"tee-**e**nen eenstalath**ee**ones espeth**ee**ales **pa**ra los meenoos**ba**leedos"
▷ what facilities do you have here?	¿qué servicios tienen aquí?	"ke ser**bee**theeos tee-**e**nen a**kee**"
▷ do you have facilities for children?	¿tienen instalaciones para niños?	"tee-**e**nen eenstalath**ee**ones **pa**ra **nee**nyos"
▷ are there facilities for mothers with babies?	¿hay alguna sala para madres con bebés?	"**a**ee al**goo**na **sa**la **pa**ra **ma**dres kon be**bes**"
▷ what sports facilities are there?	¿qué instalaciones deportivas tienen?	"ke eenstalath**ee**ones depor**tee**bas tee-**e**nen"
factor:		
▷ factor 8/15 suntan lotion	la loción bronceadora del factor 8/15	"la loth**ee**on bronthea**do**ra del fak**tor o**cho al **keen**the"
factory	la fábrica	"**fa**breeka"
▷ I work in a factory	trabajo en una fábrica	"tra**ba**kho en **oo**na **fa**breeka"
to faint	desmayarse	"desma**yar**se"
▷ she has fainted	se ha desmayado	"se a desma**ya**do"
fair (fun fair)	el parque de atracciones	"**par**ke de atrakth**ee**ones"
to fall	caer	"ka**er**"

ABSOLUTE ESSENTIALS

I don't understand	no comprendo	"no kom**pren**do"
I don't speak Spanish	no hablo español	"no **a**blo espan**yol**"
do you speak English?	¿habla inglés?	"**a**bla een**gles**"
could you help me?	¿podría ayudarme?	"po**dree**a ayoo**dar**me"

family	la familia	"fa**mee**leea"
famous	famoso	"fa**mo**so"
	famosa	"fa**mo**sa"
fan (*electric*)	el ventilador	"benteela**dor**"
(*paper*)	el abanico	"aba**neek**o"
fan belt	la correa del ventilador	"ko**rrea** del benteela**dor**"
far	lejos	"**lek**hos"
▷ **how far is it to ...?**	¿a qué distancia está ...?	"a ke dees**tan**theea es**ta**"
▷ **is it far?**	¿está lejos?	"esta **lek**hos"
fare	el precio del billete	"**pre**theeo del bee**ye**te"
▷ **what is the fare to the town centre?**	¿cuánto cuesta para ir al centro?	"**kwan**to **kwes**ta **pa**ra eer al **then**tro"
farm	la granja	"**gran**kha"
farmhouse	la granja	"**gran**kha"
fast	rápido	"**ra**peedo"
	rápida	"**ra**peeda"
▷ **he was driving too fast**	iba demasiado rápido	"**ee**ba demasee**a**do **ra**peedo"
fast food	la comida rápida	"ko**mee**da **ra**peeda"
fat	gordo	"**gor**do"
	gorda	"**gor**da"
father	el padre	"**pa**dre"
fault	la culpa	"**kool**pa"
▷ **it wasn't my fault**	no fue culpa mía	"no fwe **kool**pa **mee**a"
favourite	favorito	"fabo**ree**to"
	favorita	"fabo**ree**ta"
▷ **what's your favourite drink?**	¿cuál es tu bebida favorita?	"kwal es too be**bee**da fabo**ree**ta"
fax	el fax	"faks"

ABSOLUTE ESSENTIALS		
I would like ...	me gustaría ...	"me goosta**ree**a"
I need ...	necesito ...	"nethe**see**to"
where is ...?	¿dónde está ...?	"**don**de es**ta**"
I'm looking for ...	estoy buscando ...	"es**toee** boos**kan**do"

▷ **can I send a fax from here?**	¿puedo enviar un fax desde aquí?	"**pwe**do enbee**ar** oon faks **des**de a**kee**"
▷ **what is the fax number?**	¿cuál es el número de fax?	"kwal es el **noo**mero de faks"
February	febrero	"fe**bre**ro"
to feed	dar de comer a	"dar de ko**mer** a"
▷ **where can I feed the baby?**	¿dónde puedo dar de comer al niño?	"**don**de **pwe**do dar de ko**mer** al **nee**nyo"
to feel	sentir	"sen**teer**"
▷ **I don't feel well**	no me siento bien	"no me see-**en**to bee-**en**"
▷ **I feel sick**	estoy mareado	"es**toe**e mareado"
ferry	el transbordador	"transborda**dor**"
festival	el festival	"festee**bal**"
to fetch (*bring*) (*go and get*)	traer ir a buscar	"tra**er**" "eer a boos**car**"
fever	la fiebre	"fee-**e**bre"
▷ **he has a fever**	tiene fiebre	"tee-**e**ne fee-**e**bre"
few	pocos pocas	"**po**kos" "**po**kas"
▷ **a few**	algunos algunas	"al**goo**nos" "al**goo**nas"
fiancé(e)	el novio la novia	"**no**beeo" "**no**beea"
field	el campo	"**kam**po"
fifteen	quince	"**kween**the"
fifty	cincuenta	"theen**kwen**ta"
to fill	llenar	"ye**nar**"
to fill up (*container*)	llenar	"ye**nar**"
▷ **fill it up, please**	lleno, por favor	"**ye**no por fa**bor**"

ABSOLUTE ESSENTIALS

do you have ...?	¿tiene ...?	"tee-**e**ne"
is there ...?	¿hay ...?	"**aee**"
are there ...?	¿hay ...?	"**aee**"
how much is ...?	¿cuánto cuesta ...?	"**kwan**to **kwes**ta"

fillet	el filete	"feel**e**te"
filling	el empaste	"emp**as**te"
▷ **a filling has come out**	se me ha caído un empaste	"se me a ka**ee**do oon emp**as**te"
▷ **could you do a temporary filling?**	¿puede hacerme un empaste provisional?	"**pwe**de ath**er**me oon emp**as**te probeeseeo**nal**"
film (*in cinema*)	la película	"pel**ee**koola"
(*for camera*)	el carrete	"karr**e**te"
▷ **can you develop this film?**	¿puede revelar este carrete?	"**pwe**de rebel**ar es**te karr**e**te"
▷ **the film has jammed**	el carrete se he atascado	"el karr**e**te se aatas**ka**do"
▷ **I need a colour/black and white film for this camera**	necesito un carrete en color/en blanco y negro para esta cámara	"nethe**see**to oon karr**e**te en kol**or**/en **blan**ko ee **ne**gro para **es**ta **ka**mara"
▷ **which film is on at the cinema?**	¿qué película ponen en el cine?	"ke pel**ee**koola **po**nen en el **thee**ne"
▷ **am I allowed to film here?**	¿se me permite rodar aquí?	"se me perm**ee**te rod**ar** ak**ee**"
filter	el filtro	"**feel**tro"
filter coffee	el café de filtro	"el kaf**e** de **feel**tro"
filter-tipped	con filtro	"kon **feel**tro"
fine[1] *n*:		
▷ **how much is the fine?**	¿cuánto es la multa?	"**kwan**to es la **mool**ta"
fine[2] *adj*:		
▷ **is it going to be fine?**	¿va a hacer buen tiempo?	"ba a ath**er** bwen tee-**em**po"
to finish	acabar	"aka**bar**"
▷ **when does the show finish?**	¿cuándo termina el espectáculo?	"**kwan**do term**ee**na el espekt**a**koolo"

ABSOLUTE ESSENTIALS		
yes (please)	sí (por favor)	"see (por fa**bor**)"
no (thank you)	no (gracias)	"no (**grath**eeas)"
hello	hola	"**o**la"
goodbye	adiós	"ade**os**"

▷ when will you have finished?	¿cuándo habrá terminado?	"**kwan**do a**bra** termee**na**do"
fire	el fuego	"**fwe**go"
▷ fire!	¡fuego!	"**fwe**go"
fire brigade	los bomberos	"bom**be**ros"
fire extinguisher	el extintor	"eksteen**tor**"
firework display	los fuegos artificiales	"**fwe**gos arteefee**thee**ales"
fireworks	los fuegos artificiales	"**fwe**gos arteefee**thee**ales"
first	primero primera	"pree**me**ro" "pree**me**ra"
first aid	los primeros auxilios	"pree**me**ros owk**see**leeos"
first class	de primera clase	"de pree**me**ra **kla**se"
▷ a first class return to ...	un billete de ida y vuelta en primera a ...	"oon bee**ye**te de **ee**da ee **bwel**ta en pree**me**ra a"
first floor	el primer piso	"pree**mer pee**so"
first name	el nombre de pila	"**nom**bre de **pee**la"
fish¹ *n*	el pescado	"pes**ka**do"
to fish² *vb*	pescar	"pes**kar**"
▷ can we fish here?	¿se puede pescar aquí?	"se **pwe**de pes**kar** a**kee**"
▷ can we go fishing?	¿se puede ir a pescar?	"se **pwe**de eer a pes**kar**"
▷ where can I go fishing?	¿dónde se puede ir a pescar?	"**don**de se **pwe**de eer a pes**kar**"
fishing rod	la caña de pescar	"la **ka**nya de pes**kar**"
fit¹ *n* (*medical*)	el acceso el ataque	"ak**the**so" "a**ta**ke"
to fit² *vb* (*clothes*)	estar bien	"es**tar** bee-**en**"
▷ this dress doesn't fit me	este vestido no me está bien	"**es**te bes**tee**do no me esta bee-**en**"
five	cinco	"**theen**ko"

ABSOLUTE ESSENTIALS

I don't understand	no comprendo	"no kom**pren**do"
I don't speak Spanish	no hablo español	"no **a**blo espan**yol**"
do you speak English?	¿habla inglés?	"**a**bla een**gles**"
could you help me?	¿podría ayudarme?	"po**dree**a ayoo**dar**me"

to fix	arreglar	"arre**glar**"
▷ **where can I get this fixed?**	¿dónde me pueden arreglar esto?	"**don**de me **pwe**den arre**glar es**to"
fizzy	gaseoso	"gase**o**so"
	gaseosa	"gase**o**sa"
▷ **a fizzy drink**	un refresco con gas	"oon re**fres**ko kon gas"
flash	el flash	"flash"
▷ **the flash is not working**	el flash no funciona	"el flash no foon**thee**ona"
flask	el frasco	"**fras**ko"
▷ **a flask of coffee**	un frasco de café	"oon **fras**ko de ka**fe**"
flat (*apartment*)	el apartamento	"aparta**men**to"
flat tyre	la rueda pinchada	"**rwe**da peen**cha**da"
flavour	el sabor	"sa**bor**"
▷ **what flavours do you have?**	¿qué sabores tiene?	"ke sa**bo**res tee-**e**ne"
flight	el vuelo	"**bwe**lo"
▷ **are there any cheap flights?**	¿hay algún vuelo barato?	"**a**ee al**goon bwe**lo ba**ra**to?"
▷ **I've missed my flight**	he perdido el vuelo	"e per**dee**do el **bwe**lo"
▷ **my flight has been delayed**	han retrasado mi vuelo	"an retra**sa**do mee**bwe**lo"
flint	el pedernal	"peder**nal**"
flippers	las aletas	"a**le**tas"
flooded	inundado	"eenoon**da**do"
	inundada	"eenoon**da**da"
▷ **the bathroom is flooded**	el cuarto de baño se ha inundado	"el **kwar**to de **ba**nyo se a eenoon**da**do"
floor (*of building*)	el piso	"**pee**so"
(*of room*)	el suelo	"**swe**lo"
▷ **what floor is it on?**	¿en qué piso está?	"en ke **pee**so es**ta**"

ABSOLUTE ESSENTIALS

I would like ...	me gustaría ...	"me goosta**ree**a"
I need ...	necesito ...	"nethe**see**to"
where is ...?	¿dónde está ...?	"**don**de es**ta**"
I'm looking for ...	estoy buscando ...	"es**to**ee boos**kan**do"

▷ **on the top floor** | en el último piso | "en el **ool**teemo **pee**so"

flour | la harina | "a**ree**na"
▷ **plain flour** | la harina común | "a**ree**na ko**moon**"
▷ **self-raising flour** | la harina con levadura | "a**ree**na kon leba**doo**ra"
▷ **wholemeal flour** | la harina integral | "a**ree**na eente**gral**"

flowers | las flores | "**flo**res"
▷ **a bunch of flowers** | un ramo de flores | "oon **ra**mo de **flo**res"

flu | la gripe | "**gree**pe"
▷ **I've got flu** | tengo gripe | "**ten**go **gree**pe"

to **flush**:
▷ **the toilet won't flush** | la cisterna del wáter no funciona | "la thees**ter**na del **ba**ter no foonthee**o**na"

fly¹ *n (insect)* | la mosca | "**mos**ka"
to **fly**² *vb* | volar | "bo**lar**"

flying:
▷ **I hate flying** | no soporto volar | "no so**por**to bo**lar**"

fly sheet | el doble techo | "**do**ble **te**cho"

foggy *(day)* | nebuloso nebulosa | "neboo**lo**so" "neboo**lo**sa"
▷ **it's foggy** | hay niebla | "**a**ee nee-**e**bla"

to **follow** | seguir | "se**geer**"
▷ **follow me** | síganme | "**see**ganme"

food | el alimento | "alee**men**to"
▷ **where is the food department?** | ¿dónde está la sección de alimentación? | "**don**de esta la sekthee**on** de aleementathee**on**"

food poisoning | la intoxicación por alimentos | "eentokseekathee**on** por alee**men**tos"

foot *(measure: metric equiv = 0.30m)* | el pie el pie | "pee-**e**" "pee-**e**"

ABSOLUTE ESSENTIALS
do you have ...?	¿tiene ...?	"tee-**ene**"
is there ...?	¿hay ...?	"**a**ee"
are there ...?	¿hay ...?	"**a**ee"
how much is ...?	¿cuánto cuesta ...?	"**kwan**to **kwes**ta"

football (*game*)	el fútbol	"**foot**bol"
(*ball*)	el balón de fútbol	"ba**lon** de **foot**bol"
▷ let's play football	vamos a jugar al fútbol	"**ba**mos a khoo**gar** al **foot**bol"
for (*in exchange for*)	por	"por"
▷ for you	para usted	"**pa**ra oos**ted**"
foreign	extranjero	"ekstran**khe**ro"
	extranjera	"ekstran**khe**ra"
forest	el bosque	"**bos**ke"
to forget	olvidar	"olbee**dar**"
▷ I've forgotten my passport/the key	me he olvidado el pasaporte/la llave	"me e olbee**da**do el pasa**por**te/la **ya**be"
fork	el tenedor	"tene**dor**"
(*in road*)	la bifurcación	"beefoorkathee**on**"
fortnight	quince días	"**keen**the **dee**as"
forty	cuarenta	"kwa**ren**ta"
fountain	la fuente	"**fwen**te"
four	cuatro	"**kwa**tro"
France	Francia	"**fran**theea"
free (*not occupied*)	libre	"**lee**bre"
(*costing nothing*)	gratis	"**gra**tees"
▷ I am free tomorrow morning/for lunch	mañana estoy libre/ estoy libre para comer	"man**ya**na e**stoy**ee**lee**bre/ e**sto**ee **lee**bre **pa**ra ko**mer**"
▷ is this seat free?	¿está libre este asiento?	"esta **lee**bre **es**te asee-**en**to"
freezer	el congelador	"konkhela**dor**"
French	francés	"fran**thes**"
	francesa	"fran**the**sa"
French beans	las judías verdes	"khoo**dee**as **ber**des"

ABSOLUTE ESSENTIALS		
yes (please)	sí (por favor)	"see (por fa**bor**)"
no (thank you)	no (gracias)	"no (**gra**theeas)"
hello	hola	"**o**la"
goodbye	adiós	"ade**os**"

frequent	frecuente	"fre**kwen**te"
▷ **how frequent are the buses?**	¿con qué frecuencia pasan los autobuses?	"kon ke fre**kwen**theea **pa**san los owto**boo**ses"
fresh	fresco fresca	"**fres**ko" "**fres**ka"
▷ **are the vegetables fresh or frozen?**	¿las verduras son frescas o congeladas?	"las ber**doo**ras son **fres**kas o konkhe**la**das"
fresh air	el aire fresco	"**aeere fres**ko"
fresh vegetables	las verduras frescas	"ber**doo**ras **fres**kas"
Friday	viernes	"bee-**er**nes"
fridge	el frigorífico	"freego**ree**feeko"
fried	frito frita	"**free**to" "**free**ta"
friend	el amigo la amiga	"a**mee**go" "a**mee**ga"
from	de	"de"
▷ **I want to stay 3 nights from ... till ...**	quiero quedarme 3 noches del ... al ...	"kee-**e**ro ke**dar**me tres **no**ches del ... al"
front	la parte delantera	"**par**te delan**te**ra"
▷ **in front**	delante	"de**lan**te"
frozen (*food*)	congelado congelada	"konkhe**la**do" "konkhe**la**da"
fruit	la fruta	"**froo**ta"
fruit juice	el zumo	"**thoo**mo"
fruit salad	la macedonia de frutas	"mathe**do**neea de **froo**tas"
frying pan	la sartén	"sar**ten**"
fuel	el carburante	"karboo**ran**te"
fuel pump	el surtidor de gasolina	"soortee**dor** de gaso**lee**na"

ABSOLUTE ESSENTIALS

I don't understand	no comprendo	"no kom**pren**do"
I don't speak Spanish	no hablo español	"no **ab**lo espan**yol**"
do you speak English?	¿habla inglés?	"**ab**la een**gles**"
could you help me?	¿podría ayudarme?	"po**dree**a ayoo**dar**me"

full	lleno	"**ye**no"
	llena	"**ye**na"
▷ **I'm full (up)**	estoy lleno	"**estoe ye**no"
full board	la pensión completa	"pensee**on** kom**ple**ta"
funny (_amusing_)	divertido	"deeber**tee**do"
	divertida	"deeber**tee**da"
(_strange_)	curioso	"kooree**o**so"
	curiosa	"kooree**o**sa"
fur	la piel	"pee-el"
fuse	el fusible	"foo**see**ble"
▷ **a fuse has blown**	se ha fundido un fusible	"se a foon**dee**do oon foo**see**ble"
▷ **can you mend a fuse?**	¿puede arreglar un fusible?	"**pwe**de arre**glar** oon foo**see**ble"
gallery	la galería	"gale**ree**a"
gallon (_metric equiv = 4.55 litres_)	un galón	"ga**lon**"
gambling	el juego	"**khwe**go"
game	el juego	"**khwe**go"
▷ **a game of chess**	una partida de ajedrez	"**oo**na par**tee**da de akhe**dreth**"
gammon	el jamón	"kha**mon**"
garage	el garaje	"ga**rakhe**"
▷ **can you tow me to a garage?**	¿puede remolcarme hasta un garaje?	"**pwe**de remol**kar**me **as**ta oon ga**rakhe**"
garden	el jardín	"khar**deen**"
▷ **can we visit the gardens?**	¿se pueden visitar los jardines?	"se **pwe**den beesee**tar** los khar**dee**nes"
garlic	el ajo	"**a**kho"
▷ **is there any garlic in it?**	¿tiene ajo?	"tee-ene **a**kho"

ABSOLUTE ESSENTIALS

I would like ...	me gustaría ...	"me goosta**ree**a"
I need ...	necesito ...	"nethe**see**to"
where is ...?	¿dónde está ...?	"**don**de esta"
I'm looking for ...	estoy buscando ...	"**estoe** boos**kan**do"

gas	el gas	"gas"
▷ **I can smell gas**	huele a gas	"**we**le a gas"
gas cylinder	la bombona de gas	"bom**bo**na de gas"
gear:		
▷ **first/third gear**	primera/tercera (marcha)	"pree**me**ra/ter**the**ra (**mar**cha)"
gears	los cambios	"**kam**beeos"
gentleman	el señor	"sen**yor**"
gents'	los servicios de caballeros	"ser**bee**theeos de kaba**ye**ros"
▷ **where is the gents'?**	¿dónde están los servicios de caballeros?	"**don**de es**tan** los ser**bee**theeos de kaba**ye**ros?"
genuine	auténtico auténtica	"ow**ten**teeko" "ow**ten**teeka"
German	alemán alemana	"ale**man**" "ale**man**"
German measles	la rubeola	"roobe**o**la"
Germany	Alemania	"ale**ma**neea"
to get (*obtain*) (*receive*) (*fetch*)	obtener recibir traer	"obte**ner**" "rethee**beer**" "tra**er**"
▷ **please tell me when we get to ...**	por favor, avíseme cuando lleguemos a ...	"por fa**bor** a**bee**seme **kwan**do ye**ge**mos a"
▷ **I must get there by 8 o'clock**	tengo que llegar allí antes de las 8	"**ten**go ke es**tar** a**yee** **an**tes de las **o**cho"
▷ **please get me a taxi**	llámeme a un taxi, por favor	"**ya**meme a oon **tak**see por fa**bor**"
▷ **when do we get back?**	¿cuándo volvemos?	"**kwan**do bol**be**mos"
to get into (*house*) (*vehicle*)	entrar en subir a	"en**trar** en" "soo**beer** a"
to get off (*bus etc*)	bajarse de	"ba**khar**se de"

ABSOLUTE ESSENTIALS

do you have ...?	¿tiene ...?	"tee-**e**ne"
is there ...?	¿hay ...?	"**aee**"
are there ...?	¿hay ...?	"**aee**"
how much is ...?	¿cuánto cuesta ...?	"**kwan**to **kwes**ta"

▷ **where do I get off?**	¿dónde tengo que bajarme?	"**don**de **ten**go ke ba**khar**me"
▷ **will you tell me where to get off?**	¿puede decirme dónde tengo que bajarme?	"**pwe**de de**theer**me **don**de **ten**go ke ba**khar**me"
gift	el regalo	"re**ga**lo"
gift shop	la tienda de regalos	"tee-**en**da de re**ga**los"
giftwrap	envolver con papel de regalo	"enbol**ber** kon pa**pel** de re**ga**lo"
▷ **please giftwrap it**	envuélvalo con papel de regalo, por favor	"en**bwel**balo kon pa**pel** de re**ga**lo por fa**bor**"
gin	la ginebra	"khee**ne**bra"
▷ **a gin and tonic, please**	un gin tonic, por favor	"oon yeen **to**neek por fa**bor**"
ginger	el jengibre	"khen**khee**bre"
girl	la chica	"**chee**ka"
girlfriend	la novia	"**no**beea"
to give	dar	"dar"
to give back	devolver	"debol**ber**"
to give way	ceder el paso	"the**der** el **pa**so"
▷ **he did not give way**	no cedió el paso	"no thede**o** el **pa**so"
glass (for drinking) (for wine) (substance)	el vaso la copa el vidrio	"**ba**so" "**ko**pa" "**bee**dreeo"
▷ **a glass of lemonade, please**	una limonada, por favor	"**oo**na leemo**na**da por fa**bor**"
▷ **broken glass**	cristales rotos	"krees**ta**les **ro**tos"
glasses	las gafas	"**ga**fas"
▷ **can you repair my glasses?**	¿puede arreglarme las gafas?	"**pwe**de arre**glar**me las **ga**fas"
gloves	los guantes	"**gwan**tes"

ABSOLUTE ESSENTIALS

yes (please)	sí (por favor)	"see (por fa**bor**)"
no (thank you)	no (gracias)	"no (**gra**theeas)"
hello	hola	"**o**la"
goodbye	adiós	"adee**os**"

glucose	la glucosa	"gloo**ko**sa"
glue	la cola	"**ko**la"
gluten	el gluten	"**gloo**ten"
to **go**	ir	"eer"

I go	voy	"boy"
you go (*informal singular*)	vas	"bas"
(*formal singular*)	va	"ba"
(*plural*)	vais	"ba-**ees**"
he/she/it goes	va	"ba"
we go	vamos	"**ba**mos"
they go	van	"ban"

▷ **I'm going to the beach** me voy a la playa "me **bo**ee a la **pla**ya"
▷ **you go on ahead** sigue tú "**see**ge too"

to **go back**	volver	"bol**ber**"
▷ **I must go back now**	tengo que volver ahora	"**ten**go ke bol**ber** a**o**ra"
to **go down** (*downstairs etc*)	bajar	"ba**khar**"
to **go in**	entrar (en)	"ent**rar** (en)"
to **go out** (*leave*)	salir	"sa**leer**"
goggles (*for swimming*)	las gafas de bucear	"**ga**fas de boothe**ar**"
(*for skiing*)	las gafas de esquí	"**ga**fas de es**kee**"
gold	el oro	"**o**ro"
gold-plated	chapado en oro	"cha**pa**do en **o**ro"
	chapada en oro	"cha**pa**da en **o**ro"
golf	el golf	"golf"
▷ **where can we play golf?**	¿dónde se puede jugar al golf?	"**don**de se **pwe**de khoo**gar** al golf"
golf ball	la pelota de golf	"pe**lo**ta de golf"

ABSOLUTE ESSENTIALS

I don't understand	no comprendo	"no kom**pren**do"
I don't speak Spanish	no hablo español	"no **ab**lo espan**yol**"
do you speak English?	¿habla inglés?	"**ab**la een**gles**"
could you help me?	¿podría ayudarme?	"pod**ree**a ayoo**dar**me"

golf club (*stick*)	el palo de golf	"**pa**lo de golf"
(*association*)	el club de golf	"**kloob** de golf"
golf course	el campo de golf	"**kam**po de golf"
▷ **is there a public golf course near here?**	¿hay algún campo municipal de golf por aquí?	"**aee** al**goon kam**po mooneethee**pal** de golf por a**kee**"
good	bueno	"**bwe**no"
	buena	"**bwe**na"
good afternoon	¡buenas tardes!	"**bwe**nas **tar**des"
goodbye	¡adiós!	"adee**os**"
good evening	¡buenas tardes!	"**bwe**nas **tar**des"
Good Friday	el Viernes Santo	"bee-**er**nes **san**to"
good-looking	guapo	"**gwa**po"
	guapa	"**gwa**pa"
good morning	¡buenos días!	"**bwe**nos **dee**as"
good night	¡buenas noches!	"**bwe**nas **no**ches"
goose	el ganso	"**gan**so"
	la gansa	"**gan**sa"
gram	el gramo	"**gra**mo"
▷ **500 grams of mince meat**	500 gramos de carne picada	"keenee-**en**tos **gra**mos de **kar**ne pee**ka**da"
grandfather	el abuelo	"a**bwe**lo"
grandmother	la abuela	"a**bwe**la"
grapefruit	el pomelo	"po**me**lo"
grapefruit juice	el zumo de pomelo	"**thoo**mo de po**me**lo"
grapes	las uvas	"**oo**bas"
▷ **a bunch of grapes**	un racimo de uvas	"oon ra**thee**mo de **oo**bas"
▷ **seedless grapes**	las uvas sin pepitas	"**oo**bas seen pe**pee**tas"
grass	la hierba	"ee-**er**ba"

ABSOLUTE ESSENTIALS		
I would like ...	me gustaría ...	"me goosta**ree**a"
I need ...	necesito ...	"nethe**see**to"
where is ...?	¿dónde está ...?	"**don**de esta"
I'm looking for ...	estoy buscando ...	"estoee boos**kan**do"

gravy	la salsa	"**sal**sa"
greasy	grasiento	"grasee-**en**to"
	grasienta	"grasee- **en**ta"
▷ the food is very greasy	la comida tiene mucha grasa	"la ko**mee**da tee-**e**ne **moo**cha **gra**sa"
▷ shampoo for greasy hair	champú para cabello graso	"cham**poo** **pa**ra ca**be**yo **gra**so"
Greece	Grecia	"**gre**theea"
Greek	griego	"gree-**e**go"
	griega	"gree-**e**ga"
green	verde	"**ber**de"
green card	la carta verde	"**kar**ta **ber**de"
green pepper	el pimiento verde	"peemee-**en**to **ber**de"
grey	gris	"grees"
grilled	a la parrilla	"a la pa**rree**ya"
grocer's	la tienda de ultramarinos	"tee-**en**da de ooltrama**ree**nos"
ground	el suelo	"**swe**lo"
ground floor	la planta baja	"**plan**ta **ba**kha"
▷ could I have a room on the ground floor?	¿tiene una habitación en la planta baja?	"tee-**e**ne **oo**na abeetathee**on** en la **plan**ta **ba**kha"
groundsheet	la tela impermeable	"**te**la eempermea**ble**"
group	el grupo	"**groo**po"
▷ do you give discounts for groups?	¿hacen descuento por grupos?	"**a**then des**kwen**to por **groo**pos"
group passport	el pasaporte de grupo	"el pasa**por**te de **groo**po"
guarantee	la garantía	"garan**tee**a"
▷ it's still under guarantee	todavía está bajo garantía	"toda**bee**a es**ta ba**kho garan**tee**a"

ABSOLUTE ESSENTIALS

do you have ...?	¿tiene ...?	"tee-**e**ne"
is there ...?	¿hay ...?	"**aee**"
are there ...?	¿hay ...?	"**aee**"
how much is ...?	¿cuánto cuesta ...?	"**kwan**to **kwes**ta"

▷ a five-year guarantee	cinco años de garantía	"**theen**ko **a**nyos de garan**tee**a"
guard (*on train*)	el jefe de tren	"**khe**fe de **tren**"
▷ have you seen the guard?	¿ha visto al jefe de tren?	"a **bees**to al **khe**fe de tren"
guest (*house guest*)	el invitado	"eenbee**ta**do"
	la invitada	"eenbee**ta**da"
(*in hotel*)	el/la huésped	"**wes**ped"
guesthouse	la pensión	"pensee**on**"
guide[1] *n*	el/la guía	"**gee**a"
▷ is there an English-speaking guide?	¿hay un/una guía que hable inglés?	"**a**ee oon/**oo**na **gee**a ke **a**ble een**gles**"
to **guide**[2] *vb*	guiar	"gee**ar**"
guidebook	la guía turística	"**gee**a too**rees**teeka"
▷ do you have a guidebook in English?	¿tiene alguna guía turística en inglés?	"tee-**e**ne al**goo**na **gee**a too**rees**teeka en een**gles**"
▷ do you have a guidebook to the cathedral?	¿tiene alguna guía de la catedral?	"tee-**e**ne al**goo**na **gee**a de la kate**dral**"
guided tour	la visita con guía	"bee**see**ta kon **gee**a"
▷ what time does the guided tour begin?	¿a qué hora empieza la visita?	"a ke **o**ra empee-**e**tha la bee**see**ta"
gum	la encía	"en**thee**a"
▷ my gums are bleeding/sore	me sangran/duelen las encías	"me **san**gran/**dwe**len las en**thee**as"
gym	el gimnasio	"kheem**na**seeo"
gym shoes	las zapatillas	"thapa**tee**yas"
haddock	el abadejo	"aba**de**kho"
haemorrhoids	las hemorroides	"emo**rroe**edes"

ABSOLUTE ESSENTIALS		
yes (please)	sí (por favor)	"see (por fa**bor**)"
no (thank you)	no (gracias)	"no (**gra**theeas)"
hello	hola	"**o**la"
goodbye	adiós	"adee**os**"

▷ **I need something for haemorrhoids**	necesito algo para las hemorroides	"nethe**see**to algo para las emorro**ee**des"
hair	el pelo	"**pe**lo"
▷ **my hair is naturally curly/straight**	tengo el pelo rizado/liso	"**ten**go el **pe**lo ree**tha**do/**lee**so"
▷ **I have greasy/dry hair**	tengo el pelo graso/seco	"**ten**go el **pe**lo **gra**so/**se**ko"
hairbrush	el cepillo del pelo	"the**pee**yo del **pe**lo"
haircut	el corte de pelo	"**kor**te de **pe**lo"
hairdresser	el peluquero la peluquera	"peloo**ke**ro" "peloo**ke**ra"
hair dryer	el secador de pelo	"seka**dor** de **pe**lo"
hairgrip	la horquilla	"or**kee**ya"
hair spray	la laca	"**la**ka"
hake	la merluza	"mer**loo**tha"
half	medio media	"**me**deeo" "**me**deea"
▷ **a half bottle of ...**	una media botella de ...	"**oo**na **me**deea bo**te**ya de"
▷ **half past two/three**	las dos/tres y media	"las dos/tres ee **me**deea"
half board	la media pensión	"**me**deea pense**on**"
half fare	el medio billete	"**me**deeo bee**ye**te"
half-price	la mitad de precio	"mee**tad** de **pre**theeo"
ham	el jamón	"kha**mon**"
hamburger	la hamburguesa	"amboor**ge**sa"
hand	la mano	"**ma**no"
handbag	el bolso	"**bol**so"
▷ **my handbag's been stolen**	me han robado el bolso	"me an ro**ba**do el **bol**so"
handbrake	el freno de mano	"**fre**no de **ma**no"

ABSOLUTE ESSENTIALS

I don't understand	no comprendo	"no kom**pren**do"
I don't speak Spanish	no hablo español	"no **ab**lo espan**yol**"
do you speak English?	¿habla inglés?	"**ab**la een**gles**"
could you help me?	¿podría ayudarme?	"po**dree**a ayoo**dar**me"

handicap:

▷ my handicap is ...	mi hándicap es ...	"mee **khan**deekap es"
▷ what's your handicap?	¿cuál es tu hándicap?	"kwal es too **khan**deekap"

handicapped   minusválido — "meenoos**bal**eedo"
minusválida — "meenoos**bal**eeda"

handkerchief   el pañuelo — "pan**ywe**lo"

handle   el asa — "**asa**"

▷ the handle has come off   se ha caído el asa — "se a ka**ee**do el **asa**"

hand luggage   el equipaje de mano — "ekee**pa**khe de **ma**no"

handmade   hecho a mano — "**echo** a **ma**no"
hecha a mano — "**echa** a **ma**no"

▷ is this handmade?   ¿es hecho a mano? — "es **echo** a **ma**no"

hang-glider   el ala delta — "**ala del**ta"

hang-gliding:

▷ I'd like to go hang-gliding   me gustaría ir a volar en ala delta — "me goosta**ree**a eer a bo**lar** en **ala del**ta"

hangover   la resaca — "re**sa**ka"

to happen   pasar — "pa**sar**"

▷ what happened?   ¿qué pasó? — "ke pa**so**"
▷ when did it happen?   ¿cuándo pasó? — "**kwan**do pa**so**"

happy   feliz — "fe**leeth**"

▷ I'm not happy with ...   no estoy contento con ... — "no es**to**ee kon**ten**to kon"

harbour   el puerto — "**pwer**to"

hard   duro — "**doo**ro"
dura — "**doo**ra"

hat   el sombrero — "som**bre**ro"

ABSOLUTE ESSENTIALS

I would like ...	me gustaría ...	"me goosta**ree**a"
I need ...	necesito ...	"nethe**see**to"
where is ...?	¿dónde está ...?	"**don**de es**ta**"
I'm looking for ...	estoy buscando ...	"es**to**ee boos**kan**do"

to **have**	tener	"tener"

I have	tengo	"tengo"
you have (*informal singular*)	tienes	"tee-enes"
(*formal singular*)	tiene	"tee-ene"
(*plural*)	tenéis	"tene-ees"
he/she/it has	tiene	"tee-ene"
we have	tenemos	"tenemos"
they have	tienen	"tee-enen"

▷ **do you have ...?**	¿tiene ...?	"tee-ene"
hay fever	la fiebre del heno	"fee-ebre del eno"
hazelnut	la avellana	"abeyana"
he	él	"el"
head	la cabeza	"kabetha"
headache	el dolor de cabeza	"dolor de kabetha"
▷ **I want something for a headache**	quiero algo para el dolor de cabeza	"kee-ero algo para el dolor de kabetha"
▷ **I have a headache**	me duele la cabeza	"me dwele la kabetha"
headlights	los faros	"faros"
health food shop	la tienda de alimentos naturales	"tee-enda de aleementos natoorales"
to **hear**	oír	"oeer"
heart	el corazón	"korathon"
heart attack	el infarto	"eenfarto"
heart condition:		
▷ **I have a heart condition**	padezco de corazón	"padethko de korathon"
heater	el calentador	"kalentador"

ABSOLUTE ESSENTIALS

do you have ...?	¿tiene ...?	"tee-ene"
is there ...?	¿hay ...?	"aee"
are there ...?	¿hay ...?	"aee"
how much is ...?	¿cuánto cuesta ...?	"kwanto kwesta"

▷ the heater isn't working	el calentador no funciona	"el kalentador no foontheeona"
heating	la calefacción	"kalefaktheeon"
▷ I can't turn the heating off/on	no puedo apagar/ encender la calefacción	"no **pw**edo apa**gar**/ enthen**der** la kalefakthee**on**"
heavy	pesado	"pe**sa**do"
	pesada	"pe**sa**da"
▷ this is too heavy	esto pesa demasiado	"**es**to **pe**sa demasee**a**do"
hello	¡hola!	"**o**la"
(on telephone)	¡diga!	"**dee**ga"
help[1] n	la ayuda	"a**yoo**da"
▷ help!	¡socorro!	"so**ko**rro"
▷ fetch help quickly!	vaya a buscar ayuda, ¡deprisa!	"**ba**ya a boos**kar** a**yoo**da de**pree**sa"
to **help**[2] vb	ayudar	"ayoo**dar**"
▷ can you help me?	¿puede ayudarme?	"**pw**ede ayoo**dar**me"
▷ help yourself!	¡coje si quieres!	"**ko**khe see kee-**e**res"
her:		
▷ her car	su coche	"soo **ko**che"
▷ her socks	sus calcetines	"soos kalthe**tee**nes"
herb	la hierba	"ee-**er**ba"
here	aquí	"a**kee**"
▷ here you are!	¡aquí tiene!	"a**kee** tee-**e**ne"
herring	el arenque	"a**ren**ke"
hers	(el) suyo	"**soo**yo"
	(la) suya	"**soo**ya"
	(los) suyos	"**soo**yos
	(las) suyas	"**soo**yas"
high (price, number, temperature)	alto	"**al**to"
	alta	"**al**ta"
▷ how high is it?	¿qué altura tiene?	"ke al**too**ra tee-**e**ne"

ABSOLUTE ESSENTIALS		
yes (please)	sí (por favor)	"see (por fa**bor**)"
no (thank you)	no (gracias)	"no (**gra**theeas)"
hello	hola	"**o**la"
goodbye	adiós	"ade**os**"

▷ **200 metres high**	200 metros de alto	"dosthee-**en**tos **me**tros de **al**to"
high blood pressure	la tensión alta	"tensee**on al**ta"
high chair	la silla alta	"**see**ya **al**ta"
	la trona	"**tro**na"
highlights (*in hair*)	las mechas	"**me**chas"
high tide	la marea alta	"ma**re**a **al**ta"
▷ **when is high tide?**	¿cuándo hay marea alta?	"**kwan**do aee ma**re**a **al**ta"
hill	la colina	"ko**lee**na"
hill walking	el montañismo	"montan**yees**mo"
to hire	alquilar	"alkee**lar**"
▷ **I want to hire a car**	quiero alquilar un coche	"kee-**e**ro alkee**lar** oon **ko**che"
▷ **can I hire a deck chair?**	¿puedo alquilar una tumbona?	"**pwe**do alkee**lar** oona toom**bo**na"
his¹ *adj*:		
▷ **his car**	su coche	"soo **ko**che"
▷ **his socks**	sus calcetines	"soos kalthe**tee**nes"
his² *pron*	(el) suyo	"**soo**yo"
	(la) suya	"**soo**ya"
	(los) suyos	"**soo**yos"
	(las) suyas	"**soo**yas"
to hit (*person*)	pegar	"pe**gar**"
(*object*)	golpear	"golpe**ar**"
to hitchhike	hacer autostop	"a**ther** owtoe**stop**"
HIV-negative	seronegativo	"seronega**tee**bo"
	seronegativa	"seronega**tee**ba"
HIV-positive	seropositivo	"seroposee**tee**bo"
	seropositiva	"seroposee**tee**ba"
to hold	sostener	"soste**ner**"
(*contain*)	contener	"konte**ner**"

ABSOLUTE ESSENTIALS

I don't understand	no comprendo	"no kom**pren**do"
I don't speak Spanish	no hablo español	"no **ab**lo espan**yol**"
do you speak English?	¿habla inglés?	"**ab**la een**gles**"
could you help me?	¿podría ayudarme?	"po**dree**a ayoo**dar**me"

▷ **could you hold this for me?**	¿podría sostenerme esto?	"po**dree**a soste**ner**me **es**to"
hold-up (*traffic jam*)	el atasco	"a**tas**ko"
▷ **what is causing this hold-up?**	¿a qué se debe este atasco?	"a ke se **de**be **es**te a**tas**ko"
hole	el agujero	"agoo**khe**ro"
holiday (*public*)	las vacaciones la fiesta	"bakathee**o**nes" "fee-**es**ta"
▷ **on holiday**	de vacaciones	"de bakathee**o**nes"
▷ **I'm on holiday here**	estoy aquí de vacaciones	"es**to**ee a**kee** de bakathee**o**nes"
holiday resort	el centro turístico	"**then**tro too**rees**teeko"
holiday romance	el romance de vacaciones	"ro**man**the de bakathee**o**nes"
home	la casa	"**ka**sa"
▷ **when do you go home?**	¿cuándo te vas a casa?	"**kwan**do te bas a **ka**sa"
▷ **I'm going home tomorrow/on Tuesday**	me voy a casa mañana/el martes	"me **bo**ee a **ka**sa man**ya**na/el **mar**tes"
▷ **I want to go home**	quiero irme a casa	"kee-**e**ro **eer**me a **ka**sa"
homesick:		
▷ **to be homesick**	echar de menos la casa	"e**char** de **me**nos la **ka**sa"
honey	la miel	"mee-**el**"
honeymoon	la luna de miel	"**loo**na de mee-**el**"
▷ **we are on our honeymoon**	estamos de luna de miel	"es**ta**mos de **loo**na de mee-**el**"
to **hope**	esperar	"espe**rar**"
▷ **I hope so/not**	espero que sí/no	"es**pe**ro ke see/no"
hors d'oeuvre	los entremeses	"entre**me**ses"
horse	el caballo	"ka**ba**lo"

ABSOLUTE ESSENTIALS		
I would like ...	me gustaría ...	"me goosta**ree**a"
I need ...	necesito ...	"nethe**see**to"
where is ...?	¿dónde está ...?	"**don**de es**ta**"
I'm looking for ...	estoy buscando ...	"es**to**ee boos**kan**do"

horse riding	la equitación	"ekeetathee**on**"
▷ **to go horse riding**	ir a montar a caballo	"eer a mon**tar** a ca**bay**o"
hose	la manguera	"man**ge**ra"
hospital	el hospital	"ospee**tal**"
▷ **we must get him to hospital**	tenemos que llevarlo al hospital	"te**ne**mos ke ye**bar**lo al ospee**tal**"
▷ **where's the nearest hospital?**	¿dónde está el hospital más próximo?	"**don**de esta el ospee**tal** mas **prok**seemo"
hot	caliente	"kalee-**en**te"
(*spicy*)	picante	"pee**kan**te"
▷ **I'm hot**	tengo calor	"**ten**go ka**lor**"
▷ **it's hot** (*weather*)	hace mucho calor	"**a**the **moo**cho ka**lor**"
hotel	el hotel	"o**tel**"
▷ **can you recommend a (cheap) hotel?**	¿puede recomendarnos un hotel (barato)?	"**pwe**de rekomen**dar**nos oon o**tel** (ba**ra**to)"
hour	la hora	"**o**ra"
▷ **an hour ago**	hace una hora	"**a**the **oo**na **o**ra"
▷ **in 2 hours' time**	dentro de 2 horas	"**den**tro de dos **o**ras"
▷ **the journey takes 2 hours**	se tardan 2 horas en hacer el viaje	"se **tar**dan dos **o**ras en a**ther** el bee**ak**he"
house	la casa	"**ka**sa"
house wine	el vino de la casa	"**bee**no de la **ka**sa"
▷ **a bottle/carafe of house wine**	una botella/garrafa de vino de la casa	"**oo**na bo**tey**a/ga**rra**fa de **bee**no de la **ka**sa"
hovercraft	el aerodeslizador	"aerodesleetha**dor**"
▷ **we came by hovercraft**	vinimos en aerodeslizador	"bee**nee**mos en aerodesleetha**dor**"
how (*in what way*)	cómo	"**ko**mo"
▷ **how much?**	¿cuánto?	"**kwan**to"
▷ **how many?**	¿cuántos?	"**kwan**tos"
▷ **how are you?** (*informal*)	¿cómo estás?	"**ko**mo es**tas**"
(*formal*)	¿cómo está?	"**ko**mo es**ta**"

ABSOLUTE ESSENTIALS

do you have ...?	¿tiene ...?	"tee-**e**ne"
is there ...?	¿hay ...?	"**a**ee"
are there ...?	¿hay ...?	"**a**ee"
how much is ...?	¿cuánto cuesta ...?	"**kwan**to **kwes**ta"

▷ **how are you feeling now?**	¿cómo te encuentras ahora?	"**ko**mo te en**kwen**tras aora"
hundred	ciento	"thee-**en**to"
(*before noun*)	cien	"thee-**en**"
▷ **about a hundred people**	unas cien personas	"**oo**nas thee-**en** per**so**nas"
hungry:		
▷ **I am/we are hungry**	tengo/tenemos hambre	"**ten**go/te**ne**mos **am**bre"
hurry:		
▷ **I'm in a hurry**	tengo prisa	"**ten**go **pree**sa"
to hurt:		
▷ **he is hurt**	se ha hecho daño	"se a **e**cho **dan**yo"
▷ **my back hurts**	me duele la espalda	"me **dwe**le la es**pal**da"
▷ **he has hurt himself**	se ha hecho daño	"se a **e**cho **dan**yo"
▷ **he has hurt his leg/ arm**	se ha hecho daño en la pierna/el brazo	"se a **e**cho **dan**yo en la pee-**er**na/el **bra**tho"
husband	el marido	"ma**ree**do"
hydrofoil	el aerodeslizador	"aerodesleetha**dor**"
I	yo	"yo"
ice	el hielo	"ee-**e**lo"
ice cream	el helado	"e**la**do"
iced (*drink*)	con hielo	"kon ee-**e**lo"
▷ **iced coffee**	el café con hielo	"ka**fe** kon ee-**e**lo"
ice lolly	el polo	"**po**lo"
ice rink	la pista de patinaje	"**pees**ta de patee**na**khe"
ice skates	los patines	"pa**tee**nes"
ice skating	el patinaje sobre hielo	"patee**na**khe **so**bre ee-**e**lo"
▷ **can we go ice skating?**	¿podemos ir a patinar sobre hielo?	"po**de**mos eer a patee**nar so**bre ee-**e**lo"

ABSOLUTE ESSENTIALS		
yes (please)	sí (por favor)	"see (por fa**bor**)"
no (thank you)	no (gracias)	"no (**grat**heeas)"
hello	hola	"**o**la"
goodbye	adiós	"adee**os**"

icy	helado	"el**a**do"
	helada	"el**a**da"
▷ **are the roads icy?**	¿hay hielo en las carreteras?	"**a**ee ee-**e**lo en las karret**e**ras"
if	si	"see"
ignition	el encendido	"enthen**dee**do"
ill	enfermo	"en**fer**mo"
	enferma	"en**fer**ma"
immediately	inmediatamente	"eenmedeeata**men**te"
important	importante	"eempor**tan**te"
impossible	imposible	"eempo**see**ble"
in	en	"en"
inch (*metric equiv = 2.54cm*)	la pulgada	"pool**ga**da"
included	incluido	"eenkloo**ee**do"
	incluida	"eenkloo**ee**da"
▷ **is service included?**	¿va incluido el servicio?	"ba eenkloo**ee**do el ser**bee**theeo"
indicator (*on car*)	el indicador	"eendeeka**dor**"
▷ **the indicator isn't working**	el indicador no funciona	"el eendeeka**dor** no foonthee**o**na"
indigestion	la indigestión	"eendeekhestee**on**"
indoor:		
▷ **indoor swimming pool**	la piscina cubierta	"la pees**thee**na koobee-**er**ta"
▷ **indoor tennis**	el tenis en pista cubierta	"el **te**nees en **pees**ta koobee-**er**ta"
indoors	dentro	"**den**tro"
(*at home*)	en casa	"en **ka**sa"
infectious	contagioso/a	"kontakhee**o**so/a"

ABSOLUTE ESSENTIALS

I don't understand	no comprendo	"no kom**pren**do"
I don't speak Spanish	no hablo español	"no **a**blo espan**yol**"
do you speak English?	¿habla inglés?	"**a**bla een**gles**"
could you help me?	¿podría ayudarme?	"po**dree**a ayoo**dar**me"

▷ **is it infectious?**	¿es contagioso?	"es kontakhee**oso**"
information	la información	"eenformathee**on**"
▷ **I'd like some information about ...**	desearía información sobre ...	"desea**ree**a eenformathee**on so**bre"
information office	la oficina de turismo	"ofee**thee**na de too**rees**mo"
injection	la inyección	"eenyekthee**on**"
▷ **please give me an injection**	póngame una inyección, por favor	"**pon**game **oo**na eenyekthee**on** por fa**bor**"
injured	herido	"e**ree**do"
	herida	"e**ree**da"
▷ **he is seriously injured**	está gravemente herido	"esta grabe**men**te e**ree**do"
ink	la tinta	"**teen**ta"
insect	el insecto	"een**sek**to"
insect bite	la picadura	"peeka**doo**ra"
insect repellent	la loción contra insectos	"lothee**on kon**tra een**sek**tos"
inside	el interior	"eentere**eor**"
▷ **let's go inside**	vamos dentro	"**ba**mos **den**tro"
instant coffee	el café instantáneo	"ka**fe** eenstan**ta**neo"
instead of	en lugar de	"en loo**gar** de"
instructor	el instructor	"eenstrook**tor**"
	la instructora	"eenstrook**tora**"
insulin	la insulina	"eensoo**lee**na"
insurance	el seguro	"se**goo**ro"
▷ **will the insurance pay for it?**	¿lo paga el seguro?	"lo **pa**ga el se**goo**ro"

ABSOLUTE ESSENTIALS

I would like ...	me gustaría ...	"me goosta**ree**a"
I need ...	necesito ...	"nethe**see**to"
where is ...?	¿dónde está ...?	"**don**de esta"
I'm looking for ...	estoy buscando ...	"es**toee** boos**kan**do"

insurance certificate	la póliza de seguros	"**pol**eetha de se**goo**ros"
▷ **can I see your insurance certificate, please**	¿me enseña el seguro de su coche, por favor?	"me en**sen**ya el se**goo**ro de soo **ko**che por fa**bor**"
to insure	asegurar	"asegoo**rar**"
▷ **can I insure my luggage?**	¿puedo asegurar mi equipaje?	"**pwe**do asegoo**rar** mee ekee**pak**he"
interesting	interesante	"eentere**sante**"
▷ **can you suggest somewhere interesting to go?**	¿puede sugerirme un sitio interesante?	"**pwe**de sookhe**reer**me oon **see**teeo eentere**sante**"
international	internacional	"eenternathee**o**nal"
interpreter	el/la intérprete	"een**ter**prete"
▷ **could you act as an interpreter for us please?**	¿podría hacer de intérprete, por favor?	"po**dree**a a**ther** de een**ter**prete por fa**bor**"
into	en	"en"
invitation	la invitación	"eenbeetathee**on**"
to invite	invitar	"eenbee**tar**"
▷ **it's very kind of you to invite me**	muy amable de su parte al invitarme	"mwee a**ma**ble de soo **par**te al eenbee**tar**me"
invoice	la factura	"fak**too**ra"
Ireland	Irlanda	"eer**lan**da"
▷ **Northern Ireland**	Irlanda del Norte	"eer**lan**da del **nor**te"
▷ **Republic of Ireland**	la república de Irlanda	"la re**poo**bleeka de eer**lan**da"
Irish	irlandés	"eer**lan**des"
	irlandesa	"eer**lan**desa"
▷ **I'm Irish**	soy irlandés/irlandesa	"**so**ee eer**lan**des/ eer**lan**desa"

ABSOLUTE ESSENTIALS

do you have ...?	¿tiene ...?	"tee-**e**ne"
is there ...?	¿hay ...?	"aee"
are there ...?	¿hay ...?	"aee"
how much is ...?	¿cuánto cuesta ...?	"**kwan**to **kwes**ta"

iron[1] *n (for clothes)*	la plancha	"**plan**cha"
▷ **I need an iron**	necesito una plancha	"nethe**see**to oona **plan**cha"
▷ **I want to use my iron**	quiero utilizar mi plancha	"**kye**ro ooteelee**thar** mee **plan**cha"
to **iron**[2] *vb*	planchar	"plan**char**"
▷ **where can I get this skirt ironed?**	¿dónde me podrían planchar esta falda?	"**don**de me po**dree**an plan**char es**ta **fal**da"
ironmonger's	la ferretería	"ferrete**ree**a"
is	es	"es"
	está	"es**ta**"
▷ **the house is quite big**	la casa es bastante grande	"la **ka**sa es bas**tan**te **gran**de"
▷ **the milk is in the fridge**	la leche está en el frigorífico	"la **le**che es**ta** en el freego**ree**feeko"
island	la isla	"**ees**la"
it	lo	"lo"
	la	"la"
Italian	italiano	"eetalee**a**no"
	italiana	"eetalee**a**na"
Italy	Italia	"ee**ta**leea"
to **itch**	picar	"pee**kar**"
▷ **my leg itches**	me pica la pierna	"me **pee**ka la pee-**er**na"
jack *(for car)*	el gato	"**ga**to"
jacket	la chaqueta	"cha**ke**ta"
jam *(food)*	la mermelada	"merme**la**da"
▷ **strawberry jam**	mermelada de fresa	"merme**la**da de **fre**sa"
jammed	atascado	"atas**ka**do"
	atascada	"atas**ka**da"
▷ **the drawer is jammed**	el cajón está atascado	"el ka**hon** es**ta** atas**ka**do"

ABSOLUTE ESSENTIALS		
yes (please)	sí (por favor)	"see (por fa**bor**)"
no (thank you)	no (gracias)	"no (**grat**heeas)"
hello	hola	"**o**la"
goodbye	adiós	"adee**os**"

▷ **the controls have jammed**	los mandos se han atascado	"los **man**dos se an atas**ka**do"
January	enero	"e**ne**ro"
jar (*container*)	el tarro	"**ta**rro"
▷ **a jar of coffee**	un tarro de café	"oon **ta**rro de ka**fe**"
jazz	el jazz	"yas"
jazz festival	el festival de jazz	"festee**bal** de yas"
jeans	los vaqueros	"ba**ke**ros"
jelly (*dessert*)	la gelatina	"khela**tee**na"
jellyfish	la medusa	"me**doo**sa"
▷ **I've been stung by a jellyfish**	me ha picado una medusa	"me a pee**ka**do **oo**na me**doo**sa"
jersey	el jersey	"kher**se**-ee"
jet lag	el cambio de horario	"**kam**beeo de o**ra**reeo"
▷ **I'm suffering from jet lag**	estoy bajo los efectos del cambio de horario	"es**toe**e **ba**kho los e**fek**tos del **kam**beeo de o**ra**reeo"
jet ski	la moto acuática	"la **mo**to ak**wa**teeka"
jet skiing:		
▷ **I'd like to go jet skiing**	me gustaría ir a montar en moto acuática	"me goosta**ree**a eer a mon**tar** en **mo**to ak**wa**teeka"
jeweller's	la joyería	"khoye**ree**a"
jewellery	las joyas	"**kho**yas"
▷ **I would like to put my jewellery in a safe**	quiero poner mis joyas en una caja fuerte	"kee-**e**ro po**ner** mees**kho**yas en **oo**na **ka**ha **fwe**rte"
Jewish	judío	"khoo**dee**o"
	judía	"khoo**dee**a"
job	el trabajo	"tra**ba**kho"

ABSOLUTE ESSENTIALS

I don't understand	no comprendo	"no kom**pren**do"
I don't speak Spanish	no hablo español	"no **a**blo espan**yol**"
do you speak English?	¿habla inglés?	"**a**bla een**gles**"
could you help me?	¿podría ayudarme?	"po**dree**a ayoo**dar**me"

▷ what's your job?	¿de qué trabajas?	"de ke tra**bak**has"
jog:		
▷ to go jogging	hacer footing	"a**ther foo**teen"
joke	la broma	"**bro**ma"
journey	el viaje	"bee**akhe**"
▷ how was your journey?	¿qué tal el viaje?	"ke tal el bee**akhe**"
jug	la jarra	"**khar**ra"
▷ a jug of water	una jarra de agua	"**oo**na **khar**ra de **ag**wa"
juice	el zumo	"**thoo**mo"
jump leads	los cables para cargar la batería	"**ka**bles **pa**ra kar**gar** la bate**ree**a"
junction (road)	la bifurcación	"beefoorkathee**on**"
▷ go left at the next junction	tuerza a la izquierda en la próxima bifurcación	"**twer**tha a la eethkee-**er**da en la **prok**seema beefoorkathee**on**"
July	julio	"**khoo**lyo"
June	junio	"**khoo**nyo"
just:		
▷ just two	sólo dos	"**so**lo dos"
▷ I've just arrived	acabo de llegar	"a**ka**bo de ye**gar**"
to **keep** (retain)	guardar	"gwar**dar**"
▷ keep the door locked	tenga la puerta cerrada con llave	"**ten**ga la **pwer**ta ther**ra**da kon **ya**be"
▷ may I keep it?	¿puedo quedármelo?	"**pwe**do ke**dar**melo"
▷ could you keep me a loaf of bread?	¿podría guardarme una barra de pan?	"po**dree**a gwar**dar**me **oo**na **bar**ra de pan"
▷ how long will it keep?	¿cuánto tiempo se mantendrá fresco?	"**kwan**to tee-**em**po se manten**dra fres**ko"
▷ keep to the path	siga por el camino	"**see**ga por el ka**mee**no"
kettle	el hervidor	"erbee**dor**"

ABSOLUTE ESSENTIALS

I would like ...	me gustaría ...	"me goosta**ree**a"
I need ...	necesito ...	"nethe**see**to"
where is ...?	¿dónde está ...?	"**don**de es**ta**"
I'm looking for ...	estoy buscando ...	"es**toee** boos**kan**do"

key	la llave	"**ya**be"
▷ which is the key for the front door?	¿cuál es la llave de la puerta de entrada?	"kwal es la **ya**be de la **pwer**ta de en**tra**da"
▷ I've lost my key	he perdido la llave	"e per**dee**do la **ya**be"
▷ can I have my key, please?	¿me da la llave, por favor?	"me da la **ya**be por fa**bor**"
kidneys	los riñones	"ree**nyo**nes"
kilo	el kilo	"**kee**lo"
kilometre	el kilómetro	"kee**lo**metro"
kind¹ *n (sort, type)*	la clase	"**kla**se"
	el tipo	"**tee**po"
▷ what kind of...?	¿qué tipo de ...?	"ke **tee**po de"
kind² *adj (person)*	amable	"a**ma**ble"
▷ that's very kind of you	es muy amable de su parte	"es mwee a**ma**ble de soo **par**te"
kiss	el beso	"**be**so"
kitchen	la cocina	"ko**thee**na"
knife	el cuchillo	"koo**chee**yo"
to know *(facts)*	saber	"sa**ber**"
(be aquainted with)	conocer	"kono**ther**"
▷ do you know a good place to go?	¿conoces un buen sitio?	"ko**no**thes oon bwen **see**teeo"
▷ do you know where I can ...?	¿sabes dónde puedo ...?	"**sa**bes **don**de **pwe**do"
▷ do you know Paul?	¿conoces a Paul?	"ko**no**thes a pol"
▷ do you know how to do this?	¿sabe cómo hacer esto?	"**sa**be **ko**mo a**ther es**to"
▷ I don't know	no sé	"no se"
kosher	autorizado por la ley judía	"owtoree**tha**do por la lay khoo**dee**a"
laces *(for shoes)*	los cordones	"kor**do**nes"

ABSOLUTE ESSENTIALS

do you have ...?	¿tiene ...?	"tee-**e**ne"
is there ...?	¿hay ...?	"**aee**"
are there ...?	¿hay ...?	"**aee**"
how much is ...?	¿cuánto cuesta ...?	"**kwan**to **kwes**ta"

ladder	la escalera de mano	"eska**le**ra de **ma**no"
ladies'	los servicios de señoras	"ser**bee**theeos de sen**yo**ras"
▷ where is the ladies'?	¿dónde están los servicios de señoras?	"**don**de es**tan** los ser**bee**theeos de sen**yo**ras"
lady	la señora	"sen**yo**ra"
lager	la cerveza	"ther**be**tha"
lake	el lago	"**la**go"
lamb	el cordero	"kor**de**ro"
lamp	la lámpara	"**lam**para"
▷ the lamp is not working	la lámpara no funciona	"la **lam**para no foonthee**o**na"
lane (of motorway)	el camino el carril	"ka**mee**no" "ka**rreel**"
▷ you're in the wrong lane	se ha equivocado de carril	"se a ekeebo**ka**do de ka**rreel**"
language	el idioma	"eedee**o**ma"
▷ what languages do you speak?	¿qué idiomas habla?	"ke eedee**o**mas **a**bla"
large	grande	"**gran**de"
larger	más grande	"mas **gran**de"
▷ do you have a larger one?	¿tiene uno/una más grande?	"tee-**e**ne **oo**no/**oo**na mas **gran**de"
last	último última	"**ool**teemo" "**ool**teema"
▷ last week	la semana pasada	"se**ma**na pa**sa**da"
▷ how long will it last?	¿cuánto durará?	"**kwan**to doo**ra**ra"
late	tarde	"**tar**de"
▷ the train is late	el tren lleva retraso	"el tren **ye**ba re**tra**so"

ABSOLUTE ESSENTIALS

yes (please)	sí (por favor)	"see (por fa**bor**)"
no (thank you)	no (gracias)	"no (**gra**theeas)"
hello	hola	"**o**la"
goodbye	adiós	"adee**os**"

▷ **sorry we are late**	siento mucho haber llegado tarde	"see-**en**to **moo**cho a**ber** ye**ga**do **tar**de"
▷ **we went to bed late**	nos acostamos tarde	"nos akos**ta**mos **tar**de"
▷ **late last night**	anoche, ya tarde	"a**no**che ya **tar**de"
▷ **it's too late**	es demasiado tarde	"es demasee**a**do **tar**de"
▷ **we are 10 minutes late**	llevamos 10 minutos de retraso	"ye**ba**mos dee-**eth** mee**noo**tos de re**tra**so"
later	más tarde	"mas **tar**de"
▷ **shall I come back later?**	¿vuelvo más tarde?	"**bwel**bo mas **tar**de"
▷ **see you later**	hasta luego	"**as**ta **lwe**go"
launderette	la lavandería automática	"laban**deree**a owto**ma**teeka"
laundry service	el servicio de lavandería	"ser**bee**theeo de laban**deree**a"
▷ **is there a laundry service?**	¿hay servicio de lavandería?	"**aee** ser**bee**theeo de laban**deree**a"
lavatory (*in house*) (*in public place*)	el wáter los servicios	"**ba**ter" "ser**bee**theeos"
lawyer	el abogado la abogada	"abo**ga**do" "abo**ga**da"
laxative	el laxante	"lak**san**te"
lay-by	el área de aparcamiento	"**a**rea de aparkamee-**en**to"
lead (*electric*)	el cable	"**ka**ble"
▷ **you lead the way**	guía tú el camino	"**gee**a too el ka**mee**no"
leader (*guide*)	el jefe la jefa el guía la guía	"**khe**fe" "**khe**fa" "**gee**a" "**gee**a"
leak (*of gas, liquid*) (*in roof*)	la fuga la gotera	"**foo**ga" "go**te**ra"

ABSOLUTE ESSENTIALS

I don't understand	no comprendo	"no kom**pren**do"
I don't speak Spanish	no hablo español	"no **ab**lo espan**yol**"
do you speak English?	¿habla inglés?	"**ab**la een**gles**"
could you help me?	¿podría ayudarme?	"po**dree**a ayoo**dar**me"

▷ **there is a leak in the petrol tank**	el depósito suelta gasolina	"el de**po**seeto **swel**ta gaso**lee**na"
▷ **there is a leak in the radiator**	el radiador suelta agua	"el radeea**dor swel**ta **a**gwa"
to learn	aprender	"apren**der**"
least:		
▷ **at least**	por lo menos	"por lo **me**nos"
▷ **the least expensive item**	el artículo menos caro	"el ar**tee**koolo **me**nos **ka**ro"
leather	la piel	"pee-**el**"
	el cuero	"**kwe**ro"
to leave (*leave behind*)	dejar	"de**khar**"
(*to go*)	salir	"sa**leer**"
▷ **I've been left behind**	me han dejado atrás	"me an de**kha**do a**tras**"
▷ **I left my bags in the taxi**	me dejé las bolsas en el taxi	"me de**khe** las **bol**sas en el **tak**see"
▷ **I left the keys in the car**	me dejé las llaves en el coche	"me de**khe** las **ya**bes en el **ko**che"
▷ **when does the train leave?**	¿a qué hora sale el tren?	"a ke **o**ra **sa**le el tren"
▷ **I shall be leaving tomorrow morning at 8**	salgo mañana por la mañana a los 8	"**sal**go man**ya**na por la man**ya**na a los **o**cho"
leek	el puerro	"**pwe**rro"
left:		
▷ **on/to the left**	a la izquierda	"a la eethkee-**er**da"
▷ **take the third street on the left**	coja la primera calle a la izquierda	"**ko**kha la pree**me**ra **ka**ye a la eethkee-**er**da"
left-luggage (office)	la consigna	"kon**seeg**na"
leg	la pierna	"pee-**er**na"
lemon	el limón	"lee**mon**"
lemonade	la gaseosa	"gase**o**sa"

ABSOLUTE ESSENTIALS		
I would like ...	me gustaría ...	"me goosta**ree**a"
I need ...	necesito ...	"nethe**see**to"
where is ...?	¿dónde está ...?	"**don**de esta"
I'm looking for ...	estoy buscando ...	"es**to**ee boos**kan**do"

lemon tea	el té con limón	"**te** kon lee**mon**"
to **lend**	prestar	"pres**tar**"
▷ **could you lend me some money?**	¿podrías prestarme algo de dinero?	"po**dree**as pres**tar**me **al**go de dee**ner**o"
▷ **could you lend me a towel?**	¿podrías prestarme una toalla?	"po**dree**as pres**tar**me **oo**na to**a**ya"
lens	la lentilla	"len**tee**ya"
▷ **I wear contact lenses**	uso lentillas	"**oo**so len**tee**yas"
less	menos	"**me**nos"
lesson	la clase	"**kla**se"
▷ **do you give lessons?**	¿dan clases?	"dan **kla**ses"
▷ **can we take lessons?**	¿dan clases?	"dan **kla**ses"
to **let** (*allow*)	permitir	"permee**teer**"
(*hire out*)	alquilar	"alkee**lar**"
letter	la carta	"**kar**ta"
(*of alphabet*)	la letra	"**le**tra"
▷ **how much is a letter to England?**	¿qué franqueo llevan las cartas para Inglaterra?	"ke fran**ke**o **ye**ban las **kar**tas **pa**ra eengla**terr**a"
▷ **are there any letters for me?**	¿hay alguna carta para mí?	"**aee** al**goo**na **kar**ta **pa**ra mee"
lettuce	la lechuga	"le**choo**ga"
level crossing	el paso a nivel	"**pa**so a nee**bel**"
library	la biblioteca	"beebleeo**te**ka"
licence	el permiso	"per**mee**so"
lid	la tapa	"**ta**pa"
to **lie down**	acostarse	"akos**tar**se"
lifeboat (*on ship*)	el bote salvavidas	"**bo**te salba**bee**das"
(*shore-based*)	la lancha de salvamento	"**lan**cha de salba**men**to"
▷ **call out the lifeboat!**	¡llame a la lancha de salvamento!	"**ya**me a la **lan**cha de salba**men**to"

ABSOLUTE ESSENTIALS

do you have ...?	¿tiene ...?	"tee-**en**e"
is there ...?	¿hay ...?	"**aee**"
are there ...?	¿hay ...?	"**aee**"
how much is ...?	¿cuánto cuesta ...?	"**kwan**to **kwes**ta"

lifeguard	el vigilante	"beekhee**lan**te"
	la vigilante	"beekhee**lan**te"
▷ **get the lifeguard!**	¡llame al vigilante!	"**ya**me al beekhee**lan**te"
life jacket	el chaleco salvavidas	"cha**le**ko salba**bee**das"
lift (*in hotel etc*)	el ascensor	"asthen**sor**"
▷ **is there a lift in the building?**	¿hay ascensor en el edificio?	"**aee** asthen**sor** en el edee**fee**theeo"
▷ **can you give me a lift to the garage?**	¿me lleva hasta el garaje?	"me **ye**ba **as**ta el ga**rakhe**"
lift pass (*on ski slopes*)	el forfait	"for**faee**"
light¹ *n*	la luz	"looth"
▷ **have you got a light?**	¿tiene fuego?	"tee-**ene fwe**go"
▷ **may I take it over to the light?**	¿puedo llevarlo a la luz?	"**pwe**do ye**bar**lo a la looth"
▷ **do you mind if I turn off the light?**	¿te importa si apago la luz?	"te eem**por**ta see a**pa**go la looth"
light² *adj*	claro	"**kla**ro"
	clara	"**kla**ra"
▷ **light blue/green**	azul/verde claro	"a**thool**/**ber**de **kla**ro"
light bulb	la bombilla	"bom**bee**ya"
lighter	el encendedor	"enthende**dor**"
	el mechero	"me**che**ro"
lighter fuel	el gas para encendedores	"gas **pa**ra enthende**dor**es"
like¹ *prep*	como	"**ko**mo"
▷ **like you**	como tú	"**ko**mo **too**"
▷ **like this**	así	"a**see**"
to **like**² *vb*	gustar	"goos**tar**"
▷ **I like coffee**	me gusta el café	"me **goos**ta el ka**fe**"
▷ **I would like a newspaper**	quisiera un periódico	"keesee-**era** oon pereeo**dee**ko"

ABSOLUTE ESSENTIALS		
yes (please)	sí (por favor)	"see (por fa**bor**)"
no (thank you)	no (gracias)	"no (**gra**theeas)"
hello	hola	"**ola**"
goodbye	adiós	"adee**os**"

lime (*fruit*)	la lima	"**lee**ma"
line (*row*)	la fila	"**fee**la"
(*telephone*)	la línea	"**lee**nea"
▷ **I'd like an outside line, please**	me da línea para llamar, por favor	"me da **lee**nea **pa**ra ya**mar** por fa**bor**"
▷ **the line's engaged**	está comunicando	"esta komoonee**kan**do"
▷ **it's a bad line**	está mal la línea	"esta mal la **lee**nea"
lip salve	la crema protectora para labios	"**kre**ma protek**to**ra **pa**ra **la**beeos"
lipstick	la barra de labios	"**ba**rra de **la**beeos"
liqueur	el licor	"lee**kor**"
▷ **what liqueurs do you have?**	¿qué licores tienen?	"ke lee**ko**res tee-**e**nen"
Lisbon	Lisboa	"lees**bo**a"
to **listen (to)**	escuchar	"eskoo**char**"
litre	el litro	"**lee**tro"
little:		
▷ **a little milk**	un poco de leche	"oon **po**ko de **le**che"
▷ **a little box**	una cajita	"**oo**na ka**khee**ta"
▷ **I'm a little tired**	estoy un poco cansado	"es**to**ee oon **po**ko kan**sa**do"
to **live**	vivir	"bee**beer**"
▷ **I live in London**	vivo en Londres	"**bee**bo en **lon**dres"
▷ **where do you live?**	¿dónde vive?	"**don**de **bee**be"
liver	el hígado	"**ee**gado"
living room	el cuarto de estar	"**kwar**to de es**tar**"
loaf	la barra de pan	"**ba**rra de pan"
lobby (*in hotel*)	la recepción	"retepthee**on**"
(*in theatre*)	el vestíbulo	"bes**tee**boolo"

ABSOLUTE ESSENTIALS

I don't understand	no comprendo	"no kom**pren**do"
I don't speak Spanish	no hablo español	"no **ab**lo espan**yol**"
do you speak English?	¿habla inglés?	"**ab**la een**gles**"
could you help me?	¿podría ayudarme?	"po**dree**a ayoo**dar**me"

▷ **I'll meet you in the lobby**	nos vemos en el vestíbulo	"nos **be**mos en el bes**tee**boolo"
lobster	la langosta	"lan**gos**ta"
local (*wine, speciality*)	local	"lo**kal**"
▷ **what's the local speciality?**	¿cuál es la especialidad de la zona?	"kwal es la espetheealee**dad** de la **tho**na"
▷ **I'd like to order something local**	querría algo típico de la zona	"ke**rreea al**go **tee**peeko de la **tho**na"
lock[1] *n* (*on door,box*)	la cerradura	"therra**doo**ra"
▷ **the lock is broken**	la cerradura está rota	"la therra**doo**ra es**ta ro**ta"
to **lock**[2] *vb* (*door*)	cerrar con llave	"the**rrar** kon **ya**be"
▷ **I have locked myself out of my room**	me he dejado la llave dentro de la habitación	"me e de**kha**do la **ya**be **den**tro de la abeetathee**on**"
locker (*at station*)	la taquilla la consigna automática	"ta**kee**ya" "kon**seekh**na owto**ma**teeka"
▷ **are there any luggage lockers?**	¿hay consignas automáticas para el equipaje?	"**a**ee kon**seekh**nas owto**ma**teekas **pa**ra los ekee**pa**khe"
▷ **where are the clothes lockers?**	¿dónde están las taquillas de la ropa?	"**don**de es**tan** las ta**kee**yas de la **ro**pa"
lollipop	el pirulí	"peeroo**lee**"
London	Londres	"**lon**dres"
long	largo larga	"**lar**go" "**lar**ga"
▷ **for a long time**	durante mucho tiempo	"doo**ran**te **moo**cho tee-**em**po"
▷ **how long will it take to get to ...?**	¿cuánto se tardará en llegar a ...?	"**kwan**to se tar**da**ra en ye**gar** a"
▷ **will it be long?**	¿llevará tiempo?	"yeba**ra** tee-**em**po"
▷ **how long will it be?**	¿cuánto tardará?	"**kwan**to tar**da**ra"

ABSOLUTE ESSENTIALS		
I would like ...	me gustaría ...	"me goosta**ree**a"
I need ...	necesito ...	"nethe**see**to"
where is ...?	¿dónde está ...?	"**don**de es**ta**"
I'm looking for ...	estoy buscando ...	"es**toe** boos**kan**do"

long-sighted:

▷ **I'm long-sighted**	tengo hipermetropía	"**ten**go eepermetro**pee**a"

to look   mirar   "mee**rar**"

▷ **I'm just looking**   sólo estoy mirando   "**so**lo e**sto**ee mee**ran**do"

to look after   cuidar   "kwee**dar**"

▷ **could you look after my case for a minute please?**	por favor, ¿podría cuidarme la maleta un momento?	"por fa**bor** po**dree**a kwee**dar**me la ma**le**ta oon mo**men**to"
▷ **I need someone to look after the children tonight**	necesito a alguien que me cuide a los niños esta noche	"nethe**see**to a **al**gee-en ke me **kwee**de a los **neen**yos **es**ta **no**che"

to look for   buscar   "boos**kar**"

▷ **we're looking for a hotel/an apartment**   buscamos hotel/ apartamento   "boos**ka**mos o**tel**/ aparta**men**to"

lorry   el camión   "kamee**on**"

to lose   perder   "per**der**"

lost (*object*)   perdido   "per**dee**do"
                  perdida   "per**dee**da"

▷ **I have lost my wallet**   he perdido la cartera   "e per**dee**do la kar**te**ra"

▷ **I am lost**   me he perdido   "me e per**dee**do"

▷ **my son is lost**   mi hijo se ha perdido   "mee **ee**kho se a per**dee**do"

lost property office   la oficina de objetos perdidos   "ofee**thee**na de ob**khe**tos per**dee**dos"

lot:

▷ **a lot (of)**   mucho   "**moo**cho"
               mucha   "**moo**cha"

lotion   la loción   "lothee**on**"

loud   fuerte   "**fwer**te"

▷ **it's too loud**   está demasiado fuerte   "es**ta** demasee**a**do **fwer**te"

ABSOLUTE ESSENTIALS

do you have ...?	¿tiene ...?	"tee-**e**ne"
is there ...?	¿hay ...?	"**aee**"
are there ...?	¿hay ...?	"**aee**"
how much is ...?	¿cuánto cuesta ...?	"**kwan**to **kwes**ta"

lounge (*in hotel*)   el salón   "sa**lon**"

▷ **could we have coffee in the lounge?**   ¿podemos tomar café en el salón?   "po**de**mos to**mar** kafe en el sa**lon**"

to love (*person*)   querer   "ke**rer**"

▷ **I love swimming**   me encanta nadar   "me en**kan**ta na**dar**"

▷ **I love seafood**   me encanta el marisco   "me en**kan**ta el ma**rees**ko"

lovely   precioso   "prethee**o**so"
   preciosa   "prethee**o**sa"

▷ **it's a lovely day**   hace un día estupendo   "**a**the oon **dee**a estoo**pen**do"

low   bajo   "**ba**kho"
   baja   "**ba**kha"

low tide   la marea baja   "ma**re**a **ba**kha"

lucky   afortunado   "afortoo**na**do"
   afortunada   "afortoo**na**da"

▷ **to be lucky**   tener suerte   "te**ner swer**te"

luggage   el equipaje   "ekee**pa**khe"

▷ **can you help me with my luggage, please?**   ¿puede ayudarme a llevar las maletas, por favor?   "**pwe**de ayoo**dar**me a ye**bar** las ma**le**tas por fa**bor**"

▷ **please take my luggage to a taxi**   lléveme las maletas a un taxi, por favor   "**ye**beme las ma**le**tas a oon **tak**see por fa**bor**"

▷ **I sent my luggage on in advance**   he mandado el equipaje antes   "e man**da**do el ekee**pa**khe **an**tes"

▷ **our luggage has not arrived**   nuestro equipaje no ha llegado   "**nwes**tro ekee**pa**khe no a ye**ga**do"

▷ **where do I check in my luggage?**   ¿dónde tengo que facturar el equipaje?   "**don**de **ten**go ke faktoo**rar** el ekee**pa**khe"

▷ **could you have my luggage taken up?**   ¿puede mandar que me suban el equipaje?   "**pwe**de man**dar** ke me **soo**ban el ekee**pa**khe"

▷ **please send someone to collect my luggage**   me manda a alguien que recoja mi equipaje, por favor   "me **man**da a **al**gee-en ke re**ko**ha mee ekee**pa**khe por fa**bor**"

ABSOLUTE ESSENTIALS		
yes (please)	sí (por favor)	"see (por fa**bor**)"
no (thank you)	no (gracias)	"no (**grath**eeas)"
hello	hola	"**o**la"
goodbye	adiós	"adee**os**"

luggage allowance	el límite de equipaje	"**lee**meete de ekee**pa**khe"
▷ **what's the luggage allowance?**	¿cuál es el límite de equipaje?	"kwal es el **lee**meete de ekee**pa**khe"
luggage rack (*on car, in train*)	la rejilla	"re**khee**ya"
luggage tag	la etiqueta	"etee**ke**ta"
luggage trolley	el carrito para el equipaje	"ka**rree**to **pa**ra el ekee**pa**khe"
▷ **are there any luggage trolleys?**	¿hay carritos para el equipaje?	"aee ka**rree**tos **pa**ra el ekee**pa**khe"
lunch	el almuerzo la comida	"al**mwer**tho" "ko**mee**da"
▷ **what's for lunch?**	¿qué hay de comida?	"ke aee de ko**mee**da"
Luxembourg	Luxemburgo	"looksem**boor**go"
luxury	el lujo	"**loo**kho"
macaroni	los macarrones	"maka**rro**nes"
machine	la máquina	"**ma**keena"
mackerel	la caballa	"ka**ba**ya"
madam	la señora	"sen**yo**ra"
Madrid	Madrid	"ma**dreed**"
magazine	la revista	"re**bees**ta"
▷ **do you have any English magazines?**	¿tiene alguna revista inglesa?	"tee-**e**ne al**goo**na re**bees**ta een**gle**sa"
maid (*in hotel*)	la camarera	"kama**re**ra"
▷ **when does the maid come?**	¿cuándo viene la camarera?	"**kwan**do bee-**e**ne la kama**re**ra"
main	principal	"preenthee**pal**"
▷ **the main station**	la estación principal	"la estathee**on** preenthee**pal**"

ABSOLUTE ESSENTIALS

I don't understand	no comprendo	"no kom**pren**do"
I don't speak Spanish	no hablo español	"no **ab**lo espan**yol**"
do you speak English?	¿habla inglés?	"**ab**la een**gles**"
could you help me?	¿podría ayudarme?	"po**dree**a ayoo**dar**me"

main course	el plato principal	"**pla**to preenthee**pal**"
mains (*electric*)	la red eléctrica	"red e**lek**treeka"
▷ **turn it off at the mains**	desconecte la red eléctrica	"desko**nek**te la red e**lek**treeka"
Majorca	Mallorca	"ma**yor**ka"
to **make** (*generally*)	hacer	"a**ther**"
(*meal*)	preparar	"prepa**rar**"

I make	hago	"**ah**go"
you make (*informal singular*)	haces	"**a**thes"
(*formal singular*)	hace	"**a**the"
(*plural*)	hacéis	"a**tha**ees"
he/she/it makes	hace	"**a**the"
we make	hacemos	"a**the**mos"
they make	hacen	"**a**then"

make-up	el maquillaje	"makee**ya**khe"
make-up remover	el desmaquillador	"desmakeeya**dor**"
mallet	el mazo	"**ma**tho"
man	el hombre	"**om**bre"
manager	el gerente	"khe**ren**te"
	la gerente	"khe**ren**te"
▷ **I'd like to speak to the manager**	quisiera hablar con el gerente	"keesee-**era** a**blar** kon el khe**ren**te"
many	muchos	"**moo**chos"
	muchas	"**moo**chas"
map	el mapa	"**ma**pa"
▷ **can you show me on the map?**	¿puede indicármelo en el mapa?	"**pwe**de eendee**kar**melo en el **ma**pa"
▷ **I want a street map of the city**	quiero un plano callejero	"kee-**e**ro oon **pla**no kaye**khe**ro"

ABSOLUTE ESSENTIALS

I would like ...	me gustaría ...	"me goosta**ree**a"
I need ...	necesito ...	"nethe**see**to"
where is ...?	¿dónde está ...?	"**don**de esta"
I'm looking for ...	estoy buscando ...	"es**toe**e boos**kan**do"

▷ **I need a road map of ...**	necesito un mapa de carreteras de ...	"nethe**see**to oon **ma**pa de karre**te**ras de"
▷ **where can I buy a map of the area?**	¿dónde puedo comprar un mapa de la zona?	"**don**de **pwe**do kom**prar** oon **ma**pa de la **tho**na"
March	marzo	"**mar**tho"
margarine	la margarina	"marga**ree**na"
mark (*stain*)	la mancha	"**man**cha"
market	el mercado	"mer**ka**do"
market day	el día del mercado	"**dee**a del mer**ka**do"
▷ **when is market day?**	¿qué día ponen el mercado?	"ke **dee**a **po**nen el mer**ka**do"
marmalade	la mermelada de naranjas amargas	"merme**la**da de na**ran**khas a**mar**gas"
married	casado casada	"ka**sa**do" "ka**sa**da"
marzipan	el mazapán	"matha**pan**"
mascara	el rímel	"**ree**mel"
mass (*in church*)	la misa	"**mee**sa"
▷ **when is mass?**	¿cuándo es la misa?	"**kwan**do es la **mee**sa"
matches	las cerillas	"the**ree**yas"
material (*cloth*)	la tela	"**te**la"
▷ **what is the material?**	¿qué tela es?	"ke **te**la es"
matter:		
▷ **it doesn't matter**	no importa	"no eem**por**ta"
▷ **what's the matter?**	¿qué pasa?	"ke **pa**sa"
May	mayo	"**ma**yo"
mayonnaise	la mayonesa	"mayo**ne**sa"
meal	la comida	"ko**mee**da"

ABSOLUTE ESSENTIALS		
do you have ...?	¿tiene ...?	"tee-**e**ne"
is there ...?	¿hay ...?	"**a**ee"
are there ...?	¿hay ...?	"**a**ee"
how much is ...?	¿cuánto cuesta ...?	"**kwan**to **kwes**ta"

to **mean** (*signify*)	querer decir	"ke**rer** de**theer**"
▷ **what does this mean?**	¿qué quiere decir esto?	"ke kee-**ere** de**theer esto**"
measles	el sarampión	"sarampee**on**"
to **measure**	medir	"me**deer**"
▷ **can you measure me please?**	¿puede tomarme las medidas, por favor?	"**pwe**de to**marme** las me**dee**das por fa**bor**"
meat	la carne	"**kar**ne"
▷ **I don't eat meat**	no como carne	"no **ko**mo **kar**ne"
mechanic	el mecánico	"me**ka**neeko"
▷ **can you send a mechanic?**	¿puede mandarme un mecánico?	"**pwe**de man**darme** oon me**ka**neeko"
medicine	la medicina	"medee**thee**na"
medium	mediano	"medee**ano**"
	mediana	"medee**ana**"
medium rare	medio hecho	"**me**deeo **e**cho"
	medio hecha	"**me**deeo **e**cha"
to **meet:**		
▷ **pleased to meet you**	mucho gusto	"**moo**cho **goos**to"
▷ **shall we meet afterwards?**	¿nos vemos después?	"nos **be**mos des**pwes**"
▷ **where can we meet?**	¿dónde podemos quedar?	"**don**de po**de**mos ke**dar**"
melon	el melón	"me**lon**"
member (*of club etc*)	el socio	"**so**theeo"
	la socia	"**so**theea"
▷ **do we need to be members?**	¿hace falta ser socio?	"**athe fal**ta ser **so**theeo"
men	los hombres	"**om**bres"
to **mention:**		
▷ **don't mention it**	de nada	"de **na**da"

ABSOLUTE ESSENTIALS		
yes (please)	sí (por favor)	"see (por fa**bor**)"
no (thank you)	no (gracias)	"no (**gra**theeas)"
hello	hola	"**o**la"
goodbye	adiós	"adee**os**"

menu	la carta	"**kar**ta"
▷ **may we see the menu?**	¿nos trae la carta?	"nos **tra**-ay la **kar**ta"
▷ **do you have a special menu for children?**	¿tienen un menú especial para los niños?	"tee-**en**en oon me**noo** espethee**al pa**ra los **neen**yos"
▷ **we'll have the menu at ... pesetas**	tráiganos el plato del día de ... pesetas	"**tra**eeganos el **pla**to del **dee**a de ... pe**se**tas"
meringue	el merengue	"me**ren**ge"
message	el mensaje el recado	"men**sa**khe" "re**ka**do"
▷ **can I leave a message with his secretary?**	¿puedo dejarle un recado a su secretaria?	"**pwe**do de**khar**le oon re**ka**do a soo sekre**ta**reea"
▷ **could you take a message please?**	¿podría dejarle un mensaje a usted?	"po**dree**a de**khar**le oon men**sa**khe a oos**ted**"
metal	el metal	"me**tal**"
meter	el contador	"konta**dor**"
▷ **the meter is broken**	el contador está roto	"el konta**dor** es**ta ro**to"
▷ **do you have change for the meter?**	por favor, ¿tiene cambio para el contador?	"por fa**bor** tee-**ene kam**beeo **pa**ra el konta**dor**"
metre	el metro	"**me**tro"
migraine	la jaqueca la migraña	"ha**ke**ka" "mee**gran**ya"
mile (*metric equiv = 1.60km*)	la milla	"**mee**ya"
milk	la leche	"**le**che"
▷ **skimmed milk**	la leche desnatada	"**le**che desna**ta**da"
▷ **semi-skimmed milk**	la leche semidesnatada	"**le**che semidesna**ta**da"
milkshake	el batido de leche	"ba**tee**do de **le**che"
millimetre	el milímetro	"mee**lee**metro"
million	el millón	"mee**yon**"

ABSOLUTE ESSENTIALS

I don't understand	no comprendo	"no kom**pren**do"
I don't speak Spanish	no hablo español	"no **ab**lo espan**yol**"
do you speak English?	¿habla inglés?	"**ab**la een**gles**"
could you help me?	¿podría ayudarme?	"po**dree**a ayoo**dar**me"

mince	la carne picada	"**kar**ne pee**ka**da"

to mind:

▷ do you mind?	¿le importa?	"le eem**por**ta"
▷ do you mind if ...?	¿le importa si ...?	"le eem**por**ta see"
▷ I don't mind	no me importa	"no me eem**por**ta"

mine	(el) mío	"**mee**o"
	(la) mía	"**mee**a"
	(los) míos	"**mee**os
	(las) mías	"**mee**as

| ▷ this is not mine | esto no es mío | "**es**to no es **mee**o" |

mineral water	el agua mineral	"**agwa** meene**ral**"
minimum	el mínimo	"**mee**neemo"
minister *(church)*	el pastor	"pas**tor**"
minor road	la carretera secundaria	"karre**te**ra sekoon**da**reea"
mint *(herb)*	la hierbabuena	"yerba**bwe**na"
(sweet)	el caramelo de menta	"kara**me**lo de **men**ta"
minute	el minuto	"mee**noo**to"
▷ wait a minute	espere un segundo	"es**pe**re oon se**goon**do"
mirror	el espejo	"es**pe**kho"
Miss	la señorita	"senyo**ree**ta"
to **miss** *(train etc)*	perder	"per**der**"
▷ I've missed my train	he perdido el tren	"e per**dee**do el tren"

missing:

▷ my son is missing	mi hijo ha desaparecido	"mee **ee**kho a desapare**thee**do"
▷ my handbag is missing	se me ha perdido el bolso	"me a desapare**thee**do el **bol**so"
mistake	el error	"er**ror**"
▷ there must be a mistake	debe de haber un error	"**de**be de a**ber** oon er**ror**"

ABSOLUTE ESSENTIALS

I would like ...	me gustaría ...	"me goosta**ree**a"
I need ...	necesito ...	"nethe**see**to"
where is ...?	¿dónde está ...?	"**don**de esta"
I'm looking for ...	estoy buscando ...	"es**toee** boos**kan**do"

▷ **you've made a mistake in the change**	se ha equivocado en el cambio	"se a ekeebo**ka**do en el **kam**beeo"
misty	nebuloso	"neboo**lo**so"
	nebulosa	"neboo**lo**sa"
misunderstanding	el malentendido	"malenten**dee**do"
▷ **there's been a misunderstanding**	ha habido un malentendido	"a a**bee**do oon malenten**dee**do"
modern	moderno	"mo**der**no"
	moderna	"mo**der**na"
moisturizer	la leche hidratante	"**le**che eedra**tan**te"
monastery	el monasterio	"monas**te**reeo"
Monday	lunes	"**loo**nes"
money	el dinero	"dee**ne**ro"
▷ **I have run out of money**	me he quedado sin dinero	"me e ke**da**do seen dee**ne**ro"
▷ **I have no money**	no tengo dinero	"no **ten**go dee**ne**ro"
▷ **can I borrow some money?**	¿puedes prestarme algo de dinero?	"**pwe**des pres**tar**me **al**go de dee**ne**ro"
▷ **can you arrange to have some money sent over urgently?**	¿puede hacer los trámites para que manden dinero urgentemente?	"**pwe**de a**ther** los **tra**meetes **pa**ra que **man**den dee**ne**ro oor**khen**temente"
money belt	el cinturón-monedero	"theentoo**ron** mone**de**ro"
money order	el giro postal	"**khee**ro pos**tal**"
month	el mes	"mes"
monument	el monumento	"monoo**men**to"
mop (*for floor*)	la fregona	"fre**go**na"
more	más	"mas"
▷ **more wine, please**	más vino, por favor	"mas **bee**no por fa**bor**"
morning	la mañana	"man**ya**na"

ABSOLUTE ESSENTIALS

do you have ...?	¿tiene ...?	"tee-**e**ne"
is there ...?	¿hay ...?	"**aee**"
are there ...?	¿hay ...?	"**aee**"
how much is ...?	¿cuánto cuesta ...?	"**kwan**to **kwes**ta"

▷ **in the morning**	por la mañana	"por la ma**nya**na"
mosquito	el mosquito	"mos**kee**to"
mosquito bite	la picadura de mosquito	"peeka**doo**ra de mos**kee**to"
most	el más	"mas"
	la más	"mas"
▷ **the most popular discotheque**	la discoteca más frecuentada	"la dees**ko**teka mas frekwen**ta**da"
mother	la madre	"**ma**dre"
motor	el motor	"mo**tor**"
motor boat	la lancha motora	"**lan**cha mo**to**ra"
▷ **can we rent a motor boat?**	¿podemos alquilar una motora?	"po**de**mos alkee**lar oo**na mo**to**ra"
motor cycle	la motocicleta	"mototheek**le**ta"
motorway	la autopista	"owto**pees**ta"
▷ **how do I get onto the motorway?**	¿por dónde tengo que ir para coger la autopista?	"por **don**de **ten**go ke eer **pa**ra kok**her** la owto**pees**ta"
▷ **is there a toll on this motorway?**	¿es de peaje esta autopista?	"es de pe**akhe es**ta owto**pees**ta"
mountain	la montaña	"mon**ta**nya"
mountain bike	la bicicleta de montaña	"beetheek**le**ta de mon**ta**nya"
mousse (*dessert*)	el mousse	"moos"
mouth	la boca	"**bo**ka"
to **move**	moverse	"mo**ber**se"
▷ **it isn't moving**	no se mueve	"no se **mwe**be"
▷ **he can't move**	no puede moverse	"no **pwe**de mo**ber**se"
▷ **he can't move his leg**	no puede mover la pierna	"no **pwe**de mo**ber** la pee-**er**na"
▷ **don't move him**	no le mueva	"no le **mwe**ba"

ABSOLUTE ESSENTIALS		
yes (please)	sí (por favor)	"see (por fa**bor**)"
no (thank you)	no (gracias)	"no (**grath**eeas)"
hello	hola	"**o**la"
goodbye	adiós	"adee**os**"

▷ **could you move your car please?**	¿podría mover su coche, por favor?	"po**dree**a mo**ber** soo **ko**che por fa**bor**"
Mr	el señor	"sen**yor**"
Mrs	la señora	"sen**yo**ra"
much	mucho	"**moo**cho"
▷ **it costs too much**	cuesta demasiado	"**kwes**ta demasee**a**do"
▷ **that's too much**	eso es demasiado	"eso es demasee**a**do"
▷ **there's too much ... in it**	lleva demasiado ...	"**ye**ba demasee**a**do"
muesli	el muesli	"**mwes**lee"
mumps	las paperas	"pa**pe**ras"
museum	el museo	"moo**seo**"
▷ **the museum is open in the morning/afternoon**	el museo está abierto por la mañana/tarde	"el moo**seo** esta abee-**er**to por la man**ya**na/**tar**de"
mushroom	el champiñon	"champee**nyon**"
music	la música	"**moo**seeka"
▷ **the music is too loud**	la música está demasiado alta	"la **moo**seeka esta demasee**a**do **al**ta"
Muslim	musulmán musulmana	"moosool**man**" "moosool**ma**na"
mussel	el mejillón	"mekhee**yon**"
must	tener que	"te**ner** ke"
▷ **I must make a phone call**	tengo que hacer una llamada	"**ten**go ke a**ther oo**na ya**ma**da"
mustard	la mostaza	"mos**ta**tha"
mutton	el cordero	"kor**de**ro"
my:		
▷ **my car**	mi coche	"mee **ko**che"
▷ **my socks**	mis calcetines	"mees kalthe**tee**nes"

ABSOLUTE ESSENTIALS

I don't understand	no comprendo	"no kom**pren**do"
I don't speak Spanish	no hablo español	"no **a**blo espan**yol**"
do you speak English?	¿habla inglés?	"**a**bla een**gles**"
could you help me?	¿podría ayudarme?	"po**dree**a ayoo**dar**me"

nail (*fingernail*)	la uña	"**oo**nya"
(*metal*)	el clavo	"**kla**bo"
nail file	la lima de uñas	"**lee**ma de **oo**nyas"
nail polish	el esmalte para uñas	"es**mal**te **pa**ra **oo**nyas"
nail polish remover	el quita-esmalte	"**kee**ta es**mal**te"
naked	desnudo	"des**noo**do"
	desnuda	"des**noo**da"
name	el nombre	"**nom**bre"
▷ **what's your name?**	¿cómo se llama usted?	"**ko**mo se **ya**ma oos**ted**"
▷ **my name is ...**	me llamo ...	"me **ya**mo"
napkin	la servilleta	"serbee**ye**ta"
nappy	el pañal	"pan**yal**"
narrow	estrecho	"es**tre**cho"
	estrecha	"es**tre**cha"
nationality	la nacionalidad	"natheeonalee**dad**"
navy blue	azul marino	"a**thool** ma**ree**no"
near	cerca	"**ther**ka"
▷ **near the bank/hotel**	cerca del banco/hotel	"**ther**ka del **ban**ko/o**tel**"
necessary	necesario	"nethe**sa**reeo"
	necesaria	"nethe**sa**reea"
neck	el cuello	"**kwe**yo"
necklace	el collar	"ko**yar**"
to need	necesitar	"nethesee**tar**"
▷ **I need an aspirin**	necesito una aspirina	"nethe**see**to **oo**na aspee**ree**na"
▷ **do you need anything?**	¿necesita algo?	"nethe**see**ta **al**go"
needle	la aguja	"a**goo**kha"
▷ **needle and thread**	aguja e hilo	"a**goo**kha ay **ee**lo"

ABSOLUTE ESSENTIALS		
I would like ...	me gustaría ...	"me goosta**ree**a"
I need ...	necesito ...	"nethe**see**to"
where is ...?	¿dónde está ...?	"**don**de es**ta**"
I'm looking for ...	estoy buscando ...	"es**toee** boos**kan**do"

▷ **do you have a needle and thread?**	¿tiene aguja e hilo?	"tee-ene a**goo**kha ay **ee**lo"
negative (*photography*)	el negativo	"nega**tee**bo"
neighbour	el vecino la vecina	"be**thee**no" "be**thee**na"
never	nunca	"**noon**ka"
▷ **I never drink wine**	nunca bebo vino	"**noon**ka bebo **bee**no"
▷ **I've never been to Italy**	nunca he estado en Italia	"**noon**ka ay es**ta**do en eeta**lee**a"
new	nuevo nueva	"**nwe**bo" "**nwe**ba"
news	las noticias	"no**tee**thyas"
newsagent	el vendedor de periódicos la vendedora de periódicos	"bende**dor** de peree**o**deekos" "la bende**do**ra de peree**o**deekos"
newspaper	el periódico	"peree**o**deeko"
▷ **do you have any English newspapers?**	¿tiene algún periódico inglés?	"tee-ene al**goon** peree**o**deeko een**gles**"
New Year	el Año Nuevo	"anyo **nwe**bo"
▷ **Happy New Year!**	¡feliz Año Nuevo!	"fe**leeth** anyo **nwe**bo"
New Zealand	Nueva Zelanda	"**nwe**ba the**lan**da"
next	próximo próxima	"**prok**seemo" "**prok**seema"
▷ **the next stop**	la proxima parada	"**prok**seema pa**ra**da"
▷ **next week**	la semana que viene	"la se**ma**na ke bee-ene"
▷ **when's the next bus to town?**	¿cuándo llega el próximo autobús que va a la ciudad?	"**kwan**do yega el **prok**seemo owto**boos** ke ba a la theeoo**dad**"
▷ **take the next turning on the left**	coja el próximo desvío a la izquierda	"**ko**kha el **prok**seemo des**bee**o a la eethkee-er**da**"

ABSOLUTE ESSENTIALS

do you have ...?	¿tiene ...?	"tee-ene"
is there ...?	¿hay ...?	"aee"
are there ...?	¿hay ...?	"aee"
how much is ...?	¿cuánto cuesta ...?	"kwanto kwesta"

nice *(person)*	simpático	"seem**pat**eeko"
	simpática	"seem**pat**eeka"
(place, holiday)	bonito	"bo**nee**to"
	bonita	"bo**nee**ta"
▷ we are having a nice time	nos lo estamos pasando bien	"nos lo estamos pa**san**do bee-**en**"
▷ it doesn't taste very nice	no sabe muy bien	"no **sa**be mwee bee-**en**"
▷ yes, that's very nice	sí, eso está muy bien	"see **e**so es**ta** mwee bee-**en**"
▷ nice to have met you	encantado de haberle conocido	"enkan**ta**do de a**ber**le kono**thee**do"
night	la noche	"**no**che"
▷ at night	por la noche	"por la **no**che"
▷ on Saturday night	el sábado por la noche	"el **sa**bado por la **no**che"
▷ last night	anoche	"a**no**che"
▷ tomorrow night	mañana por la noche	"man**ya**na por la **no**che"
night club	el club nocturno	"kloob nok**toor**no"
nightdress	el camisón	"kamee**son**"
nine	nueve	"**nwe**be"
nineteen	diecinueve	"dee-etheen**we**be"
ninety	noventa	"no**ben**ta"
no	no	"no"
▷ no thank you	no gracias	"no **grat**heeas"
▷ there's no coffee	no hay café	"no **a**ee ka**fe**"
nobody	nadie	"**na**dee-e"
noisy	ruidoso	"rwee**do**so"
	ruidosa	"rwee**do**sa"
▷ it's too noisy	hay demasiado ruido	"**a**ee demasee**a**do **rwee**do"
non-alcoholic	sin alcohol	"seen al**kol**"

ABSOLUTE ESSENTIALS

yes (please)	sí (por favor)	"see (por fa**bor**)"
no (thank you)	no (gracias)	"no (**grat**heeas)"
hello	hola	"**o**la"
goodbye	adiós	"adee**os**"

▷ **what non-alcoholic drinks do you have?**	¿qué bebidas sin alcohol tiene?	"ke be**bee**das seen al**kol** tee-**e**ne"
none	ninguno ninguna	"neen**goo**no" "neen**goo**na"
▷ **there's none left**	no queda	"no **ke**da"
non-smoking (*compartment*)	no fumador	"no fooma**dor**"
▷ **is this a non-smoking area?**	¿está prohibido fumar en esta zona?	"es**ta** proee**bee**do foo**mar** en **es**ta **tho**na"
▷ **I would like a seat in a non-smoking compartment**	quiero un asiento en un compartimento de no-fumador	"kee-**e**ro oon asee-**en**to en oon komparteee**men**to de no fooma**dor**"
north	el norte	"**nor**te"
Northern Ireland	Irlanda del Norte	"eer**lan**da del **nor**te"
not	no	"no"
▷ **I don't know**	no sé	"no **se**"
▷ **I am not coming**	no voy	"no **bo**ee"
note (*bank note*) (*letter*)	el billete de banco la nota	"bee**ye**te de **ban**ko" "**no**ta"
▷ **do you have change of this note?**	¿me puede cambiar este billete?	"me **pwe**de kambee**ar es**te bee**ye**te"
note pad	el bloc	"blok"
nothing	nada	"**na**da"
▷ **nothing to declare**	nada que declarar	"**na**da ke dekla**rar**"
notice (*sign*)	el letrero	"le**tre**ro"
November	noviembre	"nobee-**em**bre"
now	ahora	"a**o**ra"
number	el número	"**noo**mero"
▷ **car number**	la matrícula	"ma**tree**koola"
▷ **what's your room number?**	¿cuál es tu número de habitación?	"kwal es too **noo**mero de abeetathee**on**"

ABSOLUTE ESSENTIALS

I don't understand	no comprendo	"no kom**pren**do"
I don't speak Spanish	no hablo español	"no **a**blo espan**yol**"
do you speak English?	¿habla inglés?	"**a**bla een**gles**"
could you help me?	¿podría ayudarme?	"po**dree**a ayoo**dar**me"

▷ **what's the telephone number?**	¿cuál es el número de teléfono?	"kwal es el **noo**mero de te**le**fono"
▷ **sorry, wrong number**	lo siento, se ha equivocado de número	"lo see-**en**to se a ekeebo**ka**do de **noo**mero"
nurse	la enfermera	"enfer**me**ra"
nursery slope	la pista para principiantes	"**pees**ta **pa**ra preentheepee**an**tes"
nut (*to eat*)	la nuez	"nweth"
(*for bolt*)	la tuerca	"**twer**ka"
occasionally	de vez en cuando	"de beth en **kwan**do"
o'clock:		
▷ **at 2 o'clock**	a las 2 en punto	"a las dos en **poon**to"
▷ **it's 10 o'clock**	son las 10 en punto	"son las dee-**eth** en **poon**to"
October	octubre	"oc**too**bre"
of	de	"de"
of course	por supuesto	"por soo**pwes**to"
off (*machine etc*)	apagado apagada	"apa**ga**do" "apa**ga**da"
▷ **this meat is off**	esta carne está pasada	"esta **kar**ne esta pa**sa**da"
▷ **let me off here, please**	déjeme aquí, por favor	"**de**kheme a**kee** por fa**bor**"
▷ **the lights are off**	las luces están apagadas	"las **loo**thes es**tan** apa**ga**das"
to **offer**	ofrecer	"ofre**ther**"
office	la oficina	"ofee**thee**na"
▷ **I work in an office**	trabajo en una oficina	"tra**ba**kho en **oo**na ofee**thee**na"
often	muchas veces	"**moo**chas **be**thes"
oil	el aceite	"a**the**-eete"

ABSOLUTE ESSENTIALS

I would like ...	me gustaría ...	"me goosta**ree**a"
I need ...	necesito ...	"nethe**see**to"
where is ...?	¿dónde está ...?	"**don**de es**ta**"
I'm looking for ...	estoy buscando ...	"es**toee** boos**kan**do"

oil filter	el filtro de aceite	"**feel**tro de **a**the-eete"
ointment	el ungüento	"oong**gwen**to"
OK	de acuerdo	"de a**kwer**do"
▷ **it's OK**	vale	"**ba**le"
old	viejo	"bee-**e**kho"
	vieja	"bee-**e**kha"
▷ **how old are you?**	¿cuántos años tienes?	"**kwan**tos **a**nyos tee-**e**nes"
old-age pensioner	el pensionista	"penseeo**nees**ta"
	la pensionista	"penseeo**nees**ta"
olive oil	el aceite de oliva	"**a**the-eete de o**lee**ba"
olives	las aceitunas	"athe-ee**too**nas"
omelette	la tortilla	"tor**tee**ya"
on¹ adj (*light, TV*)	encendido	"enthen**dee**do"
	encendida	"enthen**dee**da"
(*tap*)	abierto	"abee-**er**to"
	abierta	"abee-**er**ta"
on² prep	sobre	"**sobre**"
▷ **on the table**	sobre la mesa	"**so**bre la **me**sa"
▷ **the drinks are on me**	pago yo	"**pa**go yo"
once	una vez	"**oo**na beth"
▷ **once a day/year**	una vez al año/día	"**oo**na beth al **a**nyo/**dee**a"
one	uno	"**oo**no"
	una	"**oo**na"
one-way street	la calle de dirección única	"**ka**ye de deerekthee**on oo**neeka"
onion	la cebolla	"the**bo**ya"
only	sólo	"**so**lo"
▷ **we only want 3**	sólo queremos 3	"**so**lo ke**re**mos tres"
open¹ adj	abierto/a	"abee-**er**to/a"

ABSOLUTE ESSENTIALS

do you have ...?	¿tiene ...?	"tee-**e**ne"
is there ...?	¿hay ...?	"**a**ee"
are there ...?	¿hay ...?	"**a**ee"
how much is ...?	¿cuánto cuesta ...?	"**kwan**to **kwes**ta"

▷ **are you open?**	¿está abierto	"esta abee-**er**to"
▷ **is the castle open to the public?**	¿está abierto al público el castillo?	"esta abee-**er**to al **poo**bleeko el kas**tee**yo"
to **open**[2] *vb*	abrir	"a**breer**"
▷ **what time does the museum open?**	¿a qué hora abre el museo?	"a ke **o**ra **a**bre el moo**se**o"
▷ **I can't open the window**	no puedo abrir la ventana	"no **pwe**do a**breer** la ben**ta**na"
opera	la ópera	"**o**pera"
operator	el telefonista	"telefo**nees**ta"
	la telefonista	"telefo**nees**ta"
opposite	enfrente de	"en**fren**te de"
▷ **opposite the hotel**	enfrente del hotel	"en**fren**te del o**tel**"
or	o	"o"
orange[1] *n*	la naranja	"na**ran**kha"
orange[2] *adj*	(color) naranja	"(ko**lor**) na**ran**kha"
orange juice	el zumo de naranja	"**thoo**mo de na**ran**kha"
order[1] *n*	la orden	"**or**den"
to **order**[2] *vb*	pedir	"pe**deer**"
▷ **can you order me a taxi, please?**	¿puede pedirme un taxi, por favor?	"**pwe**de pe**deer**me oon **tak**see por fa**bor**"
▷ **can I order now please?**	¿puedo pedir ahora?	"**pwe**do pe**deer** a**o**ra"
oregano	el orégano	"o**re**gano"
original	original	"oreekhee**nal**"
other	otro	"**o**tro"
	otra	"**o**tra"
▷ **the other one**	el otro	"**o**tro"
	la otra	"**o**tra"

ABSOLUTE ESSENTIALS		
yes (please)	sí (por favor)	"see (por fa**bor**)"
no (thank you)	no (gracias)	"no (**grath**eeas)"
hello	hola	"**o**la"
goodbye	adiós	"ade**os**"

▷ **do you have any others?**	¿tiene otros?	"tee-**e**ne **o**tros"
▷ **where are the others?**	¿dónde están los otros?	"**don**de est**a**n los **o**tros"
ounce (*metric equiv =* 28.35g)	la onza	"**on**tha"

our:

▷ **our car**	nuestro coche	"**nwes**tro **ko**che"
▷ **our table**	nuestra mesa	"**nwes**tra **me**sa"
▷ **our children**	nuestros hijos	"**nwes**tros **eek**hos"
▷ **our holidays**	nuestras vacaciones	"**nwes**tras bakathee**o**nes"

ours	(el) nuestro	"**nwes**tro"
	(la) nuestra	"**nwes**tra"
	(los) nuestros	"**nwes**tros"
	(las) nuestras	"**nwes**tras"

out (*light*)	apagado	"apa**ga**do"
	apagada	"apa**ga**da"
▷ **she's out**	ha salido	"a sa**lee**do"
outdoor (*pool etc*)	al aire libre	"al **ae**ere **lee**bre"
▷ **what are the outdoor activities?**	¿cuáles son las actividades al aire libre?	"**kwa**les son las akteebee**da**des al **ae**ere **lee**bre"
outside	fuera	"**fwe**ra"
▷ **let's go outside**	vamos fuera	"**ba**mos **fwe**ra"
▷ **an outside line please**	deme línea para llamar fuera, por favor	"**de**me **lee**nea **pa**ra ya**mar fwe**ra por fa**bor**"
oven	el horno	"**or**no"
over (*on top of*)	por encima de	"por en**thee**ma de"
to **overcharge** (*in bank*)	sobrecargar la cuenta	"sobrekar**gar** la **kwen**ta"
(*when shopping*)	cobrar de más	"ko**brar** de mas"
▷ **I've been overcharged**	me han cobrado de más	"me an ko**bra**do de mas"

ABSOLUTE ESSENTIALS

I don't understand	no comprendo	"no kom**pren**do"
I don't speak Spanish	no hablo español	"no **a**blo espan**yol**"
do you speak English?	¿habla inglés?	"**a**bla een**gles**"
could you help me?	¿podría ayudarme?	"po**dree**a ayoo**dar**me"

to overheat:

▷ **the engine is overheating**	el motor se recalienta	"el mo**tor** se rekalee-**en**ta"
overnight (*travel*)	por la noche	"por la **no**che"
to owe	deber	"de**ber**"
▷ **I owe you ...**	le debo ...	"le **de**bo"
▷ **what do I owe you?**	¿qué le debo?	"ke le **de**bo"
owner	el dueño	"**dwe**nyo"
	la dueña	"**dwe**nya"
▷ **could I speak to the owner please?**	¿podría hablar con el dueño, por favor?	"po**dree**a a**blar** kon el **dwe**nyo por fa**bor**"
oyster	la ostra	"**os**tra"
to pack (*luggage*)	hacer las maletas	"**ather** las ma**le**tas"
▷ **I need to pack now**	tengo que hacer las maletas ahora	"**ten**go ke **ather** las ma**le**tas a**o**ra"
package	el paquete	"pa**ke**te"
package tour	el viaje organizado	"bee**akhe** organee**tha**do"
packed lunch	el almuerzo frío	"al**mwer**tho **free**o"
packet	el paquete	"pa**ke**te"
▷ **a packet of cigarettes**	un paquete de cigarrillos	"oon pa**ke**te de theega**rree**yos"
paddling pool	el estanque de juegos para los niños	"es**tan**ke de **khwe**gos **pa**ra los **nee**nyos"
▷ **is there a paddling pool for the children?**	¿hay un estanque de juegos para los niños?	"**aee** oon es**tan**ke de **khwe**gos **pa**ra los **nee**nyos"
paid	pagado/a	"pa**ga**do/a"
pain	el dolor	"do**lor**"
▷ **I have a pain here/in my chest**	tengo un dolor aquí/en el pecho	"**ten**go oon do**lor** a**kee**/en el **pe**cho"

ABSOLUTE ESSENTIALS		
I would like ...	me gustaría ...	"me goosta**ree**a"
I need ...	necesito ...	"nethe**see**to"
where is ...?	¿dónde está ...?	"**don**de es**ta**"
I'm looking for ...	estoy buscando ...	"es**toee** boos**kan**do"

painful	doloroso	"doloroso"
	dolorosa	"dolorosa"
painkiller	el calmante	"kalmante"
painting	la pintura	"peentoora"
pair	el par	"par"
▷ **a pair of sandals**	unas sandalias	"oonas sandaleeas"
▷ **3 pairs of shoes**	3 pares de zapatos	"tres pares de thapatos"
palace	el palacio	"palatheeo"
▷ **is the palace open to the public?**	¿está abierto al público el palacio?	"esta abee-erto al poobleeko el palatheeo"
pan	la cacerola	"katherola"
pancake	la hojuela	"okhwela"
panties	las bragas	"**brag**as"
pants (*underwear*)	los calzoncillos	"kalthon**thee**yos"
paper	el papel	"papel"
paraffin	la parafina	"parafeena"
paragliding	el ala delta	"ala delta"
▷ **where can we go paragliding?**	¿dónde podemos practicar ala delta?	"donde podemos prakteekar ala delta"
parasol	la sombrilla	"sombreeya"
parcel	el paquete	"pakete"
▷ **I want to send this parcel**	quiero mandar este paquete	"kee-ero mandar este pakete"
pardon (*I didn't understand*)	¿cómo?	"komo"
▷ **I beg your pardon**	disculpe	"deeskoolpe"
parents	los padres	"padres"
Paris	París	"parees"

ABSOLUTE ESSENTIALS

do you have ...?	¿tiene ...?	"tee-ene"
is there ...?	¿hay ...?	"aee"
are there ...?	¿hay ...?	"aee"
how much is ...?	¿cuánto cuesta ...?	"kwanto kwesta"

park¹ *n*	el parque	"**park**e"
to park² *vb*	aparcar	"apar**kar**"
▷ **can we park our caravan there?**	¿podemos aparcar la caravana/roulotte allí?	"po**de**mos apar**kar** la kara**ba**na/roo**lot** a**yee**"
▷ **where can I park?**	¿dónde puedo aparcar?	"**don**de **pwe**do apar**kar**"
▷ **can I park here?**	¿se puede aparcar aquí?	"se **pwe**de apar**kar** a**kee**"
parking disc	el disco de estacionamiento	"**dees**ko de estatheeona**mee-en**to"
parsley	el perejíl	"pere**kheel**"
part	la parte	"**part**e"
party (*group*)	el grupo	"**groo**po"
(*celebration*)	la fiesta	"fee-**es**ta"
passenger	el pasajero	"pasa**khe**ro"
	la pasajera	"pasa**khe**ra"
passport	el pasaporte	"pasa**por**te"
▷ **I have forgotten my passport**	se me ha olvidado el pasaporte	"se me a olbee**da**do el pasa**por**te"
▷ **please give me my passport back**	me devuelve el pasaporte, por favor	"me de**bwel**be el pasa**por**te por fa**bor**"
▷ **my wife/husband and I have a joint passport**	mi mujer/marido y yo tenemos un pasaporte familiar	"mee moo**kher**/ma**ree**do ee yo te**ne**mos oon pasa**por**te fameelee**ar**"
▷ **the children are on this passport**	los niños están en este pasaporte	"los **neen**yos es**tan** en **es**te pasa**por**te"
▷ **my passport number is ...**	mi número de pasaporte es ...	"mee **noo**mero de pasa**por**te es"
▷ **I've lost my passport**	he perdido el pasaporte	"e per**dee**do el pasa**por**te"
▷ **my passport has been stolen**	me han robado el pasaporte	"me an ro**ba**do el pasa**por**te"
▷ **I've got a visitor's passport**	tengo un pasaporte de visitante	"**ten**go oon pasa**por**te de beesee**tan**te"
passport control	el control de pasaportes	"kon**trol** de pasa**por**tes"
pasta	la pasta	"**pas**ta"

ABSOLUTE ESSENTIALS

yes (please)	sí (por favor)	"see (por fa**bor**)"
no (thank you)	no (gracias)	"no (**grath**eeas)"
hello	hola	"**o**la"
goodbye	adiós	"adee**os**"

pastry (cake)	la pasta el pastel	"**pas**ta" "pas**tel**"
pâté	el paté	"pa**te**"
path	el camino	"ka**mee**no"
▷ **where does this path lead?**	¿a dónde lleva este camino?	"a **don**de **ye**ba **es**te ka**mee**no"
to **pay**	pagar	"pa**gar**"
▷ **do I pay now or later?**	¿pago ahora o más tarde?	"**pa**go a**o**ra o mas **tar**de"
payment	el pago	"**pa**go"
peach	el melocotón	"meloko**ton**"
peanuts	el cacahuete	"kaka**we**te"
pear	la pera	"**pe**ra"
peas	los guisantes	"gee**san**tes"
to **peel** (fruit)	pelar	"pe**lar**"
peg (for clothes) (for tent)	la pinza la estaca	"**peen**tha" "es**ta**ka"
pen	la pluma el bolígrafo	"**ploo**ma" "bo**lee**grafo"
▷ **do you have a pen I could borrow?**	¿tiene un bolígrafo para prestarme?	"tee-**e**ne oon bo**lee**grafo **pa**ra pres**tar**me"
pencil	el lápiz	"**la**peeth"
penicillin	la penicilina	"peneethee**lee**na"
▷ **I am allergic to penicillin**	soy alérgico a la penicilina	"**so**ee a**ler**kheeko a la peneethee**lee**na"
penknife	la navaja	"na**ba**kha"
pensioner	el/la pensionista	"penseeo**nees**ta"
▷ **are there reductions for pensioners?**	¿hacen descuento a los pensionistas?	"**a**then des**kwen**to a los penseeo**nees**tas"

ABSOLUTE ESSENTIALS

I don't understand	no comprendo	"no kom**pren**do"
I don't speak Spanish	no hablo español	"no **ab**lo espan**yol**"
do you speak English?	¿habla inglés?	"**ab**la een**gles**"
could you help me?	¿podría ayudarme?	"po**dree**a ayoo**dar**me"

pepper (*spice*)	la pimienta	"peemee-**en**ta"
(*vegetable*)	el pimiento	"peemee-**en**to"
per	por	"por"
▷ **per hour**	por hora	"por **o**ra"
▷ **per week**	a la semana	"a la se**ma**na"
▷ **60 miles per hour**	60 millas por hora	"se**sen**ta **mee**yas por **o**ra"
perfect	perfecto	"per**fek**to"
	perfecta	"per**fek**ta"
performance	la actuación	"aktooathee**on**"
▷ **what time does the performance begin?**	¿a qué hora empieza la actuación?	"a ke **o**ra empee-**e**tha la aktooathee**on**"
▷ **how long does the performance last?**	¿cuánto dura la actuación?	"**kwan**to **doo**ra la aktooathee**on**"
perfume	el perfume	"per**foo**me"
perhaps	tal vez	"tal beth"
period (*of time*)	el período	"per**ee**odo"
(*menstruation*)	la regla	"**reg**la"
perm	la permanente	"perma**nen**te"
▷ **my hair is permed**	tengo hecha la permanente	"**ten**go **e**cha la perma**nen**te"
permit	el permiso	"per**mee**so"
▷ **do I need a fishing permit?**	¿me hace falta la licencia de pescar?	"me **a**the **fal**ta la lee**then**theea de pes**kar**"
person	la persona	"per**so**na"
petrol	la gasolina	"gaso**lee**na"
▷ **20 litres of unleaded petrol**	veinte litros de gasolina sin plomo	"**bay**-eente **lee**tros de gaso**lee**na seen **plo**mo"
▷ **I have run out of petrol**	me he quedado sin gasolina	"me e ke**da**do seen gaso**lee**na"
petrol station	la estación de servicio	"estathee**on** de ser**bee**theeo"

<table>
<tr><td colspan="3">ABSOLUTE ESSENTIALS</td></tr>
<tr><td>I would like ...</td><td>me gustaría ...</td><td>"me goostareea"</td></tr>
<tr><td>I need ...</td><td>necesito ...</td><td>"netheseeto"</td></tr>
<tr><td>where is ...?</td><td>¿dónde está ...?</td><td>"donde esta"</td></tr>
<tr><td>I'm looking for ...</td><td>estoy buscando ...</td><td>"estoe booskando"</td></tr>
</table>

pheasant	el faisán	"fae**esan**"
to **phone**	llamar por teléfono?	"ya**mar** por te**le**fono"
▷ **can I phone from here?**	¿puedo llamar por teléfono desde aquí?	"**pwe**do ya**mar** por te**le**fono **des**de a**kee**"
phone box	la cabina telefónica	"ka**bee**na tele**fo**neeka"
phone card:		
▷ **do you sell phone cards?**	¿venden tarjetas para llamar por teléfono?	"**ben**den tar**khe**tas **pa**ra ya**mar** por te**le**fono"
to **photocopy**	fotocopiar	"fotokopee**ar**"
▷ **where can I get some photocopying done?**	¿dónde puedo hacer unas fotocopias?	"**don**de **pwe**do a**ther** **oo**nas foto**ko**peeas"
▷ **I'd like a photocopy of this please**	una fotocopia de esto, por favor	"**oo**na foto**ko**peea de **es**to por fa**bor**"
photograph	la fotografía	"fotogra**fee**a"
▷ **when will the photos be ready?**	¿para cuándo estarán las fotos?	"**pa**ra **kwan**do esta**ran** las **fo**tos"
▷ **can I take photos in here?**	¿puedo hacer fotos aquí?	"**pwe**do a**ther fo**tos a**kee**"
▷ **would you take a photo of us?**	¿podría hacernos una foto?	"po**dree**a a**ther**nos **oo**na **fo**to"
picnic	la merienda	"meree-**en**da"
▷ **a picnic lunch**	un picnic	"oon **peek**neek"
picture (*painting*)	el cuadro	"**kwa**dro"
(*photo*)	la foto	"**fo**to"
pie	la tarta	"**tar**ta"
piece	el pedazo	"pe**da**tho"
▷ **a piece of cake**	un trozo de tarta	"oon **tro**tho de **tar**ta"
pill	la píldora	"**peel**dora"
	la pastilla	"pas**tee**ya"
▷ **to be on the pill**	estar tomando la píldora	"es**tar** to**man**do la **peel**dora"

ABSOLUTE ESSENTIALS

do you have ...?	¿tiene ...?	"tee-**en**e"
is there ...?	¿hay ...?	"aee"
are there ...?	¿hay ...?	"aee"
how much is ...?	¿cuánto cuesta ...?	"**kwan**to **kwes**ta"

pillow	la almohada	"almo**a**da"
▷ **I would like an extra pillow**	¿podría darme otra almohada?	"po**dree**a **dar**me **o**tra almo**a**da"
pillowcase	la funda	"**foon**da"
pin	el alfiler	"alfee**ler**"
pineapple	la piña	"**pee**nya"
pink	rosa	"**ro**sa"
pint (*metric equiv = 0.56l*)	la pinta	"**pee**nta"
▷ **a pint of beer**	una cerveza grande	"**oo**na ther**be**tha **gran**de"
pipe	la pipa	"**pee**pa"
pipe tobacco	el tabaco en pipa	"ta**ba**ko en **pee**pa"
pistachio	el pistacho	"pees**ta**cho"
plane	el avión	"abee**on**"
▷ **my plane leaves at ...**	mi avión sale a las ...	"mee abee**on sa**le a las"
▷ **I've missed my plane**	he perdido el avión	"e per**dee**do el abee**on**"
plaster (*sticking plaster*)	el esparadrapo	"espara**dra**po"
plastic	el plástico	"**plas**teeko"
plate	el plato	"**pla**to"
platform	el andén	"an**den**"
▷ **which platform for the train to ...?**	¿cuál es el andén para el tren de ...?	"kwal es el an**den pa**ra el tren de"
play¹ *n*	la obra de teatro	"**o**bra de te**a**tro"
to **play²** *vb* (*games*) (*instrument*)	jugar tocar	"khoo**gar**" "to**kar**"
▷ **we'd like to play tennis**	nos gustaría jugar al tenis	"nos goosta**ree**a khoo**gar** al **te**nees"
playroom	el cuarto de juego	"**kwar**to de **khwe**go"
please	por favor	"por fa**bor**"

ABSOLUTE ESSENTIALS		
yes (please)	sí (por favor)	"see (por fa**bor**)"
no (thank you)	no (gracias)	"no (**gra**theeas)"
hello	hola	"**o**la"
goodbye	adiós	"adee**os**"

▷ yes, please	sí, por favor	"see por fa**bor**"
pleased	contento	"kon**ten**to"
	contenta	"kon**ten**a"
▷ **pleased to meet you**	mucho gusto	"**moo**cho **goos**to"
pliers	los alicates	"alee**ka**tes"
plug (*electrical*)	el enchufe	"en**choo**fe"
(*for sink*)	el tapón	"ta**pon**"
plum	la ciruela	"theer**we**la"
plumber	el fontanero	"fonta**ne**ro"
points (*in car*)	los platinos	"pla**tee**nos"
police	la policía	"polee**thee**a"
▷ **police!**	¡policía!	"polee**thee**a"
▷ **we will have to report it to the police**	tendremos que dar parte a la policía	"ten**dre**mos ke dar **par**te a la polee**thee**a"
▷ **get the police**	llame a la policía	"**ya**me a la polee**thee**a"
policeman	el policía	"polee**thee**a"
police station	la comisaría de policía	"komeesa**ree**a de polee**thee**a"
▷ **where is the police station?**	¿dónde está la comisaría (de policía)?	"**don**de esta la komeesa**ree**a (de polee**thee**a)"
polish (*for shoes*)	el betún	"be**toon**"
polluted	contaminado	"kontamee**na**do"
	contaminada	"kontamee**na**da"
pony trekking	la excursión a caballo	"ekskoorsee**on** a ca**ba**yo"
▷ **we'd like to go pony trekking**	nos gustaría hacer excursiones a caballo	"nos goosta**ree**a a**ther** ekskoorsee**o**nes a ca**ba**yo"
pool (*swimming*)	la piscina	"pees**thee**na"
▷ **is there a children's pool?**	¿hay una piscina para los niños?	"**aee oo**na pees**thee**na **pa**ra los **nee**nyos"

ABSOLUTE ESSENTIALS

I don't understand	no comprendo	"no kom**pren**do"
I don't speak Spanish	no hablo español	"no **ab**lo espan**yol**"
do you speak English?	¿habla inglés?	"**ab**la een**gles**"
could you help me?	¿podría ayudarme?	"po**dree**a ayoo**dar**me"

▷ **is the pool heated?**	¿está climatizada la piscina?	"esta kleemateethada la peestheena"
▷ **is it an outdoor pool?**	¿es una piscina al aire libre?	"es oona peestheena al aeere leebre"
pork	el cerdo	"therdo"
port (*seaport*)	el puerto	"pwerto"
(*wine*)	el oporto	"oporto"
porter (*in hotel*)	el botones	"botones"
Portugal	Portugal	"portoogal"
Portuguese	portugués	"portooges"
	portuguesa	"portoogesa"
possible	posible	"poseeble"
▷ **as soon as possible**	en cuanto sea posible	"en kwanto sea poseeble"
to **post**	echar por correo	"echar por korreo"
▷ **where can I post these cards?**	¿dónde puedo echar al correo estas postales?	"donde pwedo echar al korreo estas postales"
postbox	el buzón	"boothon"
postcard	la postal	"postal"
▷ **do you have any postcards?**	¿tiene postales?	"tee-ene postales"
▷ **where can I buy some postcards?**	¿dónde puedo comprar postales?	"donde pwedo komprar postales"
postcode	el código postal	"kodeego postal"
post office	la oficina de correos	"ofeetheena de korreos"
pot (*for cooking*)	la olla	"oya"
potato	la patata	"patata"
pottery	la cerámica	"therameeka"
pound (*weight: metric equiv = 0.45kg*)	la libra	"leebra"

ABSOLUTE ESSENTIALS

I would like ...	me gustaría ...	"me goostareea"
I need ...?	necesito ...	"netheseeto"
where is ...?	¿dónde está ...?	"donde esta"
I'm looking for ...	estoy buscando ...	"estoee booskando"

powdered milk	la leche en polvo	"**le**che en **pol**bo"
pram	el cochecito de niño	"koche**thee**to de **nee**nyo"
prawn	la gamba	"**gam**ba"
to **prefer**	preferir	"prefe**reer**"
▷ **I'd prefer to go ...**	preferiría ir ...	"preferee**ree**a eer"
▷ **I prefer ... to ...**	prefiero ... a ...	"prefee-**e**ro ... a"
pregnant	embarazada	"embara**tha**da"
to **prepare**	preparar	"prepa**rar**"
prescription	la receta	"re**the**ta"
▷ **where can I get this prescription made up?**	¿dónde puedo conseguir la medicina de esta receta?	"**don**de **pwe**do konse**geer** la medee**thee**na de **es**ta re**the**ta"
present (*gift*)	el regalo	"re**ga**lo"
▷ **I want to buy a present for my husband/my wife**	quiero comprar un regalo para mi marido/mi mujer	"kee-**e**ro kom**prar** oon re**ga**lo **pa**ra mee ma**ree**do/mee moo**kher**"
pretty	bonito bonita	"bo**nee**to" "bo**nee**ta"
price	el precio	"**pre**theeo"
price list	la lista de precios	"**lees**ta de **pre**theeos"
priest	el sacerdote	"sather**do**te"
▷ **I want to see a priest**	quiero hablar con un sacerdote	"kee-**e**ro a**blar** kon oon sather**do**te"
private	privado privada	"pree**ba**do" "pree**ba**da"
▷ **can I speak to you in private?**	¿puedo hablarle en privado?	"**pwe**do a**blar**le en pree**ba**do"
▷ **this is private**	esto es privado	"**es**to es pree**ba**do"
▷ **I have private health insurance**	tengo un seguro médico privado	"**ten**go oon se**goo**ro **me**deeko pree**ba**do"

ABSOLUTE ESSENTIALS

do you have ...?	¿tiene ...?	"tee-**e**ne"
is there ...?	¿hay ...?	"aee"
are there ...?	¿hay ...?	"aee"
how much is ...?	¿cuánto cuesta ...?	"**kwan**to **kwes**ta"

probably	probablemente	"probable**mente**"
problem	el problema	"pro**ble**ma"
programme	el programa	"pro**gra**ma"
to pronounce	pronunciar	"pronoonthee**ar**"
▷ **how do you pronounce it?**	¿cómo se pronuncia?	"**ko**mo se pro**noon**theea"
Protestant	protestante	"protes**tante**"
prunes	las ciruelas pasas	"thee**rwe**las **pa**sas"
public¹ *n*	el público	"**poo**bleeko"
▷ **is the castle open to the public?**	¿está abierto al público el castillo?	"esta abee-**er**to al **poo**bleeko el kas**tee**yo"
public² *adj*	público pública	"**poo**bleeko" "**poo**bleeka"
public holiday	el día festivo	"**dee**a fes**tee**bo"
pudding	el postre	"**pos**tre"
to pull	tirar	"tee**rar**"
pullover	el jersey	"kher**se**-ee"
puncture	el pinchazo	"peen**cha**tho"
▷ **I have a puncture**	he pinchado	"e peen**cha**do"
purple	morado morada	"mo**ra**do" "mo**ra**da"
purse	el monedero	"mone**de**ro"
▷ **my purse has been stolen**	me han robado el monedero	"me an ro**ba**do el mone**de**ro"
▷ **I've lost my purse**	he perdido el monedero	"e per**dee**do el mone**de**ro"
to push	empujar	"empoo**khar**"
▷ **my car's broken down, can you give me a push?**	se me ha averiado el coche, ¿puede darle un empujón?	"se me a abere**ea**do el **ko**che, **pwe**de **dar**le oon empoo**khon**"

ABSOLUTE ESSENTIALS

yes (please)	sí (por favor)	"see (por fa**bor**)"
no (thank you)	no (gracias)	"no (**gra**theeas)"
hello	hola	"**o**la"
goodbye	adiós	"adee**os**"

to **put**	poner	"po**ner**"
to **put down**	dejar	"de**khar**"
▷ **put it down over there please**	déjelo ahí, por favor	"**dekh**elo a**ee** por fa**bor**"
pyjamas	el pijama	"pee**kha**ma"
Pyrenees	los Pirineos	"peeree**ne**os"
quarter	el cuarto	"**kwar**to"
▷ **quarter to 10**	las 10 menos cuarto	"las dee-**eth me**nos **kwar**to"
▷ **quarter past 3**	las 3 y cuarto	"las tres ee **kwar**to"
queue	la cola	"**ko**la"
▷ **is this the end of the queue?**	¿es este el final de la cola?	"es **es**te el fee**nal** de la **ko**la"
quick	rápido	"**ra**peedo"
	rápida	"**ra**peeda"
quickly	rápidamente	"**ra**peedamente"
quiet (*place*)	tranquilo	"tran**kee**lo"
	tranquila	"tran**kee**la"
quilt	el edredón	"edre**don**"
quite	bastante	"bas**tante**"
▷ **it's quite good**	es bastante bueno/buena	"es bas**tante bwe**no/**bwe**na"
▷ **it's quite expensive**	es bastante caro/cara	"es bas**tante ka**ro/**ka**ra"
rabbit	el conejo	"ko**nekh**o"
racket	la raqueta	"ra**ke**ta"
▷ **can we hire rackets?**	¿podemos alquilar raquetas?	"po**de**mos alkee**lar** ra**ke**tas"
radiator	el radiator	"radeea**dor**"
radio	la radio	"**ra**deeo"

ABSOLUTE ESSENTIALS

I don't understand	no comprendo	"no kom**pren**do"
I don't speak Spanish	no hablo español	"no **ab**lo espan**yol**"
do you speak English?	¿habla inglés?	"**ab**la een**gles**"
could you help me?	¿podría ayudarme?	"po**dree**a ayoo**dar**me"

▷ **is there a radio/radio cassette in the car?**	¿tiene radio/ radiocassette el coche?	"tee-ene **rad**eeo/ radeeoka**set** el **ko**che"
radishes	los rábanos	"**ra**banos"
railway station	la estación de ferrocarril	"estathee**on** de ferroka**rreel**"
rain	la lluvia	"**yoo**beea"
▷ **is it going to rain?**	¿va a llover?	"ba a yo**ber**"
raincoat	el impermeable	"eemper**me**able"
raining:		
▷ **it's raining**	está lloviendo	"esta yobee-**en**do"
raisin	la pasa	"**pa**sa"
rare (*unique*)	raro	"**ra**ro"
	rara	"**ra**ra"
(*steak*)	poco hecho	"**po**ko **e**cho"
	poco hecha	"**po**ko **e**cha"
rash	el sarpullido	"sarpoo**yee**do"
▷ **I have a rash**	me ha salido un sarpullido	"me a sa**lee**do oon sarpoo**yee**do"
raspberry	la frambuesa	"fram**bwe**sa"
rate	la tasa	"**ta**sa"
	la tarifa	"ta**ree**fa"
▷ **what is the daily/ weekly rate?**	¿cuál es la tarifa por día/por semana?	"kwal es la ta**ree**fa por **dee**a/por sem**a**na"
▷ **do you have a special rate for children?**	¿tienen tarifa especial para niños?	"tee-**e**nen ta**ree**fa espethee**al** para **nee**nyos"
▷ **what is the rate for sterling/dollars?**	¿a cómo está la libra esterlina/el dólar?	"a **ko**mo esta la **lee**bra ester**lee**na/el **do**lar"
▷ **rate of exchange**	tipo de cambio	"**tee**po de **kam**beeo"
raw	crudo	"**kroo**do"
	cruda	"**kroo**da"

ABSOLUTE ESSENTIALS

I would like ...	me gustaría ...	"me goosta**ree**a"
I need ...	necesito ...	"nethe**see**to"
where is ...?	¿dónde está ...?	"**don**de esta"
I'm looking for ...	estoy buscando ...	"es**too**ee boos**kan**do"

razor	la maquinilla de afeitar	"makee**nee**ya de afay-ee**tar**"
razor blades	las hojas de afeitar	"**o**khas de afay-ee**tar**"
ready	listo lista	"**lees**to" "**lees**ta"
▷ **are you ready?**	¿está listo/lista?	"esta **lees**to/**lees**ta"
▷ **I'm ready**	estoy listo/lista	"es**toee lees**to/**lees**ta"
▷ **when will lunch/dinner be ready?**	¿cuándo estará lista la comida/cena?	"**kwan**do esta**ra lees**ta la ko**mee**da/**the**na"
real	verdadero verdadera	"berda**de**ro" "berda**de**ra"
receipt	el recibo	"re**thee**bo"
▷ **I'd like a receipt, please**	¿me da un recibo, por favor?	"me da oon re**thee**bo por fa**bor**"
recently	recientemente	"rethee-ente**men**te"
reception (desk)	la recepción	"rethep**thee**on"
recipe	la receta	"re**the**ta"
to **recommend**	recomendar	"rekomen**dar**"
▷ **what do you recommend?**	¿qué recomienda usted?	"ke rekomee-**en**da oos**ted**"
▷ **can you recommend a cheap hotel/a good restaurant?**	¿puede recomendarnos un hotel barato/un buen restaurante?	"**pwe**de rekomen**dar**nos oon o**tel** ba**ra**to/oon bwen resto**wran**te"
record (music etc)	el disco	"**dees**ko"
red	rojo roja	"**ro**kho" "**ro**kha"
reduction	la rebaja	"re**ba**kha"
▷ **is there a reduction for children/for senior citizens/for a group?**	¿hay tarifa reducida para niños/pensionistas/grupos?	"**aee** ta**ree**fa redoo**thee**da para **neen**yos/penseeo**nees**tas/**groo**pos"

ABSOLUTE ESSENTIALS

do you have ...?	¿tiene ...?	"tee-**ene**"
is there ...?	¿hay ...?	"**aee**"
are there ...?	¿hay ...?	"**aee**"
how much is ...?	¿cuánto cuesta ...?	"**kwan**to **kwes**ta"

refill (for pen)	el recambio	"rekambeeo"
(for lighter)	el recambio	"rekambeeo"
▷ **do you have a refill for my gas lighter?**	¿tiene un recambio para el mechero?	"tee-ene oon rekambeeo para el mechero"
refund	el reembolso	"reembolso"
▷ **I'd like a refund**	quiero que me devuelvan el dinero	"kee-ero ke me debwelban el deenero"
to **register**	registrar	"rekheestrar"
▷ **where do I register?**	¿dónde tengo que registrarme?	"donde tengo ke rekheestrarme"
registered	certificado	"therteefeekado"
	certificada	"therteefeekada"
registered delivery	el envío certificado	"embeeo therteefeekado"
regulation	la norma	"norma"
▷ **I'm very sorry, I didn't know the regulations**	lo siento mucho, no conocía las normas	"lo see-ento moocho no konotheea las normas"
to **reimburse**	reembolsar	"ray-embolsar"
relation (family)	el pariente	"paree-ente"
to **relax**	relajarse	"relakharse"
reliable (method)	seguro	"segooro"
	segura	"segoora"
to **remain**	permanecer	"permanether"
to **remember**	acordarse de	"akordarse de"
to **rent**	alquilar	"alkeelar"
▷ **I'd like to rent a room/villa**	desearía alquilar una habitación/un chalet	"deseareea alkeelar oona abeetatheeon/oon chale"
rental	el alquiler	"alkeeler"
to **repair**	reparar	"reparar"
▷ **can you repair this?**	¿puede arreglar esto?	"pwede arreglar esto"

ABSOLUTE ESSENTIALS		
yes (please)	sí (por favor)	"see (por fabor)"
no (thank you)	no (gracias)	"no (gratheeas)"
hello	hola	"ola"
goodbye	adiós	"adeeos"

to **repeat**	repetir	"repe**teer**"
▷ **please repeat that**	¿puede repetir eso, por favor?	"**pwe**de repe**teer** **e**so por fa**bor**"
reservation	la reserva	"re**ser**ba"
▷ **I'd like to make a reservation for 7.30/ for 2 people**	quisiera reservar una mesa para las siete y media/para 2 personas	"keesee-**e**ra reser**bar** **oo**na **me**sa para las see-**e**te ee **me**deea/para dos per**so**nas"
to **reserve**	reservar	"reser**bar**"
▷ **we'd like to reserve 2 seats for tonight**	querríamos reservar 2 butacas para esta noche	"ke**rree**amos reser**bar** dos boo**ta**kas para **no**che"
▷ **I have reserved a room in the name of ...**	tengo reservada una habitación a nombre de ...	"**ten**go reser**ba**da **oo**na abeetathee**on** a **nom**bre de"
▷ **I want to reserve a single room/a double room/a hotel room**	quiero reservar una habitación individual/ una habitación doble/ una habitación en un hotel	"kee-**e**ro reser**bar** **oo**na abeetathee**on** indeebeed**wal**/**oo**na abeetathee**on** **do**ble/ **oo**na abeetathee**on** en oon o**tel**"
reserved	reservado reservada	"reser**ba**do" "reser**ba**da"
rest[1] n (repose) (remaining)	el descanso el resto	"des**kan**so" "**res**to"
▷ **the rest of the wine**	el resto del vino	"**res**to del **bee**no"
to **rest**[2] vb	descansar	"deskan**sar**"
restaurant	el restaurante	"restow**ran**te"
restaurant car	el vagón-restaurante	"ba**gon** restow**ran**te"
to **return** (go back) (give back)	volver devolver	"bol**ber**" "debol**ber**"
return ticket	el billete de ida y vuelta	"bee**ye**te de **ee**da ee **bwel**ta"

ABSOLUTE ESSENTIALS

I don't understand	no comprendo	"no kom**pren**do"
I don't speak Spanish	no hablo español	"no **ab**lo espan**yol**"
do you speak English?	¿habla inglés?	"**ab**la een**gles**"
could you help me?	¿podría ayudarme?	"po**dree**a ayoo**dar**me"

▷ **a return ticket to ...,** **first class**	un billete de ida y vuelta a ..., primera clase	"oon bee**ye**te de **ee**da ee **bwel**ta a ... pree**me**ra **kla**se"
reverse charge call	la conferencia a cobro revertido	"konfe**ren**theea a **ko**bro reber**tee**do"
▷ **I'd like to make a** **reverse charge call**	quisiera hacer ona llamada cobro revertido	"keesee-**e**ra a**ther** oona yama**da** a **ko**bro reber**tee**do"
rheumatism	el reumatismo	"reooma**tees**mo"
rhubarb	el ruibarbo	"rwee**bar**bo"
rice	el arroz	"**arroth**"
to ride	montar en	"mon**tar** en"
▷ **to go for a ride**	dar una vuelta	"dar oona **bwel**ta"
riding	la equitación	"ekeetathee**on**"
▷ **to go riding**	montar a caballo	"mon**tar** a ka**ba**yo"
▷ **can we go riding?**	¿se puede montar a caballo?	"se **pwe**de mon**tar** a ka**ba**yo"
right[1] *n (opposite of left)* *(legal etc)*	la derecha el derecho	"de**re**cha" "de**re**cho"
▷ **on/to the right**	a la derecha	"a la de**re**cha"
▷ **right of way**	derecho de paso	"de**re**cho de **pa**so"
right[2] *adj (correct)*	correcto correcta	"kor**rek**to" "kor**rek**ta"
ring	el anillo	"a**nee**yo"
ripe	maduro madura	"ma**doo**ro" "ma**doo**ra"
river	el río	"**ree**o"
▷ **can one swim in the** **river?**	¿se puede nadar en el río?	"se **pwe**de na**dar** en el **ree**o"
▷ **am I allowed to fish in** **the river?**	¿está permitido pescar en el río?	"esta permee**tee**do pes**kar** en el **ree**o"

ABSOLUTE ESSENTIALS

I would like ...	me gustaría ...	"me goosta**ree**a"
I need ...	necesito ...	"nethe**see**to"
where is ...?	¿dónde está ...?	"**don**de esta"
I'm looking for ...	estoy buscando ...	"es**too**e boos**kan**do"

road	la carretera	"karre**te**ra"
▷ **is the road to ... snowed up?**	¿está bloqueada por la nieve la carretera a ...?	"es**ta** blo**ka**yada por la nee-**e**be la karre**te**ra a"
▷ **which road do I take for ...?**	¿cuál es la carretera de ...?	"kwal es la karre**te**ra de"
▷ **when will the road be clear?**	¿cuándo estará despejada la carretera?	"**kwan**do esta**ra** despe**kha**da la karre**te**ra"
road map	el mapa de carreteras	"**ma**pa de karre**te**ras"
roast	asado asada	"a**sa**do" "a**sa**da"
to **rob**	robar	"ro**bar**"
▷ **I've been robbed**	me han robado	"me an ro**ba**do"
rock climbing:		
▷ **let's go rock climbing**	vamos a escalar	"**ba**mos a eska**lar**"
roll (*bread*)	el panecillo	"pane**thee**yo"
roller skates	los patines	"pa**tee**nes"
roller skating	el patinaje	"patee**nak**he"
▷ **where can we go roller skating?**	¿dónde se puede patinar?	"**don**de se **pwe**de patee**nar**"
Rome	Roma	"**ro**ma"
roof	el tejado	"te**kha**do"
▷ **the roof leaks**	el tejado tiene goteras	"el te**kha**do tee-**e**ne go**te**ras"
roof rack	la baca	"**ba**ka"
room (*in house, hotel*) (*space*)	la habitación el sitio	"abeetathee**on**" "**see**teeo"
room service	el servicio de habitaciones	"ser**bee**theeo de abeetathee**o**nes"
rope	la cuerda	"**kwer**da"

ABSOLUTE ESSENTIALS

do you have ...?	¿tiene ...?	"tee-**e**ne"
is there ...?	¿hay ...?	"**aee**"
are there ...?	¿hay ...?	"**aee**"
how much is ...?	¿cuánto cuesta ...?	"**kwan**to **kwes**ta"

rosé (wine)	el (vino) rosado	"el (**bee**no) ro**sa**do"
rough (sea)	agitado	"akhee**ta**do"
	agitada	"akhee**ta**da"
▷ **is the sea rough today?**	¿está el mar agitado hoy?	"es**ta** akhee**ta**do el mar **oee**"
▷ **the crossing was rough**	tuvimos una mala travesía	"too**bee**mos **oo**na **ma**la trabe**see**a"
round (shape)	redondo	"re**don**do"
	redonda	"re**don**da"
▷ **round the corner**	a la vuelta de la esquina	"a la **bwel**ta de la es**kee**na"
▷ **whose round is it?**	¿a quién le toca?	"a kee-**en** le **to**ka"
▷ **a round of golf**	un recorrido de golf	"oon reko**rree**do de golf"
route	la ruta	"**roo**ta"
▷ **is there a route that avoids the traffic?**	¿hay algún otro camino que evite el tráfico?	"**aee** al**goon o**tro ka**mee**no ke e**bee**te el **tra**feeko"
rowing boat	la barca	"**bar**ka"
▷ **can we rent a rowing boat?**	¿podemos alquilar una barca?	"po**de**mos alkee**lar oo**na **bar**ka"
rubber (material)	la goma	"**go**ma"
(eraser)	la goma de borrar	"**go**ma de bo**rrar**"
rubber band	la gomita	"go**mee**ta"
rubbish	la basura	"ba**soo**ra"
rucksack	la mochila	"mo**chee**la"
rug	la alfombra	"al**fom**bra"
rugby	el rugby	"**roog**bee"
ruins	las ruinas	"**rwee**nas"
rum	el ron	"ron"
run[1] n (skiing)	la pista	"**pees**ta"

ABSOLUTE ESSENTIALS

yes (please)	sí (por favor)	"see (por fa**bor**)"
no (thank you)	no (gracias)	"no (**gra**theeas)"
hello	hola	"**o**la"
goodbye	adiós	"adee**os**"

▷ **which are the easiest runs?**	¿cuáles son las pistas más faciles?	"**kwa**les son las **pees**tas mas **fa**theeles"
to run² *vb*	recorrer	"reko**rer**"
▷ **the bus runs every 20 minutes**	hay un autobús cada 20 minutos	"**a**ee oon owto**boos** kada **bay**-eente mee**noo**tos"
▷ **is the train running late?**	¿el tren lleva retraso?	"el tren **ye**ba re**tra**so"

running:

▷ **to go running**	ir a correr	"eer a ko**rrer**"
rush hour	las horas puntas	"**o**ras **poon**tas"
saccharine	la sacarina	"saka**ree**na"
safe¹ *n*	la caja fuerte	"**ka**ha **fwer**te"
▷ **please put this in the hotel safe**	por favor, ponga esto en la caja fuerte del hotel	"por fa**bor pon**ga **es**to en la **ka**ha **fwer**te del o**tel**"
safe² *adj (beach, medicine)*	seguro segura	"se**goo**ro" "se**goo**ra"
▷ **is it safe to swim here?**	¿se puede nadar sin peligro aquí?	"se **pwe**de na**dar** seen pe**lee**gro a**kee**"
▷ **is it safe for children?** *(medicine)*	¿lo pueden tomar los niños?	"lo **pwe**den to**mar** los **nee**nyos"
safe sex	el sexo seguro	"**sek**so se**goo**ro"
safety belt	el cinturón de seguridad	"theentoo**ron** de segooree**dad**"
safety pin	el imperdible	"eemper**dee**ble"
▷ **I need a safety pin**	necesito un imperdible	"nethe**see**to oon eemper**dee**ble"
sail¹ *n*	la vela	"**be**la"
to sail² *vb*	navegar	"nabe**gar**"
▷ **when do we sail?**	¿cuándo salimos?	"**kwan**do sa**lee**mos"
sailboard	la plancha de windsurf	"**plan**cha de **ween**soorf"

ABSOLUTE ESSENTIALS

I don't understand	no comprendo	"no kom**pren**do"
I don't speak Spanish	no hablo español	"no **a**blo espan**yol**"
do you speak English?	¿habla inglés?	"**a**bla een**gles**"
could you help me?	¿podría ayudarme?	"po**dree**a ayoo**dar**me"

sailboarding	el windsurf	"**ween**soorf"
▷ **I'd like to go sailboarding**	me gustaría hacer windsurf	"me goosta**ree**a a**ther ween**soorf"
sailing (*sport*)	la vela	"**be**la"
▷ **what time is the next sailing?**	¿a qué hora sale el próximo ferry?	"a ke **o**ra **sa**le el **prok**seemo ferree"
▷ **I'd like to go sailing**	me gustaría ir a praticar vela	"me goosta**ree**a eer a praktee**kar be**la"
salad	la ensalada	"ensa**la**da"
▷ **a mixed salad**	una ensalada mixta	"**oo**na ensa**la**da **meeks**ta"
salad dressing	la vinagreta	"beena**gre**ta"
saline solution (*for contact lenses*)	la solución salina	"sooloothee**on** sa**lee**na"
salmon	el salmón	"sal**mon**"
salt	la sal	"sal"
▷ **pass the salt, please**	páseme la sal, por favor	"**pa**seme la sal por fa**bor**"
same	mismo misma	"**mees**mo" "**mees**ma"
▷ **I'll have the same**	yo tomaré lo mismo	"yo toma**re** lo **mees**mo"
sand	la arena	"a**re**na"
sandals	las sandalias	"san**da**leeas"
sandwich	el bocadillo	"boka**dee**yo"
▷ **what kind of sandwiches do you have?**	¿qué bocadillos tiene?	"ke boka**dee**yos tee-**e**ne"
sandy	arenoso	"are**no**so"
▷ **a sandy beach**	una playa de arena	"**oo**na **pla**ya de a**re**na"
sanitary towels	las compresas	"kom**pre**sas"
sardine	la sardina	"sar**dee**na"

ABSOLUTE ESSENTIALS		
I would like ...	me gustaría ...	"me goosta**ree**a"
I need ...	necesito ...	"nethe**see**to"
where is ...?	¿dónde está ...?	"**don**de esta"
I'm looking for ...	estoy buscando ...	"es**toee** boos**kando**"

Saturday	sábado	"**sa**bado"
sauce	la salsa	"**sal**sa"
saucepan	la cacerola	"kathe**ro**la"
saucer	el platito	"pla**tee**to"
sauna	la sauna	"**sow**na"
sausage	la salchicha	"sal**chee**cha"
savoury (*not sweet*)	salado salada	"sa**la**do" "sa**la**da"
to **say**	decir	"de**theer**"
scallop	la vieira	"bee-**ay**-eera"
scampi	las gambas	"**gam**bas"
scarf	la bufanda	"boo**fan**da"
school	la escuela	"es**kwe**la"
scissors	las tijeras	"tee**khe**ras"
Scotch	el whisky escocés	"**wees**kee esko**thes**"
Scotland	Escocia	"esko**thee**a"
Scottish	escocés escocesa	"esko**thes**" "esko**the**sa"
▷ **I'm Scottish**	soy escocés/escocesa	"**so**ee esko**thes**/ esko**the**sa"
screw	el tornillo	"tor**nee**yo"
▷ **the screw has come loose**	se ha aflojado el tornillo	"se a aflo**kha**do el tor**nee**yo"
screwdriver	el destornillador	"destorneeya**dor**"
scuba diving	el submarinismo	"soobmaree**nees**mo"
▷ **where can we go scuba diving?**	¿dónde se puede hacer submarinismo?	"**don**de se **pwe**de a**ther** soobamaree**nees**mo"
sculpture (*object*)	la escultura	"eskool**too**ra"

ABSOLUTE ESSENTIALS

do you have ...?	¿tiene ...?	"tee-**en**e"
is there ...?	¿hay ...?	"**aee**"
are there ...?	¿hay ...?	"**aee**"
how much is ...?	¿cuánto cuesta ...?	"**kwan**to **kwes**ta"

sea	el mar	"mar"
seafood	los mariscos	"mareeskos"
▷ **do you like seafood?**	¿te gustan los mariscos?	"te goostan los mareeskos"
seasick	mareado mareada	"mareado" "mareada"
seasickness	el mareo	"mareo"
seaside	la costa	"kosta"
▷ **at the seaside**	en la playa	"en la playa"
season ticket	el abono	"abono"
seat (*chair*) (*in bus, train*)	la silla el asiento	"seeya" "asee-ento"
▷ **is this seat free?**	¿está libre este asiento?	"esta leebre este asee-ento"
▷ **is this seat taken?**	¿está cogido este asiento?	"esta kokheedo este asee-ento"
▷ **we'd like to reserve 2 seats for tonight**	querríamos reservar 2 butacas para esta noche	"kerreeamos reserbar dos bootakas para esta noche"
▷ **I have a seat reservation**	tengo reservado un asiento	"tengo reserbado oon asee-ento"
second	segundo segunda	"segoondo" "segoonda"
second class	de segunda clase	"de segoonda klase"
to see	ver	"ber"
▷ **see you soon**	hasta pronto	"asta pronto"
▷ **what is there to see here?**	¿qué cosas interesantes se pueden ver aquí?	"ke kosas eenteresantes se pweden ber akee"
self-service	de autoservicio	"owtoserbeetheeo"
to sell	vender	"bender"
▷ **do you sell stamps?**	¿venden sellos?	"benden seyos"

ABSOLUTE ESSENTIALS		
yes (please)	sí (por favor)	"see (por fabor)"
no (thank you)	no (gracias)	"no (gratheeas)"
hello	hola	"ola"
goodbye	adiós	"adeeos"

Sellotape®	el celo	"**the**lo"
to **send**	enviar	"embee**ar**"
▷ **please send my mail/ luggage on to this address**	por favor, mándenme el correo/equipaje a esta dirección	"por fa**bor man**denme el ko**rre**o/ekee**pa**khe a **es**ta deerekthee**on**"
senior citizen	el pensionista	"penseeoo**nees**ta"
	la pensionista	"penseeoo**nees**ta"
▷ **is there a reduction for senior citizens?**	¿hay tarifa reducida para pensionistas?	"**aee** ta**ree**fa redoo**thee**da para penseeoo**nees**tas"
semi-skimmed milk	la leche semidesnatada	"**le**che semides**na**tada"
separate	separado	"sepa**ra**do"
	separada	"sepa**ra**da"
September	septiembre	"septee-**em**bre"
serious	grave	"**gra**be"
▷ **he is seriously injured**	está gravemente herido	"es**ta** grabe**men**te e**ree**do"
to **serve**	servir	"ser**beer**"
▷ **we are still waiting to be served**	todavía estamos esperando a que nos sirvan	"toda**bee**a estamos espe**ran**do a ke nos **seer**ban"
service (*in restaurant*)	el servicio	"ser**bee**theeo"
▷ **is service included?**	¿va incluido el servicio?	"ba eenkloo**ee**do el ser**bee**theeo"
▷ **what time is the service?** (*church*)	¿a qué hora son los oficios?	"a ke **o**ra son los ofeethee**os**"
service charge	el servicio	"ser**bee**theeo"
service station	la estación de servicio	"estathee**on** de ser**bee**theeo"
set menu	el menú	"me**noo**"
▷ **we'll take the set menu**	tráiganos el plato del día	"**tra**eeganos el **pla**to del **dee**a"
▷ **do you have a set menu?**	¿tienen menú?	"tee-**e**nen me**noo**"

ABSOLUTE ESSENTIALS

I don't understand	no comprendo	"no kom**pren**do"
I don't speak Spanish	no hablo español	"no **ab**lo espan**yol**"
do you speak English?	¿habla inglés?	"**ab**la een**gles**"
could you help me?	¿podría ayudarme?	"po**dree**a ayoo**dar**me"

▷ how much is the set menu?	¿cuánto es el menú del día?	"**kwan**to es el me**noo** del **dee**a"
seven	siete	"see-**ete**"
seventeen	diecisiete	"dee-etheesee-**ete**"
seventy	setenta	"se**ten**ta"
shade	la sombra	"**som**bra"
▷ in the shade	a la sombra	"a la **som**bra"
shallow	poco profundo poco profunda	"**po**ko pro**foon**do" "**po**ko pro**foon**da"
shampoo	el champú	"cham**poo**"
▷ a shampoo and set, please	lavado y marcado, por favor	"la**ba**do ee mar**ka**do por fa**bor**"
shandy	la cerveza con gaseosa	"ther**be**tha con gase**o**sa"
to **share**	repartir	"repar**teer**"
▷ we could share a taxi	podemos compartir un taxi	"po**de**mos kompar**teer** oon **tak**see"
to **shave**	afeitarse	"afay-ee**tar**se"
shaver	la máquina de afeitar	"**ma**keena de afay-ee**tar**"
shaving brush	la brocha de afeitar	"**bro**cha de afay-ee**tar**"
shaving cream	la crema de afeitar	"**kre**ma de afay-ee**tar**"
she	ella	"**e**ya"
sheet	la sábana	"**sa**bana"
shellfish	los mariscos	"ma**rees**kos"
sherry	el jerez	"khe**reth**"
ship	el barco	"**bar**ko"
shirt	la camisa	"ka**mee**sa"

ABSOLUTE ESSENTIALS		
I would like ...	me gustaría ...	"me goosta**ree**a"
I need ...	necesito ...	"nethe**see**to"
where is ...?	¿dónde está ...?	"**don**de esta"
I'm looking for ...	estoy buscando ...	"es**to**ee boos**kan**do"

shock:

▷ **to be in shock**   estar conmocionado   "es**tar** konmotheeo**na**do"

shock absorber   el amortiguador   "amorteegwa**dor**"

shoe   el zapato   "tha**pa**to"

▷ **there is a hole in my shoe**   tengo un agujero en el zapato   "**ten**go oon agook**he**ro en el tha**pa**to"

▷ **can you reheel these shoes?**   ¿puede ponerles las tapas a estos zapatos?   "**pwe**de poner**les** las **ta**pas a **es**tos tha**pa**tos"

shoe laces   los cordones   "kor**do**nes"

shoe polish   el betún   "be**toon**"

shop   la tienda   "tee-**en**da"

▷ **what time do the shops close?**   ¿a qué hora cierran las tiendas?   "a ke **o**ra thee-**e**rran las tee-**en**das"

shopping:

▷ **to go shopping**   ir de compras   "eer de **kom**pras"

▷ **where is the main shopping area?**   ¿dónde está el zona comercial?   "**don**de esta el **tho**na komerthee**al**"

shopping centre   el centro comercial   "**then**tro komerthee**al**"

shop window   el escaparate   "el eskapa**ra**te"

▷ **in the shop window**   en el escaparate   "en el eskapa**ra**te"

short   corto   "**kor**to"
   corta   "**kor**ta"

short cut   el atajo   "a**ta**kho"

shorts   los pantalones cortos   "pantal**o**nes **kor**tos"

short-sighted   miope   "mee**o**pe"

▷ **I'm short-sighted**   soy miope   "**so**ee mee**o**pe"

shoulder   el hombro   "**om**bro"

▷ **I've hurt my shoulder**   me he hecho daño en el hombro   "me e **e**cho **da**ño en el **om**bro"

show[1] *n*   el espectáculo   "espek**ta**koolo"

ABSOLUTE ESSENTIALS

do you have ...?	¿tiene ...?	"tee-**e**ne"
is there ...?	¿hay ...?	"**a**ee"
are there ...?	¿hay ...?	"**a**ee"
how much is ...?	¿cuánto cuesta ...?	"**kwan**to **kwes**ta"

**to show² **vb	mostrar enseñar	"mos**trar**" "ense**nyar**"
▷ **could you show me please?**	¿podría mostrármelo por favor?	"po**dree**a mos**trar**melo por fa**bor**"
▷ **could you show us around the apartment?**	¿podría enseñarnos el apartamento?	"po**dree**a ensen**yar**nos el aparta**men**to"
shower	la ducha	"**doo**cha"
▷ **how does the shower work?**	¿cómo funciona la ducha?	"**ko**mo foonthee**o**na la **doo**cha"
▷ **I'd like a room with a shower**	quisiera una habitación con ducha	"keesee-**era oo**na abeetathee**on** con **doo**cha"
shrimp	el camarón	"kama**ron**"
sick (*ill*)	enfermo enferma	"en**fer**mo" "en**fer**ma"
▷ **she has been sick**	ha vomitado	"a bomee**ta**do"
▷ **I feel sick**	me mareo	"me ma**reo**"
sightseeing	el turismo	"too**rees**mo"
▷ **are there any sightseeing tours?**	¿hay excursiones turísticas?	"**a**ee ekskoorsee**o**nes too**rees**teekas"
sign¹ n	la señal	"se**nyal**"
to sign² vb	firmar	"feer**mar**"
▷ **where do I sign?**	¿dónde firmo?	"**don**de **fir**mo"
signature	la firma	"**feer**ma"
silk	la seda	"**se**da"
silver	la plata	"**pla**ta"
similar	parecido parecida	"pare**thee**do" "pare**thee**da"
simple	sencillo sencilla	"sen**thee**yo" "sen**thee**ya"

ABSOLUTE ESSENTIALS

yes (please)	sí (por favor)	"see (por fa**bor**)"
no (thank you)	no (gracias)	"no (**gra**theeas)"
hello	hola	"**o**la"
goodbye	adiós	"adee**os**"

single (*unmarried*)	soltero	"sol**te**ro"
	soltera	"sol**te**ra"
▷ **a single to ..., second class**	un billete de ida a ..., segunda clase	"oon bee**ye**te de **ee**da a ... se**goon**da **kla**se"
single bed	la cama individual	"**ka**ma eendeebee**dwal**"
single room	la habitación individual	"abeetathee**on** eendeebee**dwal**"
▷ **I want to reserve a single room**	quiero reservar una habitación individual	"kee-**e**ro reser**bar** oona abeetathee**on** eendeebee**dwal**"
sink	el fregadero	"frega**de**ro"
sir	señor	"sen**yor**"
sister	la hermana	"er**ma**na"
to **sit**	sentarse	"sen**tar**se"
▷ **please sit down**	tomen asiento, por favor	"**to**men asee-**en**to por fa**bor**"
six	seis	"**say**-ees"
sixteen	dieciséis	"dee-ethee**say**-ees"
sixty	sesenta	"se**sen**ta"
size	la talla	"**ta**ya"
▷ **I take a continental size 40**	tengo la talla 40	"**ten**go la **ta**ya kwa**ren**ta"
▷ **do you have this in a bigger/smaller size?**	¿tiene esto en una talla más grande/pequeña?	"tee-**e**ne **es**to en oona **ta**ya mas **gran**de/ pe**ke**nya"
skateboard	el monopatín	"monopa**teen**"
skateboarding:		
▷ **I'd like to go skateboarding**	me gustaría montar en monopatín	"me goosta**ree**a mon**tar** en monopa**teen**"
skates	los patines	"pa**tee**nes"

ABSOLUTE ESSENTIALS

I don't understand	no comprendo	"no kom**pren**do"
I don't speak Spanish	no hablo español	"no **a**blo espan**yol**"
do you speak English?	¿habla inglés?	"**a**bla een**gles**"
could you help me?	¿podría ayudarme?	"po**dree**a ayoo**dar**me"

▷ **where can we hire skates?**	¿dónde se pueden alquilar patines?	"**don**de se **pwe**den alkee**lar** pa**tee**nes"
skating	el patinaje	"patee**nakhe**"
▷ **where can we go skating?**	¿dónde podemos ir a patinar sobre hielo?	"**don**de po**de**mos eer a patee**nar so**bre ee-**e**lo"
ski[1] *n*	el esquí	"es**kee**"
▷ **can we hire skis here?**	¿podemos alquilar esquís aquí?	"po**de**mos alkee**lar** es**kees** a**kee**"
to **ski**[2] *vb*	esquiar	"eskee**ar**"
ski boot	la bota de esquí	"**bo**ta de es**kee**"
skid	patinar	"patee**nar**"
▷ **the car skidded**	el coche patinó	"el **ko**che patee**no**"
skiing (*downhill*) (*cross-country*)	el esquí el esquí de fondo	"es**kee**" "es**kee** de **fon**do"
▷ **I'd like to go skiing**	me gustaría ir a esquiar	"me goosta**ree**a eer a eskee**ar**"
skiing lessons	las clases de esquí	"**kla**ses de es**kee**"
▷ **do you organize skiing lessons?**	¿organizan clases de esquí?	"orga**nee**than **kla**ses de es**kee**"
ski instructor	el monitor de esquí la monitora de esquí	"monee**tor** de es**kee**" "monee**to**ra de es**kee**"
ski jacket	la cazadora de esquí	"katha**do**ra de es**kee**"
ski lift	el forfait	"for**fa**ee"
skimmed milk	la leche desnatada	"**le**che desna**ta**da"
skin	la piel	"pee-**el**"
skin diving	el escafandrismo	"eskafan**drees**mo"
ski pants	los pantalones de esquí	"panta**lo**nes de es**kee**"
ski pass	el pase de esquí	"**pa**se de es**kee**"
ski pole	el palo de esquí	"**pa**lo de es**kee**"

ABSOLUTE ESSENTIALS

I would like ...	me gustaría ...	"me goosta**ree**a"
I need ...	necesito ...	"nethe**see**to"
where is ...?	¿dónde está ...?	"**don**de es**ta**"
I'm looking for ...	estoy buscando ...	"es**toee** boos**kan**do"

ski resort	la estación de esquí	"estat**hee**on de es**kee**"
skirt	la falda	"**fal**da"
ski run	la pista de esquí	"**pees**ta de es**kee**"
ski suit	el traje de esquí	"**tra**khe de es**kee**"
sledge	el trineo	"tree**ne**o"
sledging:		
▷ **where can we go sledging?**	¿dónde se puede montar en trineo?	"**don**de se **pwe**de mon**tar** en tree**ne**o"
to **sleep**	dormir	"dor**meer**"
▷ **I can't sleep for the noise/heat**	no puedo dormir con el ruido/calor	"no **pwe**do dor**meer** kon el **rwee**do/ka**lor**"
sleeper (*in train*)	la litera	"lee**te**ra"
▷ **can I reserve a sleeper?**	¿puedo reservar una litera?	"**pwe**do reser**bar** oona lee**te**ra"
sleeping bag	el saco de dormir	"**sa**ko de dor**meer**"
sleeping car	el coche-cama	"**ko**che **ka**ma"
sleeping pill	el somnífero	"som**nee**fero"
slice (*of bread*) (*of meat*)	la rebanada la tajada	"reba**na**da" "ta**kha**da"
slide (*photograph*)	la diapositiva	"deeaposee**tee**ba"
slipper	la zapatilla	"thapa**tee**ya"
slow	lento lenta	"**len**to" "**len**ta"
▷ **slow down!**	¡más despacio!	"mas des**pa**theeo"
slowly	lentamente	"lenta**men**te"
▷ **please speak slowly**	por favor, hable despacio	"por fa**bor** **a**ble des**pa**theeo"
small	pequeño pequeña	"pe**ke**nyo" "pe**ke**nya"

ABSOLUTE ESSENTIALS

do you have ...?	¿tiene ...?	"tee-**e**ne"
is there ...?	¿hay ...?	"**a**ee"
are there ...?	¿hay ...?	"**a**ee"
how much is ...?	¿cuánto cuesta ...?	"**kwan**to **kwes**ta"

smaller	más pequeño	"mas pe**ke**nyo"
	más pequeña	"mas pe**ke**nya"
smell	el olor	"o**lor**"
smoke[1] *n*	el humo	"**oo**mo"
to **smoke**[2] *vb*	fumar	"foo**mar**"
▷ **do you mind if I smoke?**	¿le importa que fume?	"le eem**por**ta ke **foo**me"
▷ **do you smoke?**	¿fuma?	"**foo**ma"
smoked	ahumado	"aoo**ma**do"
	ahumada	"aoo**ma**da"

smoking:

| ▷ **I'd like a no smoking seat** | quisiera un asiento de no-fumador | "keesee-**e**ra oon asee-**en**to de no fooma**dor**" |
| ▷ **I'd like a seat in the smoking area** | quiero un asiento en la zona de fumadores | "kee-**e**ro oon asee-**en**to en la **tho**na de fooma**do**res" |

smoky:

▷ **it's too smoky here**	hay demasiado humo aquí	"**aee** demasee**a**do **oo**mo a**kee**"
snack bar	la cafetería	"kafete**ree**a"
snorkel	el tubo	"**too**bo"

snorkelling:

▷ **let's go snorkelling**	vamos a bucear	"**ba**mos a boothe**ar**"
snow	la nieve	"nee-**e**be"
▷ **the snow is very icy/ heavy**	la nieve está muy helada/dura	"la nee-**e**be es**ta** mwee e**la**da/**doo**ra"
▷ **what are the snow conditions?**	¿cuál es el estado de la nieve?	"kwal es el es**ta**do de la nee-**e**be"
▷ **is it going to snow?**	¿va a nevar?	"ba a ne**bar**"
snowboard	la plancha para la nieve	"**plan**cha **pa**ra la nee-**e**be"
snowed up	encerrado/a por la nieve	"enthe**rra**do/a por la nee-**e**be"

ABSOLUTE ESSENTIALS

yes (please)	sí (por favor)	"see (por fa**bor**)"
no (thank you)	no (gracias)	"no (**gra**theeas)"
hello	hola	"**o**la"
goodbye	adiós	"adee**os**"

snowing:

▷ **it's snowing**	está nevando	"esta ne**ban**do"
snowplough	el quitanieves	"keetanee-**e**bes"
so	tan	"tan"
▷ **so much**	tanto	"**tan**to"
	tanta	"**tan**ta"
soaking solution (*for contact lenses*)	la solución limpiadora	"soolooth**eon** leempeea**do**ra"
soap	el jabón	"kha**bon**"
▷ **there is no soap**	no hay jabón	"no **a**ee kha**bon**"
soap powder	el jabón en polvo	"kha**bon** en **pol**bo"
sober	sobrio	"**so**breeo"
	sobria	"**so**breea"
socket	el enchufe	"en**choo**fe"
▷ **where is the socket for my electric razor?**	¿dónde está el enchufe para la máquina de afeitar?	"**don**de esta el en**choo**fe **pa**ra la **ma**keena de afay-ee**tar**"
socks	los calcetines	"kalthe**tee**nes"
soda	la soda	"**so**da"
soft	blando	"**blan**do"
	blanda	"**blan**da"
soft drink	la bebida sin alcohol	"be**bee**da seen al**kol**"
sole (*fish*)	la suela	"**swe**la"
soluble aspirin	la aspirina soluble	"aspee**ree**na so**loo**ble"
solution	la solución	"soolooth**eon**"
▷ **saline solution**	solución salina	"soolooth**eon** sa**lee**na"

ABSOLUTE ESSENTIALS

I don't understand	no comprendo	"no kom**pren**do"
I don't speak Spanish	no hablo español	"no **a**blo espan**yol**"
do you speak English?	¿habla inglés?	"**a**bla een**gles**"
could you help me?	¿podría ayudarme?	"po**dree**a ayoo**dar**me"

▷ **cleansing solution for contact lenses**	solución limpiadora para las lentes de contacto	"solootheeon leempeeadora para las lentes de kontakto"
▷ **soaking solution for contact lenses**	solución salina para las lentes de contacto	"solootheeon saleena para las lentes de kontakto"
some	algunos algunas	"algoonos" "algoonas"
someone	alguien	"algee-en"
something	algo	"algo"
sometimes	a veces	"a bethes"
son	el hijo	"eekho"
song	la canción	"kantheeon"
soon	pronto	"pronto"
sore:		
▷ **my back is sore**	me duele la espalda	"me dwele la espalda"
▷ **I have a sore throat**	me duele la garganta	"me dwele la garganta"
▷ **my eyes/feet are sore**	me duelen los ojos/pies	"me dwelen los okhos/pee-es"
sorry:		
▷ **sorry!**	¡perdón!	"perdon"
▷ **I'm sorry!**	¡lo siento!	"lo see-ento"
sort	el tipo	"teepo"
▷ **what sort of cheese?**	¿qué tipo de queso?	"ke teepo de keso"
▷ **a sort of chapel**	una especie de capilla	"oona espethee-e de kapeeya"
▷ **sort of**	algo así	"algo asee"
soup	la sopa	"sopa"
▷ **what is the soup of the day?**	¿cuál es la sopa de día?	"kwal es la sopa del deea"
south	el sur	"soor"

ABSOLUTE ESSENTIALS

I would like ...	me gustaría ...	"me goostareea"
I need ...	necesito ...	"netheseeto"
where is ...?	¿dónde está ...?	"donde esta"
I'm looking for ...	estoy buscando ...	"estoee booskando"

souvenir	el recuerdo	"re**kwer**do"
space	el espacio	"es**pa**theeo"
▷ **parking space**	el sitio para aparcar	"**see**teeo para apar**kar**"
spade	la pala	"**pa**la"
Spain	España	"es**pa**nya"
▷ **what part of Spain do you come from?**	¿de qué de España eres?	"de ke de es**pa**nya **e**res"
Spanish	español	"espa**nyol**"
	española	"espa**nyo**la"
▷ **I don't speak Spanish**	no hablo español	"no **a**blo espa**nyol**"
spanner	la llave inglesa	"**ya**be een**gle**sa"
spare wheel	la rueda de repuesto	"**rwe**da de re**pwes**to"
sparkling wine	el vino espumoso	"**bee**no espoo**mo**so"
spark plug	la bujía	"boo**khee**a"
to **speak**	hablar	"a**blar**"
▷ **can I speak to ...?** (on telephone)	¿puedo hablar con ...?	"**pwe**do a**blar** kon"
	¿se puede poner ...?	"se **pwe**de po**ner**"
▷ **please speak louder/ more slowly**	hable más alto/despacio por favor	"**a**ble mas **al**to/des**pa**theeo por fa**bor**"
special	especial	"espe**theeal**"
▷ **do you have a special menu for children?**	¿tienen menú especial para niños?	"tee-**e**nen me**noo** espe**theeal** para **nee**nyos"
speciality	la especialidad	"espetheealee**dad**"
▷ **is there a local speciality?**	¿hay alguna especialidad local?	"**aee** al**goo**na espetheealee**dad** lo**kal**"
▷ **what is the chef's speciality?**	¿cuál es la especialidad del chef?	"kwal es la espetheealee**dad** del chef"
speed	la velocidad	"belothee**dad**"

ABSOLUTE ESSENTIALS

do you have ...?	¿tiene ...?	"tee-**e**ne"
is there ...?	¿hay ...?	"**aee**"
are there ...?	¿hay ...?	"**aee**"
how much is ...?	¿cuánto cuesta ...?	"**kwan**to **kwes**ta"

speed limit:

▷ **what is the speed limit on this road?**	¿cuál es el límite de velocidad de esta carretera?	"kwal es el **lee**meete de belothee**dad** de **es**ta karre**te**ra"
speedometer	el velocímetro	"belo**thee**metro"
to **spell**	deletrear	"deletre**ar**"
▷ **how do you spell it?**	¿cómo se escribe?	"**ko**mo se es**kree**be"
spicy	picante	"pee**kan**te"
spinach	las espinacas	"espee**na**kas"
spirits	el alcohol	"al**kol**"
sponge	la esponja	"es**pon**kha"
spoon	la cuchara	"koo**cha**ra"
sport	el deporte	"de**por**te"
▷ **which sports activities are available here?**	¿qué actividades deportivas ofrecen aquí?	"ke akteebee**da**des deporte**ee**bas ofre**then** a**kee**"
spring (*season*)	la primavera	"preema**be**ra"
square (*in town*)	la plaza	"**pla**tha"
squash (*drink*)	el zumo	"**thoo**mo"
(*game*)	el squash	"es**kwosh**"
stain	la mancha	"**man**cha"
▷ **this stain is coffee/ blood**	esta mancha es de café/ sangre	"**es**ta **man**cha es de ka**fe**/ **san**gre"
▷ **can you remove this stain?**	¿puede quitar esta mancha?	"**pwe**de kee**tar es**ta **man**cha"
stairs	la escalera	"eska**le**ra"
stalls (*theatre*)	la butaca	"boo**ta**ka"
stamp (*postage*)	el sello	"**se**yo"
▷ **do you sell stamps?**	¿venden sellos?	"**ben**den **se**yos"

ABSOLUTE ESSENTIALS		
yes (please)	sí (por favor)	"see (por fa**bor**)"
no (thank you)	no (gracias)	"no (**gra**theeas)"
hello	hola	"**o**la"
goodbye	adiós	"adee**os**"

▷ **I'd like stamps for 6 postcards to Great Britain, please**	me da sellos para enviar 6 postales a Gran Bretaña, por favor	"me da **se**yos para embe**ar** say-ees postales a gran bre**tan**ya por fa**bor**"
▷ **twelve 45-peseta stamps, please**	doce sellos de cuarenta y cinco pesetas, por favor	"**do**the **se**yos de kwa**ren**ta ee **theen**ko pe**se**tas por fa**bor**"
▷ **where can I buy stamps?**	¿dónde venden sellos?	"**don**de **ben**den **se**yos"
to **start**	comenzar	"komen**thar**"
▷ **when does the film/ show start?**	¿cuándo empieza la película/el espectáculo?	"**kwan**do empee-**e**tha la pe**lee**koola/el espek**ta**koolo"
starter (*at meal*) (*in car*)	el entremés el motor de arranque	"entre**mes**" "mo**tor** de a**rran**ke"
station	la estación	"estathee**on**"
▷ **to the station, please**	a la estación, por favor	"a la estathee**on** por fa**bor**"
stationer's	la papelería	"papele**ree**a"
to **stay** (*remain*)	quedarse alojarse	"ke**dar**se" "alo**khar**se"
▷ **I'm staying at a hotel**	me alojo en un hotel	"me a**lo**kho en oon o**tel**"
▷ **I want to stay an extra night**	quiero quedarme una noche más	"kee-**e**ro ke**dar**me oona **no**che mas"
▷ **where are you staying?**	¿dónde se aloja?	"**don**de se a**lo**kha"
steak	el filete	"fee**le**te"
steep	escarpado escarpada	"eskar**pa**do" "eskar**pa**da"
sterling:		
▷ **pounds sterling**	las libras esterlinas	"**lee**bras ester**lee**nas"
▷ **what is the rate for sterling?**	¿a cómo está la libra esterlina?	"a **ko**mo esta la **lee**bra ester**lee**na"
sterling silver	la plata de ley	"**pla**ta de **le**-ee"

ABSOLUTE ESSENTIALS

I don't understand	no comprendo	"no kom**pren**do"
I don't speak Spanish	no hablo español	"no **ab**lo espan**yol**"
do you speak English?	¿habla inglés?	"**ab**la een**gles**"
could you help me?	¿podría ayudarme?	"pod**ree**a ayoo**dar**me"

stew	el estofado	"esto**fa**do"
steward	el camarero	"kama**re**ro"
stewardess	la azafata	"atha**fa**ta"
sticking plaster	el esparadrapo	"espara**dra**po"
still	todavía	"toda**bee**a"
sting	la picadura	"peeka**doo**ra"
stockings	las medias	"**me**deeas"
stolen	robado	"ro**ba**do"
	robada	"ro**ba**da"
▷ **my passport/watch has been stolen**	me han robado el pasaporte/reloj	"me an ro**ba**do el pasa**por**te/re**lo**"
stomach	el estómago	"es**to**mago"
stomach ache	el dolor de estómago/ barriga	"do**lor** de es**to**mago/ ba**rree**ga"
stomach upset	el trastorno estomacal	"tras**tor**no estoma**kal**"
▷ **I have a stomach upset**	tengo el estómago malo	"**ten**go el es**to**mago **ma**lo"
to stop	parar	"pa**rar**"
▷ **stop here/at the corner**	pare aquí/en la esquina	"**pa**re a**kee**/en la es**kee**na"
▷ **do we stop at ...?**	¿paramos en ...?	"pa**ra**mos en"
▷ **where do we stop for lunch?**	¿dónde paramos para comer?	"**don**de pa**ra**mos para ko**mer**"
▷ **please stop the bus**	por favor, pare el autobús	"por fa**bor** **pa**re el owto**boos**"
stopover	la escala	"es**ka**la"
storm	la tormenta	"tor**men**ta"
stormy:		
▷ **it's (very) stormy**	hay (mucha) tormenta	"**aee** (**moo**cha) tor**men**ta"
straight on	todo recto	"**to**do **rek**to"

ABSOLUTE ESSENTIALS

I would like ...	me gustaría ...	"me goosta**ree**a"
I need ...	necesito ...	"nethe**see**to"
where is ...?	¿dónde está ...?	"**don**de es**ta**"
I'm looking for ...	estoy buscando ...	"es**toee** boos**kan**do"

strap	la correa	"ko**rre**a"
▷ **I need a new strap**	me hace falta una correa nueva	"me **athe falta oo**na ko**rre**a **nwe**ba"
straw (*for drinking*)	la pajita	"pa**khee**ta"
strawberry	la fresa	"**fre**sa"
street	la calle	"**ka**ye"
street map	el plano de la ciudad	"**pla**no de la theeoo**dad**"
string	la cuerda	"**kwer**da"
striped	rayado	"ra**ya**do"
	rayada	"ra**ya**da"
	a rayas	"a **ra**yas"
strong	fuerte	"**fwer**te"
stuck	atascado	"atas**ka**do"
	atascada	"atas**ka**da"
▷ **it's stuck**	está atascado	"es**ta** atas**ka**do"
student	el estudiante	"estoodee**an**te"
	la estudiante	"estoodee**an**te"
stung	picado	"pee**ka**do"
	picada	"pee**ka**da"
▷ **he has been stung**	le han picado	"le an pee**ka**do"
stupid	tonto	"**ton**to"
	tonta	"**ton**ta"
suddenly	de repente	"de re**pen**te"
suede	el ante	"**an**te"
sugar	el azúcar	"a**thoo**kar"
suit	el traje	"**tra**khe"
suitcase	la maleta	"ma**le**ta"
▷ **my suitcase was damaged in transit**	se me ha estropeado la maleta en el viaje	"se me a estrope**a**do la ma**le**ta en el bee**a**khe"

ABSOLUTE ESSENTIALS

do you have ...?	¿tiene ...?	"tee-**e**ne"
is there ...?	¿hay ...?	"**aee**"
are there ...?	¿hay ...?	"**aee**"
how much is ...?	¿cuánto cuesta ...?	"**kwan**to **kwes**ta"

▷ **my suitcase is missing**	me falta la maleta	"me **fal**ta la ma**le**ta"
summer	el verano	"be**ra**no"
sun	el sol	"sol"
to **sunbathe**	tomar el sol	"to**mar** el sol"
sunbed	la cama solar	"**ka**ma so**lar**"
sunburn	la quemadura del sol	"kema**doo**ra del sol"
▷ **can you give me anything for sunburn?**	¿podría darme algo para las quemaduras del sol?	"po**dree**a **dar**me **al**go **pa**ra las kema**doo**ras del sol"
sunburnt	quemado quemada	"ke**ma**do" "ke**ma**da"
▷ **I am sunburnt**	me he quemado	"me e ke**ma**do"
Sunday	domingo	"do**meen**go"
sunglasses	las gafas de sol	"**ga**fas de sol"
sun lounger	la tumbona	"toom**bo**na"
sunny	soleado soleada	"sole**a**do" "sole**a**da"
▷ **it's sunny**	hace sol	"**a**the sol"
sunshade	la sombrilla	"som**bree**ya"
sunstroke	la insolación	"eensolathe**on**"
suntan lotion	la loción bronceadora	"lothe**on** bronthe**a**dora"
supermarket	el supermercado	"soopermer**ka**do"
supper (*dinner*)	la cena	"**the**na"
supplement	el suplemento	"soople**men**to"
▷ **is there a supplement to pay?**	¿hay que pagar algún suplemento?	"**aee** ke pa**gar** al**goon** soople**men**to"
sure	seguro segura	"se**goo**ro" "se**goo**ra"

ABSOLUTE ESSENTIALS		
yes (please)	sí (por favor)	"see (por fa**bor**)"
no (thank you)	no (gracias)	"no (**grath**eeas)"
hello	hola	"**o**la"
goodbye	adiós	"ad**ee**os"

surface mail:

▷ **by surface mail**	por vía terrestre	"por **bee**a te**rres**tre"
surfboard	la plancha de surf	"**plan**cha de soorf"
▷ **can I rent a surfboard?**	¿puedo alquilar una plancha de surf?	"**pwe**do alkee**lar** oona **plan**cha de soorf"
surfer	el surfista	"soor**fees**ta"
	la surfista	"soor**fees**ta"
surfing	el surf	"soorf"
▷ **I'd like to go surfing**	me gustaría hacer surf	"me goosta**ree**a a**ther** soorf"
surname	el apellido	"ape**yee**do"
suspension	la suspensión	"soospensee**on**"
sweater	el suéter	"**swe**ter"
	el jersey	"kher**se**-ee"
sweet	dulce	"**dool**the"
sweetener	el edulcorante	"edoolko**rante**"
sweets	los caramelos	"kara**me**los"
to **swim**	nadar	"na**dar**"
▷ **can one swim in the river?**	¿se puede nadar en el río?	"se **pwe**de na**dar** en el **ree**o"
▷ **is it safe to swim here?**	¿se puede nadar sin peligro aquí?	"se **pwe**de na**dar** seen pe**lee**gro a**kee**"
▷ **can you swim?**	¿sabe nadar?	"**sa**be na**dar**"
swimming	la natación	"natathee**on**"
▷ **let's go swimming**	vamos a bañarnos	"**ba**mos a ban**yar**nos"
swimming pool	la piscina	"pees**thee**na"
▷ **is there a swimming pool?**	¿hay piscina?	"**a**ee pees**thee**na"
▷ **where is the municipal swimming pool?**	¿dónde está la piscina municipal?	"**don**de esta la pees**thee**na mooneethee**pal**"

ABSOLUTE ESSENTIALS

I don't understand	no comprendo	"no kom**pren**do"
I don't speak Spanish	no hablo español	"no **a**blo espan**yol**"
do you speak English?	¿habla inglés?	"**a**bla een**gles**"
could you help me?	¿podría ayudarme?	"po**dree**a ayoo**darme**"

swimsuit	el bañador	"ba**nya**dor"
	el traje de baño	"**tra**khe de **ba**nyo"
Swiss	suizo	"**swee**tho"
	suiza	"**swee**tha"
switch	el interruptor	"eenterroop**tor**"
to **switch off** (*engine*)	parar	"pa**rar**"
▷ **can I switch the light/ radio off?**	¿puedo apagar la luz/ radio?	"**pwe**do apa**gar** la looth/ **ra**deeo"
to **switch on**	encender	"enthen**der**"
▷ **can I switch the light/ radio on?**	¿puedo encender la luz/ radio?	"**pwe**do enthen**der** la looth/**ra**deeo"
Switzerland	Suiza	"**swee**tha"
synagogue	la sinagoga	"seena**go**ga"
table	la mesa	"**me**sa"
▷ **a table for four, please**	una mesa para cuatro, por favor	"**oo**na **me**sa para **kwa**tro por fa**bor**"
▷ **the table is booked for ... o'clock this evening**	la mesa está reservada para esta noche a las ...	"la **me**sa esta reser**ba**da para **es**ta **no**che a las"
tablecloth	el mantel	"man**tel**"
tablespoon	la cuchara	"koo**cha**ra"
tablet	la pastilla	"pas**tee**ya"
table tennis	el ping-pong	"**peen**pon"
to **take**	tomar	"to**mar**"
▷ **how long does it take?**	¿cuánto tiempo lleva?	"**kwan**to tee-**em**po **ye**ba"
▷ **how long does the journey take?**	cuánto tiempo se tarda en hacer el viaje?	"**kwan**to tee-**em**po se **tar**da en a**ther** el bee**akhe**"
▷ **I take a continental size 40**	gasto una talla 40 europea	"**gas**to **oo**na **ta**ya kwa**ren**ta eooro**pea**"

ABSOLUTE ESSENTIALS

I would like ...	me gustaría ...	"me goosta**ree**a"
I need ...	necesito ...	"nethe**see**to"
where is ...?	¿dónde está ...?	"**don**de esta"
I'm looking for ...	estoy buscando ...	"es**toee** boos**kan**do"

▷ **I'd like to take a shower**	me gustaría ducharme	"me goostar**ee**a doo**char**me"
▷ **could you take a photograph of us?**	¿podría hacernos una foto?	"po**dree**a ha**cer**nos una **fo**to"
talc	los polvos de talco	"**pol**bos de **tal**ko"
to **talk**	hablar	"a**blar**"
tall	alto alta	"**al**to" "**al**ta"
▷ **how tall are you/is it?**	¿cuánto mide?	"**kwan**to **mee**de"
▷ **I am 1m 80 tall**	mido 1m 80	"**mee**do oon **me**tro o**chen**ta"
▷ **it is 10m tall**	mide 10m	"**mee**de dee-**eth me**tros"
tampons	los tampones	"tam**pon**es"
tan	el bronceado	"bron**the**ado"
tap	el grifo	"**gree**fo"
tape (*cassette, ribbon*) (*video*)	la cinta la cinta de vídeo	"**theen**ta" "**theen**ta de **bee**deo"
tape recorder	el magnetofón	"magneto**fon**"
tart (*cake*)	la tarta	"**tar**ta"
tartar sauce	la salsa tártara	"**sal**sa **tar**tara"
taste[1] *n*	el sabor	"sa**bor**"
to **taste**[2] *vb*	*vb* probar	"pro**bar**"
▷ **can I taste it?**	¿puedo probarlo?	"**pwe**do pro**bar**lo"
tax	el impuesto	"eem**pwes**to"
taxi	el taxi	"**tak**see"
▷ **can you order me a taxi, please?**	¿puede llamarme un taxi, por favor?	"**pwe**de ya**mar**me oon **tak**see por fa**bor**"
taxi rank	la parada de taxis	"pa**ra**da de **tak**sees"
tea	el té	"tay"

ABSOLUTE ESSENTIALS

do you have ...?	¿tiene ...?	"tee-**en**e"
is there ...?	¿hay ...?	"**aee**"
are there ...?	¿hay ...?	"**aee**"
how much is ...?	¿cuánto cuesta ...?	"**kwan**to **kwes**ta"

tea bag	la bolsita de té	"bol**see**ta de tay"
to **teach**	enseñar	"ense**nyar**"
teacher	el profesor	"profe**sor**"
	la profesora	"profe**sor**a"
team	el equipo	"e**kee**po"
team games	los juegos de equipo	"**khwe**gos de e**kee**po"
teapot	la tetera	"te**ter**a"
teaspoon	la cucharilla	"koocha**ree**ya"
teat	la tetina	"te**tee**na"
tee shirt	la camiseta	"kamee**se**ta"
teeth	los dientes	"dee-**en**tes"
telegram	el telegrama	"tele**gra**ma"
▷ **where can I send a telegram from?**	¿dónde se puede mandar un telegrama?	"**don**de se **pwe**de man**dar** oon tele**gra**ma"
▷ **I want to send a telegram**	quiero poner un telegrama	"kee-**e**ro po**ner** oon tele**gra**ma"
telephone	el teléfono	"te**le**fono"
▷ **how much is it to telephone Britain/the USA?**	¿cuánto cuesta llamar por teléfono a Gran Bretaña/los Estados Unidos?	"**kwan**to **kwes**ta ya**mar** por te**le**fono a gran bre**ta**nya/los es**ta**dos oo**nee**dos"
telephone book	la guía telefónica	"**gee**a tele**fo**neeka"
telephone box	la cabina telefónica	"ka**bee**na tele**fo**neeka"
telephone call	la llamada telefónica	"ya**ma**da tele**fo**neeka"
▷ **I want to make a telephone call**	quiero hacer una llamada telefónica	"kee-**e**ro a**ther** **oo**na ya**ma**da tele**fo**neeka"
telephone directory	la guía telefónica	"**gee**a tele**fo**neeka"
television	la televisión	"telebee**see**on"
television lounge	la sala de televisión	"**sa**la de telebee**see**on"

ABSOLUTE ESSENTIALS

yes (please)	sí (por favor)	"see (por fa**bor**)"
no (thank you)	no (gracias)	"no (**gra**theeas)"
hello	hola	"**o**la"
goodbye	adiós	"adee**os**"

▷ **is there a television lounge?**	¿hay sala de televisión?	"aee sala de telebeeseeon"
television set	el televisor	"telebeesor"
telex	el télex	"teleks"
to **tell**	decir	"detheer"
temperature	la temperatura	"temperatoora"
▷ **to have a temperature**	tener fiebre	"tener fee-ebre"
▷ **what is the temperature?**	¿qué temperatura hace?	"ke temperatoora athe"
temporary	provisional	"probeeseeonal"
ten	diez	"dee-eth"
tennis	el tenis	"tenees"
▷ **where can we play tennis?**	¿dónde podemos jugar al tenis?	"donde podemos khoogar al tenees"
tennis ball	la pelota de tenis	"pelota de tenees"
tennis court	la pista de tenis	"peesta de tenees"
▷ **how much is it to hire a tennis court?**	¿cuánto cuesta alquilar la pista de tenis?	"kwanto kwesta alkeelar la peesta de tenees"
tennis racket	la raqueta de tenis	"raketa de tenees"
tent	la tienda de campaña	"tee-enda de kampanya"
▷ **can we pitch our tent here?**	¿podemos montar la tienda aquí?	"podemos montar la tee-enda akee"
tent peg	la estaca la piqueta de tienda	"estaka" "peeketa de tee-enda"
terminus	la estacíon terminal	"estatheeon termeenal"
terrace	la terraza	"terratha"
▷ **can I eat on the terrace?**	¿se puede comer en la terraza?	"se pwede komer en la terratha"
than	que	"ke"

ABSOLUTE ESSENTIALS

I don't understand	no comprendo	"no komprendo"
I don't speak Spanish	no hablo español	"no ablo espanyol"
do you speak English?	¿habla inglés?	"abla eengles"
could you help me?	¿podría ayudarme?	"podreea ayoodarme"

▷ **more than**	más que	"mas ke"
▷ **less than**	menos de	"**me**nos de"
▷ **better than this**	mejor que esto	"me**khor** ke **es**to"

thank you	gracias	"**gra**theeas"
▷ **thank you very much**	muchas gracias	"**moo**chas **gra**theeas"
▷ **no thank you**	no gracias	"no **gra**theeas"

that	eso	"**es**o"
▷ **that book**	ese libro	"**es**e **lee**bro"
▷ **that table**	esa mesa	"**es**a **me**sa"
▷ **that one**	ése	"**es**e"
	ésa	"**es**a"

to thaw	deshelar	"dese**lar**"
▷ **it's thawing**	deshiela	"desee-**e**la"

theatre	el teatro	"te**a**tro"

their:		
▷ **their car**	su coche	"soo **ko**che"
▷ **their socks**	sus calcetines	"soos kalthe**tee**nes"

theirs	(el) suyo	"**soo**yo"
	(la) suya	"**soo**ya"
	(los) suyos	"**soo**yos"
	(las) suyas	"**soo**yas"

then	entonces	"enton**thes**"
▷ **they will be away then**	no estarán durante estas fechas	"no esta**ran** doo**rante** estas **fe**chas"

there	allí	"a**yee**"
▷ **there is/there are...**	hay...	"**aee**"

thermometer	el termómetro	"ter**mo**metro"

these	estos	"**es**tos"
	estas	"**es**tas"

ABSOLUTE ESSENTIALS

I would like ...	me gustaría ...	"me goosta**ree**a"
I need ...	necesito ...	"nethe**see**to"
where is ...?	¿dónde está ...?	"**don**de esta"
I'm looking for ...	estoy buscando ...	"es**toee** boos**kan**do"

they	ellos	"**e**yos"
	ellas	"**e**yas"
thief	el ladrón	"la**dron**"
thing	la cosa	"**ko**sa"
▷ **my things**	mis cosas	"mees **ko**sas"
to **think**	pensar	"pen**sar**"
third	tercero/a	"ter**the**ro/a"
thirsty:		
▷ **I'm/we're thirsty**	tengo/tenemos sed	"**ten**go/te**ne**mos sed"
thirteen	trece	"**tre**the"
thirty	treinta	"**tray**nta"
this	este	"**es**te"
	esta	"**es**ta"
▷ **this one**	éste	"**es**te"
	ésta	"**es**ta"
those	esos	"**e**sos"
	esas	"**e**sas"
thousand	mil	"meel"
thread	el hilo	"**ee**lo"
three	tres	"tres"
throat	la garganta	"gar**gan**ta"
▷ **I want something for a sore throat**	quiero algo para la garganta	"kee-**e**ro **al**go **pa**ra la gar**gan**ta"
throat lozenge	la pastilla para la garganta	"pas**tee**ya **pa**ra la gar**gan**ta"
through	por	"por"
▷ **I can't get through**	no contestan	"no kon**tes**tan"
▷ **is it/this a through train?**	¿es este tren directo?	"es **es**te tren dee**rek**to"
thunder	el trueno	"troo**e**no"

ABSOLUTE ESSENTIALS

do you have ...?	¿tiene ...?	"tee-**e**ne"
is there ...?	¿hay ...?	"**a**ee"
are there ...?	¿hay ...?	"**a**ee"
how much is ...?	¿cuánto cuesta ...?	"**kwan**to **kwes**ta"

▷ **I think it's going to thunder**	creo que va a tronar	"kreo ke ba a tronar"
thunderstorm	la tormenta	"tormenta"
▷ **will there be a thunderstorm?**	¿va a haber tormenta?	"ba a aber tormenta"
Thursday	jueves	"khwebes"
ticket	el billete	"beeyete"
(for show)	la entrada	"entrada"
▷ **can you book the tickets for us?** *(travelling)*	¿puede reservarnos los billetes?	"pwede reserbarnos los beeyetes"
▷ **where do I buy a ticket?** *(for theatre etc)*	¿dónde se compran las entradas?	"donde se kompran las entradas"
▷ **can I buy the tickets here?** *(for theatre etc)*	¿puedo sacar las entradas aquí?	"pwedo sakar las entradas akee"
▷ **a single ticket**	un billete de ida	"oon beeyete de eeda"
▷ **a return ticket**	un billete de ida y vuelta	"oon beeyete de eeda ee bwelta"
▷ **2 tickets for the opera/theatre**	2 entradas para la ópera/el teatro	"dos entradas para la opera/el teatro"
ticket collector	el revisor	"rebeesor"
ticket office	el despacho de billetes	"despacho de beeyetes"
tie	la corbata	"korbata"
tights	las medias	"medeeas"
till[1] *n*	la caja	"kaha"
till[2] *prep*	hasta	"asta"
▷ **I want to stay 3 nights from ... till ...**	quiero quedarme 3 noches del ... al ...	"kee-ero kedarme tres noches del ... al"
time	el tiempo	"tee-empo"
▷ **this time**	esta vez	"esta beth"
▷ **what time is it?**	¿qué hora es?	"ke ora es"

ABSOLUTE ESSENTIALS		
yes (please)	sí (por favor)	"see (por fabor)"
no (thank you)	no (gracias)	"no (gratheeas)"
hello	hola	"ola"
goodbye	adiós	"adeeos"

▷ do we have time to visit the town?	¿tenemos tiempo para visitar la ciudad?	"tenemos tee-**em**po para beeseetar la theeoo**dad**"
▷ what time do we get to ...?	¿a qué hora llegamos a ...?	"a ke **o**ra ye**ga**mos a"
▷ is it time to go?	¿ya es hora de irnos?	"ya es **o**ra de**eer**nos"
timetable	la tabla de los horarios	"**ta**bla de los o**ra**reeos"
▷ can I have a timetable?	¿puede darme una tabla de los horarios?	"**pwe**de **da**rme **oo**na **ta**bla de los o**ra**reeos"
timetable board	el tablero de los horarios	"tab**le**ro de los o**ra**reeos"
tin	la lata	"**la**ta"
tinfoil	el papel de aluminio	"pa**pel** de aloo**mee**neeo"
tin-opener	el abrelatas	"abre**la**tas"
tinted	teñido teñida	"ten**yee**do" "ten**yee**da"
▷ my hair is tinted	tengo el pelo teñido	"**ten**go el **pe**lo ten**yee**do"
tip (*to waiter etc*)	la propina	"pro**pee**na"
▷ is it usual to tip?	¿está bien dar de propina?	"es**ta** bee-**en** dar de pro**pee**na"
▷ how much should I tip?	¿cuánto tengo que dar de propina?	"**kwan**to **ten**go ke dar de pro**pee**na"
▷ is the tip included?	¿está incluida la propina?	"es**ta** eenkloo**ee**da la pro**pee**na"
tipped	con filtro	"kon **feel**tro"
tired	cansado cansada	"kan**sa**do" "kan**sa**da"
tiring	cansado cansada	"kan**sa**do" "kan**sa**da"
tissues	los pañuelos de papel	"panyoo**e**los de pa**pel**"
to	a	"a"

ABSOLUTE ESSENTIALS

I don't understand	no comprendo	"no kom**pren**do"
I don't speak Spanish	no hablo español	"no **a**blo espan**yol**"
do you speak English?	¿habla inglés?	"**a**bla een**gles**"
could you help me?	¿podría ayudarme?	"po**dree**a ayoo**dar**me"

toast	el pan tostado	"pan tostado"
▷ **2 slices of toast**	2 tostadas	"dos tostadas"
tobacco	el tabaco	"tabako"
tobacconist's	el estanco	"estanko"
today	hoy	"oee"
▷ **is it open today?**	¿está abierto hoy?	"esta abee-erto oee"
together	juntos	"khoontos"
	juntas	"khoontas"
toilet	los servicios	"serbeetheeos"
▷ **is there a toilet for the disabled?**	¿hay wáter especial para minusválidos?	"aee bater espetheeal para meenoosbaleedos"
▷ **where are the toilets, please?**	por favor, ¿dónde están los servicios?	"por fabor donde estan los serbeetheeos"
▷ **is there a toilet on board the coach?**	¿hay servicio en el autocar?	"aee serbeetheeo en el owtokar"
▷ **the toilet won't flush**	no funciona la cisterna del wáter	"no foontheeona la theesterna del bater"
toilet paper	el papel higiénico	"papel eekhee-eneeko"
▷ **there is no toilet paper**	no hay papel higiénico	"no aee papel eekhee-eneeko"
toll	el peaje	"peakhe"
▷ **is there a toll on this motorway?**	¿es de peaje esta autopista?	"es de peakhe esta owtopeesta"
tomato	el tomate	"tomate"
tomato juice	el zumo de tomate	"thoomo de tomate"
tomato soup	la sopa de tomate	"sopa de tomate"
tomorrow	mañana	"manyana"
▷ **tomorrow morning**	mañana por la mañana	"manyana por la manyana"
▷ **tomorrow afternoon**	mañana por la tarde	"manyana por la tarde"
▷ **tomorrow night**	mañana por la noche	"manyana por la noche"

ABSOLUTE ESSENTIALS		
I would like ...	me gustaría ...	"me goostareea"
I need ...	necesito ...	"netheseeto"
where is ...?	¿dónde está ...?	"donde esta"
I'm looking for ...	estoy buscando ...	"estoee booskando"

▷ **is it open tomorrow?**	¿está abierto mañana?	"**esta** abee-**er**to man**ya**na"
tongue	la lengua	"**len**gwa"
tonic water	la tónica	"**to**neeka"
tonight	esta noche	"**es**ta **no**che"
too (*also*)	también	"tambee-**en**"
▷ **it's too big**	es demasiado grande	"es demasee**a**do **gran**de"
tooth	el diente	"dee-**en**te"
▷ **I've broken a tooth**	me he roto un diente	"me e **ro**to oon dee-**en**te"
toothache	el dolor de muelas	"do**lor** de **mwe**las"
▷ **I have toothache**	me duelen las muelas	"me **dwe**len las **mwe**las"
▷ **I want something for toothache**	quiero algo para el dolor de muelas	"kee-**ero al**go para el do**lor** de **mwe**las"
toothbrush	el cepillo de dientes	"the**pee**yo de dee-**en**tes"
toothpaste	la pasta de dientes	"**pas**ta de dee-**en**tes"
toothpick	el palillo de dientes	"pa**lee**yo de dee-**en**tes"
top[1] *n*	la cima	"**thee**ma"
▷ **on top of ...**	sobre ...	"**so**bre"
top[2] *adj*:		
▷ **the top floor**	el último piso	"**ool**teemo **pee**so"
torch	la linterna	"leen**ter**na"
torn	rasgado	"ras**ga**do"
	rasgada	"ras**ga**da"
total	el total	"to**tal**"
tough (*meat*)	duro	"**doo**ro"
	dura	"**doo**ra"
tour (*trip*)	la excursión	"ekskoorsee**on**"
(*of museum etc*)	la visita	"bee**see**ta"
▷ **how long does the tour take?**	¿cuánto tiempo dura la excursión?	"**kwan**to tee-**em**po **doo**ra la ekskoorsee**on**"

ABSOLUTE ESSENTIALS

do you have ...?	¿tiene ...?	"tee-**ene**"
is there ...?	¿hay ...?	"**aee**"
are there ...?	¿hay ...?	"**aee**"
how much is ...?	¿cuánto cuesta ...?	"**kwan**to **kwes**ta"

▷ **when is the bus tour of the town?**	¿a qué hora sale el autobús que hace el recorrido turístico por la ciudad?	"a ke **ora sale** el owto**boos** ke **a**the el rekor**ree**do too**rees**teeko por la theeoo**dad**"
▷ **the tour starts at about ...**	la excursión empieza sobre las ...	"la ekskoorsee**on** empee-**e**tha **so**bre las"
tourist	el/la turista	"too**rees**ta"
tourist office	la oficina de turismo	"ofee**thee**na de too**rees**mo"
▷ **I'm looking for the tourist information office**	busco la oficina de turismo	"**boo**sko la ofee**thee**na de too**rees**mo"
tourist ticket	un billete turístico	"bee**ye**te too**rees**teeko"
to tow	remolcar	"remol**kar**"
▷ **can you tow me to a garage?**	¿puede remolcarme hasta un garage?	"**pwe**de remol**kar**me asta oon ga**rakhe**"
towel	la toalla	"to**a**ya"
▷ **the towels have run out**	se han acabado las toallas	"se an aka**ba**do las to**a**yas"
town	la ciudad	"theeoo**dad**"
town centre	el centro de la ciudad	"**then**tro de la theeoo**dad**"
town plan	el plano de la ciudad	"**pla**no de la theeoo**dad**"
tow rope	el cable de remolque	"**ka**ble de re**mol**ke"
toy	el juguete	"khoo**ge**te"
toy shop	la tienda de juguetes	"tee-**en**da de khoo**ge**tes"
traditional	tradicional	"tradeethee**onal**"
traffic	la circulación	"theerkoolathee**on**"
▷ **is the traffic heavy on the motorway?**	¿hay mucho tráfico en la autopista?	"**a**ee **moo**cho **tra**feeko en la owto**pees**ta"

ABSOLUTE ESSENTIALS

yes (please)	sí (por favor)	"see (por fa**bor**)"
no (thank you)	no (gracias)	"no (**gra**theeas)"
hello	hola	"**o**la"
goodbye	adiós	"adee**os**"

▷ **is there a route that avoids the traffic?**	¿hay algún otro camino que evite el tráfico?	"**aee** al**goon o**tro ka**mee**no ke e**bee**te el **traf**eeko"
traffic jam	el atasco	"a**tas**ko"
trailer	el remolque	"re**mol**ke"
train	el tren	"tren"
▷ **is this the train for ...?**	¿es éste el tren de ...?	"es **es**te el tren de"
▷ **what times are the trains?**	¿cuál es el horario de los trenes?	"kwal es el o**ra**reeo de los **tre**nes"
▷ **are there any cheap train fares?**	¿hay algunas tarifas de tren baratas?	"**aee** al**goo**nas ta**ree**fas de tren ba**ra**tas?"
▷ **does this train go to ...?**	este tren ¿va a ...?	"**es**te tren ba a"
▷ **how frequent are the trains to town?**	¿con qué frecuencia pasan los trenes para el centro?	"kon ke fre**kwen**theea **pa**san los **tre**nes para el **then**tro"
▷ **does this train stop at ...?**	¿este tren para en ...?	"**es**te tren **pa**ra en"
▷ **when is the first/next/ last train to ...?**	¿cuándo sale el primer/ próximo/último tren para ...?	"**kwan**do **sa**le el pree**mer**/**prok**seemo/ **ool**teemo tren **pa**ra"
training shoes	las zapatillas de deporte	"thapa**tee**yas de de**por**te"
tram	el tranvía	"tran**bee**a"
trampoline	la cama elástica	"**ka**ma e**las**teeka"
transfer (*travelling*)	transferir hacer transbordo	"transfe**reer**" "a**ther** trans**bor**do"
▷ **I should like to transfer some money from my account**	quisiera hacer una transferencia de mi cuenta	"keesee-**e**ra a**ther oo**na transfe**ren**theea de mee **kwen**ta"
▷ **you have to transfer at ...**	tiene que hacer transbordo en ...	"tee-**e**ne ke a**ther** trans**bor**do en"
to translate	traducir	"tradoo**theer**"
▷ **could you translate this for me?**	¿podría traducirme esto?	"po**dree**a tradoo**theer**me **es**to"

ABSOLUTE ESSENTIALS

I don't understand	no comprendo	"no kom**pren**do"
I don't speak Spanish	no hablo español	"no **ab**lo espan**yol**"
do you speak English?	¿habla inglés?	"**ab**la een**gles**"
could you help me?	¿podría ayudarme?	"po**dree**a ayoo**dar**me"

translation	la traducción	"tradooktheeon"
to travel	viajar	"beeakhar"
▷ **I am travelling alone**	viajo solo	"beeakho solo"
travel agent	el agente de viajes	"akhente de beeakhes"
	la agente de viajes	"akhente de beeakhes"
traveller's cheque	el cheque de viaje	"cheke de beeakhe"
▷ **do you accept traveller's cheques?**	¿aceptan cheques de viaje?	"atheptan chekes de beeakhe"
▷ **can I change my traveller's cheques here?**	¿puedo cambiar mis cheques de viaje aquí?	"pwedo kambeear mees chekes de beeakhe akee"
travel-sick:		
▷ **I get travel-sick**	me mareo en los viajes	"me mareo en los beeakhes"
tray	la bandeja	"bandekha"
tree	el árbol	"arbol"
trim (haircut)	el recorte	"rekorte"
▷ **can I have a trim?**	¿puede recortarme el pelo?	"pwede rekortarme el pelo"
trip	la excursión	"ekskoorseeon"
▷ **this is my first trip to ...**	este es mi primer viaje a ...	"este es mee preemer beeakhe a"
▷ **a business trip**	un viaje de negocios	"oon beeakhe de negotheeos"
▷ **do you run day trips to ...?**	¿organizan excursiones a ...?	"organeethan ekskoorseeones a"
trolley	el carrito	"karreeto"
trouble	los problemas	"problemas"
▷ **I am in trouble**	estoy en un apuro	"estoee en oon apooro"
▷ **I'm sorry to trouble you**	perdone las molestias	"perdone las molesteeas"

ABSOLUTE ESSENTIALS

I would like ...	me gustaría ...	"me goostareea"
I need ...	necesito ...	"netheseeto"
where is ...?	¿dónde está ...?	"donde esta"
I'm looking for ...	estoy buscando ...	"estoee booskando"

▷ **I'm having trouble with the phone/the key**	tengo problemas con el teléfono/la llave	"**ten**go pro**ble**mas kon el tele**fo**no/la **ya**be"
trousers	los pantalones	"panta**lo**nes"
trout	la trucha	"**troo**cha"
true	verdadero verdadera	"berda**de**ro" "berda**de**ra"
trunk (*luggage*)	el baúl	"ba**ool**"
▷ **I'd like to send my trunk on ahead**	quisiera mandar mi baúl antes	"keesee-**e**ra man**dar** mee ba**ool an**tes"
trunks	el bañador (de hombre)	"banya**dor** (de **om**bre)"
to **try**	(*attempt*) intentar	"eenten**tar**"
to **try on**	probarse	"pro**bar**se"
▷ **may I try on this dress?**	¿puedo probarme este vestido?	"**pwe**do pro**bar**me **es**te bes**tee**do"
T-shirt	la camiseta	"kamee**se**ta"
Tuesday	martes	"**mar**tes"
tuna	el atún	"a**toon**"
tunnel	el túnel	"**too**nel"
▷ **the Channel tunnel**	el Eurotúnel	"el eooro**too**nel"
turkey	el pavo	"**pa**bo"
to **turn** (*rotate*)	volver girar	"bol**ber**" "khee**rar**"
▷ **it's my turn**	me toca a mí	"me **to**ka a mee"
▷ **it's her turn**	le toca a ella	"le **to**ka a **e**ya"
to **turn down** (*sound, heating etc*)	bajar	"ba**khar**"
to **turn off** (*light etc*) (*tap*) (*engine*)	apagar cerrar parar	"apa**gar**" "the**rrar**" "pa**rar**"

ABSOLUTE ESSENTIALS

do you have ...?	¿tiene ...?	"tee-**e**ne"
is there ...?	¿hay ...?	"**a**ee"
are there ...?	¿hay ...?	"**a**ee"
how much is ...?	¿cuánto cuesta ...?	"**kwan**to **kwes**ta"

▷ **I can't turn the heating off**	no puedo apagar la calefacción	"no **pwe**do apa**gar** la kalefakthee**on**"
to turn on (*light etc*)	encender	"enthen**der**"
(*tap*)	abrir	"a**breer**"
(*engine*)	poner	"po**ner**"
▷ **I can't turn the heating on**	no puedo encender la calefacción	"no **pwe**do enthen**der** la kalefakthee**on**"

turning:

▷ **is this the turning for ...?**	¿se va por aquí a ...?	"se ba por a**kee** a"
▷ **take the second/third turning on your left/ right**	coga la segunda/tercera a la izquierda/derecha	"**ko**ha la se**goon**da/ ter**the**ra a la eethkee-**er**da/de**re**cha"
turnip	el nabo	"**na**bo"
to turn up (*sound, heating etc*)	subir	"soo**beer**"
tweezers	las pinzas	"**peen**thas"
twice	dos veces	"dos **be**thes"
twin-bedded room	la habitación con dos camas	"abeetathee**on** kon dos **ka**mas"
twenty	veinte	"**bay**-eente"
twenty-one	veintiuno	"bay-eente-**oo**no"
twenty-two	veintidós	"bay-eentee**dos**"
two	dos	"dos"
typical	típico	"**tee**peeko"
	típica	"**tee**peeka"
▷ **have you anything typical of this town/ region?**	¿tienen algo típico de esta ciudad/región?	"tee-**enen al**go **tee**peeko de **es**ta theeoo**dad**/ rekhee**on**"
tyre	el neumático	"neoo**ma**teeko"

ABSOLUTE ESSENTIALS

yes (please)	sí (por favor)	"see (por fa**bor**)"
no (thank you)	no (gracias)	"no (**grat**heeas)"
hello	hola	"**ola**"
goodbye	adiós	"adee**os**"

up

tyre pressure	la presión de los neumáticos	"preseeon de los neoomateekos"
▷ **what should the tyre pressure be?**	¿qué presión deberían tener los neumáticos?	"ke preseeon debereean tener los neoomateekos"
UK	el Reino Unido	"ray-eeno ooneedo"
umbrella (for rain) (on beach)	el paraguas la sombrilla	"paragwas" "sombreeya"
uncomfortable	incómodo incómoda	"eenkomodo" "eenkomoda"
▷ **the bed is uncomfortable**	la cama es incómoda	"la kama es eenkomoda"
unconscious	inconsciente	"eenkonsthee-ente"
under	debajo de	"debakho de"
underground	el metro	"metro"
underground station	la estación de metro	"estatheeon de metro"
underpass	el paso subterráneo	"paso soobterraneo"
to understand	comprender	"komprender"
▷ **I don't understand**	no comprendo	"no komprendo"
underwear	la ropa interior	"ropa eentereeor"
United States	los Estados Unidos	"estados ooneedos"
university	la universidad	"ooneeberseedad"
unleaded petrol	la gasolina sin plomo	"gasoleena seen plomo"
to unpack	deshacer	"desather"
▷ **I have to unpack**	tengo que deshacer las maletas	"tengo ke desather las maletas"
up	arriba	"arreeba"
▷ **up there**	allí arriba	"ayee arreeba"

ABSOLUTE ESSENTIALS

I don't understand	no comprendo	"no komprendo"
I don't speak Spanish	no hablo español	"no ablo espanyol"
do you speak English?	¿habla inglés?	"abla eengles"
could you help me?	¿podría ayudarme?	"podreea ayoodarme"

upstairs	arriba	"**arree**ba"
urgent	urgente	"oor**khen**te"
USA	EE. UU.	"estados oo**nee**dos"
to use	usar	"oo**sar**"
	utilizar	"ooteelee**thar**"
▷ **may I use your phone?**	¿puedo usar su teléfono?	"**pwe**do oo**sar** soo te**le**fono"
useful	útil	"**oo**teel"
usual	acostumbrado	"akostoom**bra**do"
	acostumbrada	"akostoom**bra**da"
usually	por lo general	"por lo khe**ne**ral"
vacancy (*in hotel*)	la habitación libre	"abeetathee**on lee**bre"
▷ **do you have any vacancies?** (*campsite*)	¿tienen sitio?	"tee-**e**nen **see**teeo"
to vacate	desalojar	"desalo**khar**"
▷ **when do I have to vacate the room?**	¿cuándo tengo que desalojar la habitación?	"**kwan**do **ten**go ke desalo**khar** la abeetathee**on**"
vacuum cleaner	la aspiradora	"aspeera**do**ra"
valid	válido	"**ba**leedo"
	válida	"**ba**leeda"
valley	el valle	"**ba**ye"
valuable	de valor	"de ba**lor**"
valuables	los objetos de valor	"ob**khe**tos de ba**lor**"
van	la furgoneta	"foorgo**ne**ta"
vase	el florero	"flo**re**ro"
VAT	el IVA	"**ee**ba"
▷ **does the price include VAT?**	¿va el IVA incluido en el precio?	"ba el **ee**ba eenkloo**ee**do en el **pre**theeo"

ABSOLUTE ESSENTIALS

I would like ...	me gustaría ...	"me goosta**ree**a"
I need ...	necesito ...	"nethe**see**to"
where is ...?	¿dónde está ...?	"**don**de esta"
I'm looking for ...	estoy buscando ...	"es**too**ee boos**kan**do"

veal	la ternera	"ter**ne**ra"
vegan	el vegetariano estricto	"bekhetaree**a**no es**treek**to"
	la vegetariana estricta	"bekhetaree**a**na es**treek**ta"
▷ **is this suitable for vegans?**	¿lo pueden comer los vegetarianos?	"lo **pwe**den ko**mer** los bekhetaree**a**nos"
▷ **do you have any vegan dishes?**	¿tienen platos vegetarianos?	"tee-**e**nen **pla**tos bekhetaree**a**nos"
vegetables	las verduras	"ber**doo**ras"
▷ **are the vegetables included?**	¿lleva verduras?	"**ye**ba ber**doo**ras"
vegetarian	vegetariano	"bekhetaree**a**no"
	vegetariana	"bekhetaree**a**na"
▷ **is this suitable for vegetarians?**	¿lo pueden comer los vegetarianos?	"lo **pwe**den ko**mer** los bekhetaree**a**nos"
▷ **do you have any vegetarian dishes?**	¿tienen platos vegetarianos?	"tee-**e**nen **pla**tos bekhetaree**a**nos"
venison	la carne de venado	"**kar**ne de be**na**do"
ventilator	el ventilador	"benteela**dor**"
vermouth	el vermut	"ber**moot**"
vertigo	el vértigo	"**ber**teego"
▷ **I suffer from vertigo**	padezco vértigo	"pa**deth**ko **ber**teego"
very	muy	"mwee"
vest	la camiseta	"kamee**se**ta"
via	por	"por"
video	el vídeo	"**bee**deo"
video camera	la cámara de vídeo	"**ka**mara de **bee**deo"
video cassette	la videocassette	"beedeoka**set**"
video recorder	el vídeo	"**bee**deo"

ABSOLUTE ESSENTIALS		
do you have ...?	¿tiene ...?	"tee-**e**ne"
is there ...?	¿hay ...?	"**aee**"
are there ...?	¿hay ...?	"**aee**"
how much is ...?	¿cuánto cuesta ...?	"**kwan**to **kwes**ta"

view	la vista	"**bees**ta"
▷ **I'd like a room with a view of the sea/the mountains**	quiero una habitación con vistas al mar/a las montañas	"kee-**e**ro **oo**na abeetathee**on** kon **bees**tas al mar/a las montane**e**as"
villa (*in country*)	la casa de campo	"**ka**sa de **kam**po"
(*by sea*)	la casa en la playa	"**ka**sa en la **pla**ya"
village	el pueblo	"**pwe**blo"
vinegar	el vinagre	"bee**na**gre"
vineyard	la viña	"**bee**nya"
visa	el visado	"bee**sa**do"
▷ **I have an entry visa**	tengo un visado de entrada	"**ten**go oon bee**sa**do de en**tra**da"
visit	la visita	"bee**see**ta"
▷ **can we visit the vineyard/church?**	¿podemos ver las viñas/la iglesia?	"po**de**mos ber las **bee**nyas/la ee**gle**seea"
vitamin	la vitamina	"beeta**mee**na"
vodka	el vodka	"**bod**ka"
volleyball	el voleybol	"bolay-ee**bol**"
voltage	el voltaje	"bol**ta**khe"
▷ **what's the voltage?**	¿qué voltaje lleva?	"ke bol**ta**khe **ye**ba"
waist	la cintura	"theen**too**ra"
waistcoat	el chaleco	"cha**le**ko"
to wait (for)	esperar	"espe**rar**"
▷ **can you wait here for a few minutes?**	¿puede esperar aquí unos minutos?	"**pwe**de espe**rar** a**kee** **oo**nos mee**noo**tos"
▷ **please wait for me**	espéreme, por favor	"es**pe**reme por fa**bor**"
waiter	el camarero	"kama**re**ro"
waiting room	la sala de espera	"**sa**la de es**pe**ra"

ABSOLUTE ESSENTIALS

yes (please)	sí (por favor)	"see (por fa**bor**)"
no (thank you)	no (gracias)	"no (**grat**heeas)"
hello	hola	"**o**la"
goodbye	adiós	"adee**os**"

waitress	la camarera	"kama**re**ra"
to **wake**	despertar	"desper**tar**"
▷ **please wake me at 8.00**	por favor, despiérteme a las ocho en punto	"por fa**bor** despee-**er**teme a las **o**cho en **poon**to"
to **wake up**	despertarse	"desper**tar**se"
▷ **wake up!**	¡despierta!	"despee-**er**ta"
Wales	el País de Gales	"pa**ees** de **ga**les"
walk¹ *n*	el paseo	"pa**seo**"
▷ **to go for a walk**	dar un paseo	"dar oon pa**seo**"
▷ **are there any interesting walks nearby?**	¿sabe de alguna ruta interesante para pasear por aquí cerca?	"**sa**be de al**goo**na **roo**ta eentere**san**te para pase**ar** por a**kee ther**ka"
to **walk²** *vb*	andar	"an**dar**"
wallet	la cartera	"kar**te**ra"
walnut	la nuez	"nweth"
to **want**	querer	"ke**rer**"
warm (*climate*)	cálido	"**ka**leedo"
	cálida	"**ka**leeda"
(*clothes*)	abrigado	"abree**ga**do"
	abrigada	"abree**ga**da"
(*person, object*)	caliente	"kalee-**en**te"
warning triangle	el triángulo de avería	"tree**an**goolo de abe**ree**a"
to **wash**	lavar	"la**bar**"
▷ **to wash oneself**	lavarse	"la**bar**se"
▷ **where can I wash my hands?**	¿dónde puedo lavarme las manos?	"**don**de **pwe**do la**bar**me las **ma**nos"
▷ **where can I wash my clothes?**	¿dónde puedo lavar la ropa?	"**don**de **pwe**do la**bar** la **ro**pa"
washable	lavable	"la**ba**blay"
▷ **is it washable?**	¿se lava?	"se **la**ba"
washbasin	el lavabo	"la**ba**bo"

ABSOLUTE ESSENTIALS

I don't understand	no comprendo	"no kom**pren**do"
I don't speak Spanish	no hablo español	"no **a**blo espan**yol**"
do you speak English?	¿habla inglés?	"**a**bla een**gles**"
could you help me?	¿podría ayudarme?	"po**dree**a ayoo**dar**me"

▷ **the washbasin is dirty**	el lavabo está sucio	"el la**ba**bo es**ta soo**theeo"
▷ **do I have to pay extra to use the washbasin?**	¿tengo que pagar para usar el lavabo?	"**ten**go ke pa**gar** para oo**sar** el la**ba**bo"
washing	la colada	"ko**la**da"
▷ **where can I do some washing?**	¿dónde puedo lavar?	"**don**de **pwe**do la**bar**"
washing machine	la lavadora	"laba**do**ra"
▷ **how do you work the washing machine?**	¿cómo funciona la lavadora?	"**ko**mo foon**thee**o**na la laba**do**ra"
washing powder	el jabón en polvo	"kha**bon** en **pol**bo"
washing up	el fregado	"fre**ga**do"
▷ **to do the washing up**	fregar los platos	"fre**gar** los **pla**tos"
washing-up liquid	el lavavajillas	"lababa**khee**yas"
wasp	la avispa	"a**bees**pa"
waste bin	el cubo de la basura	"**koo**bo de la ba**soo**ra"
watch¹ *n*	el reloj	"re**lo**"
▷ **I think my watch is slow/fast**	creo que mi reloj está atrasado/adelantado	"**kre**o ke mee re**lo** esta atra**sa**do/adelan**ta**do"
▷ **my watch has stopped**	se me ha parado el reloj	"se me a pa**ra**do el re**lo**"
to watch² *vb (look at)*	mirar	"mee**rar**"
▷ **could you watch my bag for a minute please?**	¿podría vigilarme la bolsa un momento?	"po**dree**a beekhee**lar**me la **bol**sa oon mo**men**to"
water	el agua	"**a**gwa"
▷ **there is no hot water**	no hay agua caliente	"no aee **a**gwa kalee-**en**te"
▷ **a glass of water**	un vaso de agua	"oon **ba**so de **a**gwa"
waterfall	la cascada	"kas**ka**da"
water heater	el calentador de agua	"kalenta**dor** de **a**gwa"
watermelon	la sandía	"san**dee**a"
waterproof	impermeable	"eemper**me**able"

ABSOLUTE ESSENTIALS		
I would like ...	me gustaría ...	"me goosta**ree**a"
I need ...	necesito ...	"nethe**see**to"
where is ...?	¿dónde está ...?	"**don**de es**ta**"
I'm looking for ...	estoy buscando ...	"es**toe**e boos**kan**do"

water-skiing	el esquí acuático	"es**kee** akwa**teek**o"
▷ **is it possible to go water-skiing here?**	¿se puede hacer esquí acuático aquí?	"se **pwe**de a**ther** es**kee** akwa**teek**o a**kee**"
wave (*on sea*)	la ola	"**o**la"
wax	la cera	"**ther**a"
way (*manner*)	la manera	"ma**ner**a"
(*route*)	el camino	"ka**meen**o"
▷ **this way**	por aquí	"por a**kee**"
▷ **which is the way to ...?**	¿por dónde se va a ...?	"por **don**de se ba a"
▷ **what's the best way to get to ...?**	¿cuál es la mejor manera de ir a ...?	"kwal es la me**khor** ma**ner**a de eer a"
▷ **that way**	por ahí	"por a**ee**"
we	nosotros	"no**so**tros"
	nosotras	"no**so**tras"
weak (*person*)	débil	"**deb**eel"
(*coffee*)	flojo	"**flo**kho"
	floja	"**flo**kha"
to wear	llevar	"ye**bar**"
▷ **what should I wear?**	¿qué me pongo?	"ke me **pon**go"
weather	el tiempo	"tee-**em**po"
▷ **what dreadful weather!**	¡qué tiempo tan horrible!	"ke tee-**em**po tan or**ree**ble"
▷ **is the weather going to change?**	¿va a cambiar el tiempo?	"ba a kambee**ar** el tee-**em**po"
weather forecast	el pronóstico del tiempo	"pro**nos**teeko del tee-**em**po"
▷ **what's the weather forecast for tomorrow?**	¿cuál es el pronóstico del tiempo para mañana?	"kwal es el pro**nos**teeko del tee-**em**po **pa**ra man**ya**na"
wedding	la boda	"**bo**da"
▷ **we are here for a wedding**	hemos venido a una boda	"**e**mos be**nee**do a **oo**na **bo**da"

ABSOLUTE ESSENTIALS

do you have ...?	¿tiene ...?	"tee-**en**e"
is there ...?	¿hay ...?	"aee"
are there ...?	¿hay ...?	"aee"
how much is ...?	¿cuánto cuesta ...?	"**kwan**to **kwes**ta"

Wednesday	miércoles	"mee-**er**koles"
week	la semana	"se**ma**na"
▷ **this week**	esta semana	"**es**ta se**ma**na"
▷ **last week**	la semana pasada	"la se**ma**na pa**sa**da"
▷ **next week**	la semana que viene	"la se**ma**na ke bee-**e**ne"
▷ **for 2 weeks**	durante 2 semanas	"doo**ran**te dos se**ma**nas"
weekday	el día laborable	"**dee**a labo**ra**ble"
weekend	el fin de semana	"feen de se**ma**na"
weekly rate	la tarifa semanal	"ta**ree**fa sema**nal**"
weight	el peso	"**pe**so"
welcome	bienvenido	"bee-enben**ee**do"
	bienvenida	"bee-enben**ee**da"
▷ **you're welcome**	de nada	"de **na**da"
well	bien	"bee-**en**"
▷ **he's not well**	no está bien	"no es**ta** bee-**en**"
well done (*steak*)	muy hecho	"mwee **e**cho"
	muy hecha	"mwee **e**cha"
Welsh	galés	"ga**les**"
	galesa	"ga**les**a"
▷ **I'm Welsh**	soy galés/galesa	"**so**ee ga**les**/ga**les**a"
west	el oeste	"o**es**te"
wet	mojado	"mo**kha**do"
	mojada	"mo**kha**da"
(*weather*)	lluvioso	"yoobee**o**so"
	lluviosa	"yoobee**o**sa"
wetsuit	el traje de bucear	"**tra**khe de booth**ear**"
what	¿qué?	"ke"
▷ **what is it?**	¿qué es?	"ke es"
wheel	la rueda	"**rwe**da"

ABSOLUTE ESSENTIALS		
yes (please)	sí (por favor)	"see (por fa**bor**)"
no (thank you)	no (gracias)	"no (**grat**heeas)"
hello	hola	"**o**la"
goodbye	adiós	"adee**os**"

wheelchair	la silla de ruedas	"**see**ya de **rwe**das"
when	cuando	"**kwan**do"
▷ **when?**	¿cuándo?	"**kwan**do"
where	donde	"**don**de"
▷ **where?**	¿dónde?	"**don**de"
▷ **where are you from?**	¿de dónde es?	"de **don**de es"
which:		
▷ **which is it?**	¿cuál es?	"kwal es"
▷ **which man?**	¿qué hombre?	"ke **om**bre"
▷ **which woman?**	¿qué mujer?	"ke moo**kher**"
▷ **which book?**	¿qué libro?	"ke**lee**bro"
while¹ *n:*		
▷ **in a (short) while**	dentro de un rato	"**den**tro de oon **ra**to"
while² *conj*	mientras	"mee-**en**tras"
▷ **can you do it while I wait?**	¿puede hacerlo ahora?	"**pwe**de a**ther**lo a**o**ra"
whipped cream	la nata batida	"**na**ta ba**tee**da"
whisky	el whisky	"**wees**kee"
▷ **I'll have a whisky**	tráigame un whisky	"**tra**eegame oon **wees**kee"
▷ **whisky and soda**	whisky con soda	"**wees**kee kon **so**da"
white	blanco	"**blan**ko"
	blanca	"**blan**ka"
who	quien	"kee-**en**"
(*plural*)	quienes	"kee-**en**es"
▷ **who is it?**	¿quién es?	"kee-**en** es"
whole	entero	"en**te**ro"
	entera	"en**te**ra"
wholemeal bread	el pan integral	"pan eente**gral**"
whose:		
▷ **whose is it?**	¿de quién es?	"de kee-**en** es"

ABSOLUTE ESSENTIALS

I don't understand	no comprendo	"no kom**pren**do"
I don't speak Spanish	no hablo español	"no **ab**lo espan**yol**"
do you speak English?	¿habla inglés?	"**ab**la een**gles**"
could you help me?	¿podría ayudarme?	"po**dree**a ayoo**dar**me"

why?	¿por qué?	"por ke"
wide	ancho	"**an**cho"
	ancha	"**an**cha"
wife	la esposa	"es**po**sa"
window	la ventana	"ben**ta**na"
(shop)	el escaparate	"eskapa**ra**te"
(in car, train)	la ventanilla	"benta**nee**ya"
▷ **I'd like a window seat**	quiero un asiento al lado de la ventanilla	"kee-**e**ro oon asee-**en**to al **la**do de la benta**nee**ya"
▷ **I can't open the window**	no puedo abrir la ventana	"no **pwe**do a**breer** la ben**ta**na"
▷ **I have broken the window**	he roto la ventana	"e **ro**to la ben**ta**na"
▷ **may I open the window?**	¿puedo abrir la ventana?	"**pwe**do a**breer** la ben**ta**na"
▷ **shop window**	el escaparate	"el eskapa**ra**te"
▷ **in the window**	en el escaparate	"en el eskapa**ra**te"
windscreen	el parabrisas	"para**bree**sas"
▷ **could you clean the windscreen?**	¿podría limpiarme el parabrisas?	"po**dree**a leempee**ar**me el para**bree**sas"
▷ **the windscreen has shattered**	el parabrisas se ha hecho añicos	"el para**bree**sas se a **e**cho an**yee**kos"
windscreen washers	los limpiaparabrisas	"leempeeapara**bree**sas"
▷ **can you top up the windscreen washers?**	¿puede llenar los limpiaparabrisas?	"**pwe**de ye**nar** los leempeeapara**bree**sas"
windscreen wiper	el limpiaparabrisas	"leempeeapara**bree**sas"
windsurfer *(person)*	el surfista	"soor**fees**ta"
	la surfista	"soor**fees**ta"
(board)	la tabla de windsurf	"**ta**bla de **ween**soorf"
▷ **can I hire a windsurfer?**	¿se puede alquilar una tabla de windsurf?	"se **pwe**de alkee**lar** oona **ta**bla de **ween**soorf"
windsurfing	el windsurfing	"**ween**soor**feen**"

ABSOLUTE ESSENTIALS

I would like ...	me gustaría ...	"me goosta**ree**a"
I need ...	necesito ...	"nethe**see**to"
where is ...?	¿dónde está ...?	"**don**de esta"
I'm looking for ...	estoy buscando ...	"es**toee** boos**kan**do"

▷ **can I go windsurfing?**	¿se puede hacer windsurfing?	"se **pwe**de a**ther** ween**soor**feen"
windy:		
▷ **it's windy**	hace viento	"**athe** bee-**en**to"
▷ **it's (too) windy**	hace (demasiado) viento	"**athe** (demasee**a**do) bee-**en**to"
wine	el vino	"**bee**no"
▷ **this wine is not chilled**	este vino no está frío	"**este bee**no no esta **free**o"
▷ **can you recommend a good red/white/rosé wine?**	¿puede recomendarnos un tinto/blanco/rosado bueno?	"**pwe**de rekomen**dar**nos oon **teen**to/**blan**ko/rosado **bwe**no"
▷ **a bottle/carafe of house wine**	una botella/garrafa de vino de la casa	"**oo**na bo**te**ya/gar**ra**fa de **bee**no de la **ka**sa"
▷ **red/white wine**	vino tinto/blanco	"**bee**no **teen**to/**blan**ko"
▷ **rosé/sparkling wine**	vino rosado/espumoso	"**bee**no ro**sa**do/espoo**mo**so"
▷ **sweet/medium-sweet wine**	vino dulce/semidulce	"**bee**no **dool**the/semee**dool**the"
▷ **dry/medium-dry wine**	vino seco/semiseco	"**bee**no **se**ko/semee**se**ko"
wine list	la carta de vinos	"**kar**ta de **bee**nos"
▷ **may we see the wine list, please?**	¿nos trae la carta de vinos, por favor?	"nos **tra**-ay la **kar**ta de **bee**nos por fa**bor**"
winter	el invierno	"eenbee-**er**no"
with	con	"kon"
without	sin	"seen"
woman	la mujer	"moo**kher**"
wood (*material*) (*forest*)	la madera el bosque	"ma**de**ra" "**bos**ke"
wool	la lana	"**la**na"
word	la palabra	"pa**la**bra"
▷ **what is the word for ...?**	¿cómo se dice ...?	"**ko**mo se **dee**the"

ABSOLUTE ESSENTIALS

do you have ...?	¿tiene ...?	"tee-**e**ne"
is there ...?	¿hay ...?	"**a**ee"
are there ...?	¿hay ...?	"**a**ee"
how much is ...?	¿cuánto cuesta ...?	"**kwan**to **kwes**ta"

to **work** (*person*)	trabajar	"traba**khar**"
(*machine, car*)	funcionar	"foonthee**o**nar"
▷ **this does not work**	esto no funciona	"**es**to no foonthee**o**na"
▷ **how does this work?**	¿cómo funciona esto?	"**ko**mo foonthee**o**na **es**to"
▷ **where do you work?**	¿dónde trabaja?	"**don**de traba**kha**"

| **worried** | preocupado | "preokoo**pa**do" |
| | preocupada | "preokoo**pa**da" |

| **worse** | peor | "pe**or**" |

worth:

| ▷ **it's worth ...** | vale ... | "**ba**le" |
| ▷ **how much is it worth?** | ¿cuánto vale? | "**kwan**to **ba**le" |

| to **wrap (up)** | envolver | "enbol**ber**" |
| ▷ **could you wrap it up for me, please?** | ¿podría envolvérmelo, por favor? | "po**dree**a enbol**ber**melo por fa**bor**" |

| **wrapping paper** | el papel de envolver | "pa**pel** de enbol**ber**" |

| to **write** | escribir | "eskree**beer**" |
| ▷ **could you write that down please?** | ¿podría escribirlo, por favor? | "po**dree**a eskree**beer**lo por fa**bor**" |

| **writing paper** | el papel de escribir | "pa**pel** de eskree**beer**" |

wrong	equivocado	"ekeebo**ka**do"
	equivocada	"ekeebo**ka**da"
▷ **there is something wrong with the brakes**	los frenos no van bien	"los **fre**nos no ban bee-**en**"
▷ **there is something wrong with the electrics**	algo va mal en el sistema eléctrico	"**al**go ba mal en el sees**te**ma el**ek**treeko"
▷ **I think you've given me the wrong change**	creo que me ha dado mal el cambio	"**kre**o ke me a **da**do mal el **kam**beeo"
▷ **what's wrong?**	¿qué pasa?	"ke **pa**sa"

| **yacht** | el yate | "**ya**te" |

| **year** | el año | "**a**nyo" |
| ▷ **this year** | este año | "**es**te **a**nyo" |

ABSOLUTE ESSENTIALS		
yes (please)	sí (por favor)	"see (por fa**bor**)"
no (thank you)	no (gracias)	"no (**gra**theeas)"
hello	hola	"**o**la"
goodbye	adiós	"ade**os**"

▷ **last year**	el año pasado	"el **a**nyo pa**sa**do"
▷ **next year**	el año que viene	"el **a**nyo ke bee-**e**ne"
▷ **every year**	cada año	"**ka**da **a**nyo"
yellow	amarillo	"ama**ree**yo"
	amarilla	"ama**ree**ya"
yes	sí	"see"
▷ **yes please**	sí por favor	"see por fa**bor**"
yesterday	ayer	"a**yer**"
yet	todavía	"toda**bee**a"
▷ **not yet**	todavía no	"toda**bee**a no"
yoghurt	el yogur	"yo**goor**"
you (*informal*)	tú	"too"
(*plural*)	vosotros	"bo**so**tros"
	vosotras	"bo**so**tras"
(*formal singular*)	usted	"oos**ted**"
(*formal plural*)	ustedes	"oos**te**des"
young	joven	"**kho**ben"
your	tu	"too"
	tus	"toos"
(*plural*)	vuestro	"**bwes**tro"
	vuestra	"**bwes**tra"
	vuestros	"**bwes**tros"
	vuestras	"**bwes**tras"
(*polite form*)	su	"soo"
	sus	"soos"
yours	(el) tuyo	"**too**yo"
	(la) tuya	"**too**ya"
	(los) tuyos	"**too**yos"
	(las) tuyas	"**too**yas"
(*plural*)	(el) vuestro	"**bwes**tro"
	(la) vuestra	"**bwes**tra"
	(los) vuestros	"**bwes**tros"
	(las) vuestras	"**bwes**tras"
(*polite form*)	(el) suyo	"**soo**yo"

ABSOLUTE ESSENTIALS

I don't understand	no comprendo	"no kom**pren**do"
I don't speak Spanish	no hablo español	"no **a**blo espan**yol**"
do you speak English?	¿habla inglés?	"**a**bla een**gles**"
could you help me?	¿podría ayudarme?	"po**dree**a ayoo**dar**me"

	(la) suya	"**soo**ya"
	(los) suyos	"**soo**yos"
	(las) suyas	"**soo**yas"
youth hostel	el albergue de juventud	"al**ber**ge de khooben**tood**"
▷ **is there a youth hostel?**	¿hay un albergue de juventud?	"**aee** oon al**ber**ge de khooben**tood**"
zebra crossing	el paso de cebra	"**pa**so de **the**bra"
zero	el cero	"**the**ro"
zip	la cremallera	"krema**ye**ra"
zoo	el zoo	"tho"

ABSOLUTE ESSENTIALS

I would like ...	me gustaría ...	"me goosta**ree**a"
I need ...	necesito ...	"nethe**see**to"
where is ...?	¿dónde está ...?	"**don**de esta"
I'm looking for ...	estoy buscando ...	"es**to**ee boos**kan**do"

In the pronunciation system used in this book, Spanish sounds are represented by spellings of the nearest possible sounds in English. Hence, when you read out the pronunciation – shown in the third column, after the translation – sound the letters as if you were reading an English word. Whenever we think it is not sufficiently clear where to stress a word or phrase, we have used **bold** to highlight the syllable to be stressed. The following notes should help you:

	REMARKS	EXAMPLE	PRONUNCIATION
e	Midway between gate and got	**puede**	**pwe**de
o	Midway between goat and got	**como**	**ko**mo
y	As in yet	**llegar**	ye**gar**
th	As in thick	**centro**	**then**tro
kh	As in Scottish loch	**gente**	**khen**te
ny	As in onion	**niño**	**nee**nyo

Spelling in Spanish is very regular and, with a little practice, you will soon be able to pronounce Spanish words from their spelling alone. The only letters which are unlike English are:

v, w	As b in bed	**curva**	**koor**ba
c	Before a, o, u as in cat	**calle**	**ka**ye
	Before e, i as th in thin	**centro**	**then**tro
g	Before a, o, u as in got	**gato**	**ga**to
	Before e, i as ch in loch	**gente**	**khen**te
h	Silent	**hombre**	**om**-bre
j	As ch in loch	**jueves**	**khwe**-bes
ñ	As ni in onion	**niño**	**nee**nyo
z	As th in thin	**zumo**	**thoo**mo

The letter 'r' is always rolled; the double 'r' is rolled even more strongly. Spanish vowels are single sounds: when you find two together, pronounce both of them in quick succession as in **aceite** a**thay**-eete.

In the weight and length charts the middle figure can be either metric or imperial. Thus 3.3 feet = 1 metre, 1 foot = 0.3 metres, and so on.

feet		metres	inches		cm	lbs		kg
3.3	1	0.3	0.39	1	2.54	2.2	1	0.45
6.6	2	0.61	0.79	2	5.08	4.4	2	0.91
9.9	3	0.91	1.18	3	7.62	6.6	3	1.4
13.1	4	1.22	1.57	4	10.6	8.8	4	1.8
16.4	5	1.52	1.97	5	12.7	11.0	5	2.2
19.7	6	1.83	2.36	6	15.2	13.2	6	2.7
23.0	7	2.13	2.76	7	17.8	15.4	7	3.2
26.2	8	2.44	3.15	8	20.3	17.6	8	3.6
29.5	9	2.74	3.54	9	22.9	19.8	9	4.1
32.9	10	3.05	3.9	10	25.4	22.0	10	4.5
			4.3	11	27.9			
			4.7	12	30.1			

°C	0	5	10	15	17	20	22	24	26	28	30	35	37	38	40	50	100
°F	32	41	50	59	63	68	72	75	79	82	86	95	98.4	100	104	122	212

Km	10	20	30	40	50	60	70	80	90	100	110	120
Miles	6.2	12.4	18.6	24.9	31.0	37.3	43.5	49.7	56.0	62.0	68.3	74.6

Tyre pressures

lb/sq in	15	18	20	22	24	26	28	30	33	35
kg/sq cm	1.1	1.3	1.4	1.5	1.7	1.8	2.0	2.1	2.3	2.5

Liquids

gallons	1.1	2.2	3.3	4.4	5.5		pints	0.44	0.88	1.76
litres	5	10	15	20	25		litres	0.25	0.5	1

CAR PARTS

accelerator	el acelerador	"athelera**dor**"
air conditioning	el aire acondicionado	"a**ee**re akondeethee**o**nado"
antifreeze	el anticongelante	"anteekonkhe**lan**te"
automatic	automático	"owto**ma**teeko"
	automática	"owto**ma**teeka"
battery	la batería	"bate**ree**a"
boot	el maletero	"male**te**ro"
brake fluid	el líquido de frenos	"**lee**keedo de **fre**nos"
brakes	el freno	"**fre**no"
car	el coche	"**ko**che"
carburettor	el carburador	"karboora**dor**"
car number	la matrícula	"ma**tree**koola"
chain	la cadena	"ka**de**na"
de-ice	deshelar	"dese**lar**"
diesel	el gasoil	"ga**so**eel"
engine	el motor	"mo**tor**"
exhaust pipe	el tubo de escape	"**too**bo de es**ka**pe"
fan belt	la correa del ventilador	"ko**rre**a del benteela**dor**"
fuel pump	el surtidor de gasolina	"soortee**dor** de gaso**lee**na"
garage	el garaje	"ga**ra**khe"
gear	la marcha	"**mar**cha"
headlights	los faros	"**fa**ros"
indicator	el indicador	"eendeeka**dor**"
jack	el gato	"**ga**to"
jump leads	los cables para cargar la batería	"**ka**bles **pa**ra kar**gar** la bate**ree**a"
leak	la fuga	"**foo**ga"
luggage rack	la rejilla	"re**khee**ya"
oil filter	el filtro de aceite	"**feel**tro de **athee**-eete"
petrol	la gasolina	"gaso**lee**na"
points	los platinos	"pla**tee**nos"
radiator	el radiador	"radeea**dor**"
roof rack	la baca	"**ba**ka"
shock absorber	el amortiguador	"amorteegwa**dor**"
spare wheel	la rueda de repuesto	"**rwe**da de re**pwes**to"
spark plug	la bujía	"boo**khee**a"
speedometer	el velocímetro	"belo**thee**metro"
suspension	la suspensión	"soospensee**on**"
tyre	el neumático	"neoo**ma**teeko"
tyre pressure	la presión de los neumáticos	"pressee**on** de los neoo**ma**teekos"
warning triangle	el triángulo de avería	"tree**an**goolo de abe**ree**a"
windscreen	el parabrisas	"para**bree**sas"
windscreen washers	los limpiaparabrisas	"leempeeapara**bree**sas"
windscreen wiper	el limpiaparabrisas	"leempeeapara**bree**sas"

COLOURS

black	negro	"**neg**ro"
	negra	"**neg**ra"
blue	azul	"a**thool**"
brown	marrón	"ma**rron**"
colour	el color	"ko**lor**"
dark	oscuro	"os**koo**ro"
	oscura	"os**koo**ra"
green	verde	"**ber**de"
grey	gris	"grees"
light	claro	"**kla**ro"
navy blue	azul marino	"a**thool** ma**ree**no"
orange	naranja	"na**ran**kha"
pink	rosa	"**ro**sa"
purple	morado	"mo**ra**do"
	morada	"mo**ra**da"
red	rojo	"**rok**ho"
	roja	"**rok**ha"
white	blanco	"**blan**ko"
	blanca	"**blan**ka"
yellow	amarillo	"ama**ree**yo"
	amarilla	"ama**ree**ya"

COUNTRIES

America	América del Norte	"**amer**eeka del **nor**te"
Australia	Australia	"owst**ral**eea"
Austria	Austria	"**ows**treea"
Belgium	Bélgica	"**bel**kheeka"
Britain	Gran Bretaña	"gran bret**an**ya"
Canada	Canadá	"kana**da**"
England	Inglaterra	"eengla**ter**ra"
Europe	Europa	"eoo**ro**pa"
France	Francia	"**fran**theea"
Germany	Alemania	"alem**an**eea"
Greece	Grecia	"**gre**theea"
Ireland	Irlanda	"eer**lan**da"
Italy	Italia	"eet**al**eea"
Luxembourg	Luxemburgo	"looksem**boor**go"
New Zealand	Nueva Zelanda	"**nwe**ba the**lan**da"
Northern Ireland	Irlanda del Norte	"eer**lan**da del **nor**te"
Portugal	Portugal	"portoo**gal**"
Scotland	Escocia	"es**ko**theea"
Spain	España	"es**pan**ya"
Switzerland	Suiza	"**swee**tha"
United States	los Estados Unidos	"est**ad**os oo**nee**dos"
USA	EE. UU.	"est**ad**os oo**nee**dos"
Wales	el País de Gales	"pa**ees** de **ga**les"

DRINKS

alcohol	el alcohol	"al**kol**"
alcoholic	alcohólico	"al**ko**leeko"
	alcohólica	"al**ko**leeka"
apéritif	el aperitivo	"apere**tee**bo"
beer	la cerveza	"ther**be**tha"
brandy	el coñac	"ko**nyak**"
champagne	el champán	"cham**pan**"
cider	la sidra	"**see**dra"
cocktail	el cóctel	"**kok**tel"
cocoa	el cacao	"ka**kao**"
coffee	el café	"ka**fe**"
coke®	la coca cola	"**koka kola**"
draught beer	la cerveza de barril	"ther**be**tha de ba**rreel**"
drinking chocolate	el chocolate en polvo	"choko**late** en **pol**vo"
drinking water	el agua potable	"**agwa po**table"
fruit juice	el zumo	"**thoo**mo"
gin	la ginebra	"khee**ne**bra"
gin and tonic	el gin tonic	"yeen**to**neek"
grapefruit juice	el zumo de pomelo	"**thoo**mo de po**me**lo"
juice	el zumo	"**thoo**mo"
lager	la cerveza	"ther**be**tha"
lemonade	la gaseosa	"gase**o**sa"
lemon tea	el té con limón	"**te** kon lee**mon**"
liqueur	el licor	"lee**kor**"
milk	la leche	"**le**che"
milkshake	el batido de leche	"ba**tee**do de **le**che"
mineral water	el agua mineral	"**agwa** meene**ral**"
non-alcoholic	sin alcohol	"seen al**kol**"
orange juice	el zumo de naranja	"**thoo**mo de na**ran**kha"
rosé (wine)	el rosado	"ro**sa**do"
shandy	la cerveza con gaseosa	"ther**be**tha kon gase**o**sa"
sherry	el jerez	"khe**reth**"
skimmed milk	la leche desnatada	"**le**che desna**ta**da"
soda	la soda	"**so**da"
soft drink	la bebida sin alcohol	"be**bee**da seen al**kol**"
spirits	el alcohol	"al**kol**"
squash	el zumo	"**thoo**mo"
tea	el té	"tay"
tomato juice	el zumo de tomate	"**thoo**mo de to**ma**te"
tonic water	la tónica	"**to**neeka"
vermouth	el vermut	"ber**moot**"
vodka	el vodka	"**bod**ka"
whisky	el whisky	"**wee**skee"
wine	el vino	"**bee**no"

FISH AND SEAFOOD

anchovy	la anchoa	"an**cho**a"
caviar	el caviar	"kabee**ar**"
cod	el bacalao	"baka**lao**"
crab	el cangrejo	"kan**gre**kho"
fish	el pescado	"pes**ka**do"
haddock	el abadejo	"aba**de**kho"
hake	la merluza	"mer**loo**tha"
herring	el arenque	"**a**renke"
lobster	la langosta	"lan**gos**ta"
mackerel	la caballa	"ka**ba**ya"
mussel	el mejillón	"mekhee**yon**"
oyster	la ostra	"**os**tra"
prawn	la gamba	"**gam**ba"
salmon	el salmón	"sal**mon**"
sardine	la sardina	"sar**dee**na"
scallop	la vieira	"bee-**ay**-eera"
scampi	las gambas	"**gam**bas"
seafood	los mariscos	"ma**rees**kos"
shellfish	los mariscos	"ma**rees**kos"
shrimp	el camarón	"kama**ron**"
sole	la suela	"**swe**la"
trout	la trucha	"**troo**cha"
tuna	el atún	"a**toon**"

FRUIT AND NUTS

English	Spanish	Pronunciation
almond	la almendra	"al**men**dra"
apple	la manzana	"man**tha**na"
apricot	el albaricoque	"albaree**ko**ke"
banana	el plátano	"**pla**tano"
blackcurrants	los arándanos	"a**ran**danos"
cherry	la cereza	"the**re**tha"
chestnut	la castaña	"kas**ta**nya"
coconut	el coco	"**ko**ko"
currant	la pasa de Corinto	"**pa**sa de ko**reen**to"
date	el dátil	"**da**teel"
fig	el higo	"**ee**go"
fruit	la fruta	"**froo**ta"
grapefruit	el pomelo	"po**me**lo"
grapes	las uvas	"**oo**bas"
hazelnut	la avellana	"abe**ya**na"
lemon	el limón	"lee**mon**"
lime	la leema	"**lee**ma"
melon	el melón	"me**lon**"
nut	la nuez	"nweth"
olives	las aceitunas	"athee-ee**too**nas"
orange	la naranja	"na**ran**kha"
peach	el melocotón	"meloko**ton**"
peanut	el cacahuete	"kaka**we**te"
pear	la pera	"**pe**ra"
pineapple	la piña	"**pee**nya"
pistachio	el pistacho	"pees**ta**cho"
plum	la ciruela	"thee**rwe**la"
prunes	las ciruelas pasas	"thee**rwe**las **pa**sas"
raisin	la pasa	"**pa**sa"
raspberry	la frambuesa	"fram**bwe**sa"
strawberry	la fresa	"**fre**sa"
walnut	la nuez	"nweth"
watermelon	la sandía	"san**dee**a"

MEATS

bacon	el beicon	"**bay**-eekon"
beef	la carne de vaca	"**kar**ne de **ba**ka"
beefburger	la hamburguesa (de carne de vaca)	"amboor**ges**a (de **kar**ne de **ba**ka)"
breast	la pechuga	"pe**choo**ga"
cheeseburger	la hamburguesa con queso	"amboor**ges**a kon **kes**o"
chicken	el pollo	"**po**yo"
chop	la chuleta	"choo**let**a"
cold meat	las fiambres	"fee**am**bres"
duck	el pato	"**pa**to"
goose	el ganso	"**gan**so"
ham	el jamón	"kha**mon**"
hamburger	la hamburguesa	"amboor**ges**a"
kidneys	los riñones	"ree**nyo**nes"
liver	el higado	"**ee**gado"
meat	la carne	"**kar**ne"
mince	la carne picada	"**kar**ne pee**ka**da"
mutton	el cordero	"kor**de**ro"
pâté	el paté	"pa**te**"
pheasant	el faisán	"faee**san**"
pork	el cerdo	"**ther**do"
rabbit	el conejo	"ko**nek**ho"
salami	el salami	"sala**mee**"
sausage	la salchicha	"sal**chee**cha"
steak	el filete	"fee**le**te"
stew	el estofado	"esto**fa**do"
turkey	el pavo	"**pa**bo"
veal	la ternera	"ter**ne**ra"

SHOPS

baker's	la panadería	"panader**eea**"
barber	el peluquero	"peloo**ke**ro"
bookshop	la librería	"leebrer**eea**"
butcher's	la carnicería	"karneether**eea**"
café	el café	"ka**fe**"
chemist's	la farmacia	"far**ma**theea"
dry-cleaner's	la tintorería	"teentorer**eea**"
duty-free shop	la tienda "duty free"	"tee-**en**da dootee**free**"
grocer's	la tienda de ultramarinos	"tee-**en**da de ooltrama**ree**nos"
hairdresser	el peluquero	"peloo**ke**ro"
	la peluquera	"peloo**ke**ra"
health food shop	la tienda de alimentos naturales	"tee-**en**da de alee**men**tos natoo**ra**les"
ironmonger's	la ferretería	"ferreter**eea**"
jeweller's (shop)	la joyería	"khoyer**eea**"
launderette	la lavandería automática	"labander**eea** owto**ma**teeka"
market	el mercado	"mer**ka**do"
newsagent	el vendedor de periódicos	"bende**dor** de peree**o**deekos"
	la vendedora de periódicos	"bende**do**ra de peree**o**deekos"
post office	la oficina de correos	"ofee**thee**na de ko**rre**os"
shop	la tienda	"tee-**en**da"
stationer's	la papelería	"papeler**eea**"
supermarket	el supermercado	"soopermer**ka**do"
tobacconist's	el estanco	"es**tan**ko"
toy shop	la tienda de juguetes	"tee**en**da de khoo**ge**tes"

VEGETABLES

English	Spanish	Pronunciation
artichoke	la alcachofa	"alka**cho**fa"
asparagus	los espárragos	"es**pa**rragos"
aubergine	la berenjena	"beren**khe**na"
avocado	el aguacate	"agwa**ka**te"
bean	la judía	"khoo**dee**a"
beetroot	la remolacha	"remo**la**cha"
broccoli	el brécol	"**bre**kol"
Brussels sprouts	las coles de Bruselas	"**ko**les de broo**se**las"
cabbage	la col	"kol"
carrot	la zanahoria	"thana**o**reea"
cauliflower	la coliflor	"kolee**flor**"
celery	el apio	"**a**peeo"
chives	los cebollinos	"thebo**yee**nos"
courgettes	los calabacines	"kalaba**thee**nes"
cucumber	el pepino	"pe**pee**no"
French beans	las judías verdes	"khoo**dee**as **ber**des"
garlic	el ajo	"**a**kho"
green pepper	el pimiento verde	"peemee-**en**to **ber**de"
onion	la cebolla	"the**bo**ya"
parsley	el perejíl	"pere**kheel**"
peas	los guisantes	"gee**san**tes"
pepper	el pimiento	"peemee-**en**to"
potato	la patata	"pa**ta**ta"
radishes	los rábanos	"**ra**banos"
spinach	las espinacas	"espee**na**kas"
tomato	el tomate	"to**ma**te"
turnip	el nabo	"**na**bo"
vegan	el vegetariano estricto	"bekhetaree**a**no es**treek**to"
	la vegetariana estricta	"bekhetaree**a**na es**treek**ta"
vegetables	las verduras	"ber**doo**ras"
vegetarian	el vegetariano	"bekhetaree**a**no"
	la vegetariana	"bekhetaree**a**na"

13

SPANISH–ENGLISH

A

a: a la estación to the station; **a las 4** at 4 o'clock; **de lunes a viernes** from Monday to Friday; **a 30 kilómetros** 30 kilometres away; **a la izquierda/derecha** on/to the left/right

abadejo m haddock

abadía f abbey

abajo below, downstairs; **hacia abajo** downward(s); **el de abajo** the bottom one

abandonar to give up

abeja f bee

abeto m fir (tree)

abierto(a) open; on (water supply)

abogado m lawyer

abolladura f dent, bump

abonado(a) m/f subscriber

abonados mpl subscribers; season-ticket holders

abonar to credit; **abonarse** to subscribe; to buy a season ticket

abono m subscription; season ticket

abonos mpl deposits

abrazo m hug; **un fuerte abrazo** with best wishes (on letter)

abrebotellas m bottle opener

abrelatas m can-opener

abrigo m coat; **el abrigo de pieles** fur coat

abril m April

abrir to open; to turn on (water); **abrir (con llave)** to unlock; **abrir por aquí** open here

abrochar to fasten

absceso m abscess

absoluto(a) absolute; **en absoluto** not in the least

abstener: abténgase de visitas turísticas durante la celebración del culto please do not visit the church during services

abuela f grandmother

abuelo m grandfather; **los abuelos** grandparents

aburrido(a) boring; **estoy aburrido** I'm bored

acabado(a) complete; finished

acabar to finish; to complete

academia f academy; school

acampar to camp

acaso perhaps

acceso m: **acceso andenes** (to) platforms; **acceso prohibido a peatones** no pedestrians; **acceso vías** to platforms

accesorios mpl accessories

accidente m accident; **el accidente corporal** injury

acedía f heartburn

aceite m oil; **el aceite bronceador** suntan oil; **el aceite del coche** car oil; **el aceite de oliva** olive oil; **el aceite para niños** baby oil

aceituna f olive; **las aceitunas aliñadas** olives seasoned with a variety of herbs

acelerador m accelerator

acelerar to speed up; to accelerate

acelgas fpl chard; **las acelgas en menestra** boiled chard, fried with potatoes, garlic and egg

acera f pavement

acercarse to approach

ácido m acid

acogida f welcome

acomodador(a) m/f usher, usherette

acompañar to accompany

aconsejar to advise

acordarse de to remember

acortar to shorten

acostarse to go to bed; to lie down

acotado: acotado de pesca fishing restricted

actividad f activity

activo(a) active; energetic

acto m act; **en el acto** while you wait

actor m actor

actriz f actress

actual present(-day)
acuerdo *m* agreement; **estar de acuerdo con alguien** to agree with somebody; **ponerse de acuerdo** to come to an agreement
acuse de recibo *m* receipt
adecuado(a) suitable
adelantado(a) advanced; **por adelantado** in advance
adelantar to overtake; to advance (*money*)
adelante forwards; ahead
adelgazar to slim
además in addition
adentro indoors; **ir adentro** to go inside
adiós goodbye
administración *f* management; manager's office
admitirse: no se admiten cambios goods cannot be exchanged; **no se admiten cheques** no cheques; **no se admiten comidas de fuera** food purchased elsewhere may not be consumed on the premises; **no se admiten devoluciones** no refunds will be given; **no se admiten propinas** please do not tip the staff; **no se admiten tarjetas de crédito** no credit cards accepted; **se admiten huéspedes** accommodation available
adobado(a) marinated in garlic, vinegar and herbs
adobo *m* marinade
adolescente *m/f* teenager
adonde where
adorno *m* decoration; ornament
adquirir to acquire
aduana *f* customs

aduanero *m* customs officer
adulto(a) grown-up; **para adultos** adult
advertir to warn
aéreo(a) air; aerial
aerobús *m* air bus
aerodeslizador *m* hovercraft
aerolínea *f* airline
aeropuerto *m* airport
afeitadora *f* electric razor
afeitarse to shave; **la máquina de afeitar** electric razor
afilado(a) sharp
afuera outside
afueras *fpl* outskirts; the suburbs
agencia *f* agency; **la agencia de la propiedad inmobiliaria** estate agent; **la agencia de seguros** insurance company; **la agencia de viajes** travel agency
agente *m* agent; **el agente de tráfico** traffic warden; **el agente de viajes** travel agent
agitado(a) rough
agitar to shake; **agítese antes de usar** shake well before use
agosto *m* August
agotado(a) sold out; out of stock
agradable pleasant
agradecer to thank; **agradecer a alguien** to thank someone
agradecido(a) grateful
agricultor *m* farmer
agridulce sweet and sour
agrietarse to crack
agrio(a) sour
agua *f* water; **el agua destilada** distilled water; **el agua del grifo** tap water; **el agua mineral**

mineral water; **el agua no potable** not drinking water; **el agua potable** drinking water; **el agua de seltz** soda water; **sin agua** neat
aguacate *m* avocado; **el aguacate con gambas** avocado stuffed with prawns
aguacero *m* shower (*rain*)
aguardar: aguarde su turno please wait your turn
agudo(a) sharp; pointed
aguja *f* needle; **la aguja e hilo** needle and thread; **la aguja (palada)** swordfish; **la aguja a la plancha** grilled swordfish
agujero *m* hole
ahí there
ahogarse to drown
ahora now; **por ahora** for the time being
ahorrar to save
ahumado(a) smoked
aire *m* air; **al aire libre** open-air
aire acondicionado *m* air-conditioning
ajedrez *m* chess
ají *m* chilli
ajillo *m*: **al ajillo** in a garlic sauce
ajo *m* garlic; **el ajo blanco** cold soup made with garlic, almonds, bread, olive oil, vinegar and water; **el ajo de las manos** boiled potatoes and red peppers mixed with a garlic, oil and vinegar dressing
ajustado(a) tight (*clothes*)
al = **a** + **el**
ala *f* wing
a la carta à la carte
alarma *f* alarm; **la alarma de incendios** fire

alarm; **prohibido hacer uso de las alarmas sin causa justificada** do not use the alarm except in case of emergency

alba f dawn

albahaca f basil

albaricoque m apricot

albergue m hostel; **el albergue de carretera** state-run roadside hotel; **el albergue de juventud** youth hostel

albóndiga f meatball

álbum m L.P.; **álbum de fotos** photo album

alcachofa f artichoke; **las alcachofas con jamón** artichokes fried with chopped ham

alcalde m mayor

alcance m reach; **manténgase fuera del alcance de los niños** keep out of reach of children

alcaparras fpl capers

alcoba f bedroom

alcohol m alcohol; **el alcohol desnaturalizado** methylated spirits; **sin alcohol** soft

alcohólico(a) alcoholic (drink)

aldea f village

alegre happy

alegría f joy

alejado(a) de away from

alemán(mana) German

Alemania f Germany

alergia f allergy

alérgico(a) a allergic to

aletas fpl flippers

alfarería f pottery

alfiler m pin

alfombra f rug

algas fpl seaweed

algo something; **¿algo más?** anything else?

algodón m cotton; **el algodón hidrófilo** cotton

wool

alguien somebody; someone

algún, alguno(a) some, any; **alguna vez** ever

Alicante m strong, full-bodied red wine

aliento m breath

alimentación f nourishment; grocery shop

alimentar to feed

alimento m food; **los alimentos infantiles** baby foods; **los alimentos de régimen** diet foods

alioli m garlic-flavoured mayonnaise

alivio m relief

allá there

allí there

all i oli m garlic-flavoured mayonnaise

almacén m store; **los grandes almacenes** department stores

almeja f clam; mussel; **las almejas a la marinera** steamed clams with a parsley, olive oil and garlic sauce

almendra f almond; **las almendras garrapiñadas** sugar-coated almonds

almíbar m syrup

almohada f pillow

almohadón m bolster

almuerzo m lunch

alojamiento m accommodation

alpargata f espadrille

alpinismo m mountaineering

alquilar to rent; to hire; **se alquila** to let

alquiler m rent; rental; **el alquiler de coches sin conductor** self-drive car hire; **el alquiler de coches con conductor**

chauffeur-driven car hire

alrededor de around

alrededores mpl outskirts

alternador m alternator

alto(a) high; **alta tensión** high voltage

altoparlante m loudspeaker

altura f altitude; height; **de 6 metros de altura** 6 metres high

alubia f: **las alubias blancas** butter beans; **las alubias pintas** red kidney beans

alumno(a) m/f pupil

ama de casa f housewife

amable pleasant; kind

amanecer m dawn

amargo(a) bitter

amarillo(a) yellow

amarrar to moor

ambiente m atmosphere

ambos(as) both

ambulancia f ambulance

ambulatorio m National Health clinic

americana f jacket

americano(a) American

amigdalitis f tonsillitis

amigo(a) m/f friend

amistoso(a) friendly

amontillado m a medium dry sherry

amor m love

amortiguador m shock absorber

amperio m amp

ampliación f enlargement

ampolla f blister

amueblado(a) furnished

amueblar to furnish

análisis m analysis; **el análisis de sangre/orina** blood/urine test; **los análisis clínicos** medical tests

ananás f pineapple

anaranjado(a) orange(-coloured)

ancas *fpl*: **las ancas de rana** frog's legs
ancho(a) broad; wide
anchoa *f* anchovy
anchura *f* width
ancla *f* anchor
Andalucía *f* Andalusia
andaluz(a) Andalucian
andar to walk
andén *m* platform
anestésico *m* anaesthetic
anfiteatro *m* circle (*theatre*)
anfitrión *m* host
anguila *f* eel
angula *f* baby eel
anillo *m* ring; **el anillo de boda** wedding ring; **el anillo de compromiso** engagement ring
animal *m* animal
anís *m* aniseed
anisete *m* aniseed-flavoured liqueur
aniversario *m* anniversary
anoche last night
anochecer *m* dusk
ante *m* suede
anteayer the day before yesterday
antebrazo *m* forearm
antena *f* antenna; aerial
anteojos *mpl* binoculars; goggles
antes before
antiadherente non-stick
antibiótico *m* antibiotic
antichoque shockproof
anticipado(a) in advance
anticonceptivo *m* contraceptive
anticongelante *m* antifreeze
anticuario(a) *m/f* antique dealer
antídoto *m* antidote
antigüedades *fpl* antiques
antiguo(a) old
antihistamínico *m*

antihistamine
antiséptico *m* antiseptic
anular to cancel
anunciar to announce; to advertise
anuncio *m* advertisement; notice
anzuelo *m* hook
año *m* year; **Año Nuevo** New Year's Day; **¿cuántos años tiene?** how old are you?
apagado(a) off
apagar to switch off; to turn off
apagón *m* power cut
aparato *m* appliance; **los aparatos de sordo** hearing aids
aparcamiento *m* parking-lot; car park; **el aparcamiento cubierto** covered parking; **el aparcamiento subterráneo** underground car park
aparcar to park; **¿se puede aparcar aquí?** can I park here?; **por favor no aparcar** no parking
aparecer to appear
apartadero *m* lay-by
apartado de Correos *m* P.O. Box
apartamento *m* apartment
aparte apart
apdo. *see* **apartado de Correos**
apeadero *m* halt (*railway*)
apellido *m* surname; **el apellido de soltera** maiden name
apenas scarcely
aperitivo *m* aperitif
apertura *f*: **apertura de cuentas** new accounts (*in banks*)
apetecer: **¿le apetece un café?** do you feel like a coffee?

apetito *m* appetite
apio *m* celery; **el apio nabo** celeriac
aplauso *m* applause
aplazar to postpone
apoplejía *f* stroke (*illness*)
apostar to bet
apoyabrazos *m* armrest
apoyacabezas *m* headrest
apoyarse en to lean on
aprender to learn
aprendiz *m* trainee; **el aprendiz de conductor** learner(-driver)
apretar to press; to push
aprovechar: **¡que aproveche!** enjoy your meal!
aproximado(a) approximate
apto U (*film*)
apurarse to hurry; **¡apúrate!** hurry up!
aquel that; **aquél** that one
aquella that; **aquélla** that one
aquellas those; **aquéllas** those ones
aquello that
aquellos those; **aquéllos** those ones
aquí here; **por aquí, por favor** this way please; **venga aquí** come over here; **está aquí de vacaciones** he's over here on holiday
árabe *m/f* Arab
araña *f* spider
árbitro *m* referee (*sports*)
árbol *m* tree; **el árbol de Navidad** Christmas tree
arcén *m* verge; hard shoulder
arco *m* arch
arco iris *m* rainbow
arder to blaze; **la casa está ardiendo** the house is on fire

ardilla *f* squirrel
ardor de estómago *m* indigestion; heartburn
área *f*: **el área de servicio** service area; **área oficial** staff only
arena *f* sand
arenque *m* herring
argot *m* slang
arma *f* weapon; **las armas de fuego** firearms
armar to assemble; to pitch
armario *m* cupboard; wardrobe
armería *f* hunting and fishing gear
arquitecto *m* architect
arrancar to switch on (*engine*)
arranque *m* starter
arrebatar to snatch
arreglar to arrange
arreglo *m* arrangement
arrendamiento *m* lease
arrendatario(a) *m/f* tenant; lessee
arriba upstairs; **hacia arriba** upward(s); **de arriba** overhead
arroyo *m* stream
arroz *m* rice; **el arroz a banda** a mixture of cooked fish and shellfish served with rice boiled in fish stock; **el arroz blanco** plain boiled rice; **el arroz a la cubana** rice topped with fried egg and banana; **el arroz a la española** rice cooked in fish stock, chicken livers, pork and tomatoes; **el arroz con leche** rice pudding; **el arroz a la levantina** rice with shellfish, onions, artichokes, peas, tomatoes and saffron; **el arroz a la milanesa** fried rice with onion,

chicken livers, ham, tomatoes, peas and grated cheese; **el arroz murciano** rice with pork, tomatoes, red peppers and garlic; **el arroz a la primavera** boiled rice and vegetables served with a hot hollandaise sauce
arrugado(a) creased
arruinar to ruin; to wreck (*plans*)
arte *f* art
arteria *f* artery
artesanía *f* craft shop; **de artesanía** handmade
artesanías *fpl* crafts
artesano *m* craftsman
articulación *f* joint (*of body*)
artículo *m*: **artículos de fumador** smoker's requisites; **artículos del hogar** household goods; **artículos de tocador** toiletries; **artículos de ocasión** bargains; **artículos de piel** leather goods; **los artículos de viaje** travel goods
artificial artificial
artista *m/f* artist
artritis *f* arthritis
asadero de pollos *m* roast chicken take-away
asado *m* roast meat
asado(a) roast
asaltar to mug; to assault
asalto *m* raid
asar to roast; **asar a la parrilla** to grill
ascender to amount to; **asciende a 5000 pesetas** it amounts to 5000 pesetas
ascensor *m* lift
asegurado(a) insured
asegurar to insure
aseos *mpl* toilets
así thus; in this way

asiento *m* seat
asistencia *f*: **asistencia técnica** repairs
asistir a to attend
asma *f* asthma
asno *m* donkey
asociación *f* association
asomarse: **es peligroso asomarse** do not lean out of the window
áspero(a) rough
aspiradora *f* vacuum cleaner
aspirina *f* aspirin
asunto *m* subject; matter
atacar to attack
atajo *m* short cut
ataque *m* attack; fit; **el ataque cardíaco** heart attack
atar to tie up
atasco *m* blockage; traffic jam
atención *f*: **atención a su luz** mind your lights; **atención, obras** drive carefully – roadworks ahead; **atención al tren** look out, trains
aterrizaje *m* landing; **el aterrizaje forzoso** emergency landing
aterrizar to land (*plane*)
Atlántico *m* Atlantic Ocean
atomizador *m* spray
atrás behind; **hacia atrás** backwards; **mirar hacia atrás** to look behind
atrasado(a) late
atrasar to hold up
atraso *m* delay
atravesar to pierce; to cross
atreverse a to dare to
atropellar to run down/over
A.T.S. *see* **Ayudante**
atún *m* tuna fish; **el atún encebollado** casseroled tuna fish with onion,

tomato, garlic, parsley and walnuts; **el atún a la vinagreta** casseroled tuna fish with onions, garlic, parsley, lemon juice and vinegar

audífono *m* hearing aid

aumentar to increase

aumento *m* rise; increase

aun even

aún still

aunque although

auricular *m* receiver

auriculares *mpl* headphones

auténtico(a) genuine

auto *m* car

autoadhesivo(a) self-adhesive

autobús *m* bus

autocar *m* coach

autolavado *m* car wash

automático(a) automatic; **el coche automático** an automatic

automotor *m* short-distance diesel train

automovilista *m/f* motorist

autopista *f* motorway; **la autopista de peaje** toll road

autor(a) *m/f* author

autorizado(a) authorized; **autorizado subir y bajar viajeros** no stopping except to set down or pick up passengers

autoservicio *m* self-service

autostop *m*: **hacer autostop** to hitchhike

autostopista *m/f* hitchhiker

auxilio *m* help; **Auxilio en Carretera** police breakdown patrol

Av., Avda. see **avenida**

avance *m* trailer (*film*); **avance informativo** news brief

avanzar to advance

ave *f* bird

avellana *f* hazelnut

avena *f* oats

avenida *f* avenue

avería *f* breakdown; **la avería del motor** engine trouble; **en caso de avería, diríjanse a ...** in case of breakdown, contact ...

averiarse to break down

aves *fpl* poultry; **aves y caza** poultry and game

avión *m* aircraft; aeroplane; **en avión** by air

avisar to inform

aviso *m* notice; warning

ayer yesterday

ayuda *f* help

Ayudante *m*: **Ayudante Técnico Sanitario (A.T.S.)** male nurse

ayudar to help; **¿puede ayudarme?** can you help me?

ayuntamiento *m* town hall

azafata *f* air hostess

azafrán *m* saffron

azúcar *m* sugar

azucarado(a) sweet

azucena *f* lily

azul blue; **azul marino** navy blue

B

baca *f* roof rack

bacalao *m* cod; **el bacalao encebollado** stewed cod with onion and beaten eggs; **bacalao al pil-pil** garlic-fried cod

bahía *f* bay

bailaor(a) *m/f* flamenco dancer

bailar to dance

baile *m* dance

bajamar *f* low tide

bajar to go down; to fall; **bajar la radio** to turn down the radio

bajo(a) low; short; soft; **más bajo** lower

balandro *m* sailing boat

balanza *f* scales

balcón *m* balcony

balneario *m* spa

balón *m* ball

baloncesto *m* basketball

bañador *m* swimming costume; bather

bañarse to go swimming; **prohibido bañarse** bathing prohibited; **prohibido bañarse sin gorro** bathing caps must be worn

banca *f* banking; **la Banca** the banks

bancario(a) bank

banco *m* bench; bank

banda *f* ribbon; band (*musical*)

bandeja *f* tray

bandera *f* flag

banderilla *f* banderilla

bañera *f* bath(tub)

baño *m* bath; bathroom; **con baño** with bath

bar *m* bar

baraja *f* pack (*of cards*)

barandilla *f* banisters

barato(a) cheap; **más barato** cheaper

barba *f* beard

barbería *f* barber's

barbero *m* barber

barbilla *f* chin

barca *f* boat; **la barca de pasaje** ferry

barco *m* ship; boat; **el barco a vela** dinghy

barquillo *m* ice-cream cone

barra *f* bar; counter; **la barra de labios** lipstick

barrer to sweep

barrera *f* barrier; crash barrier

barriga *f* stomach

barrio *m* district; suburb; **el barrio chino** red light district

barro *m* mud

báscula *f* scales

base *f* basis; base

bastante enough; quite; rather; **bastante agua** enough water

bastar to be enough; **basta** that's enough

basura *f* rubbish

basurero *m* rubbish dump

bata *f* dressing gown

batata *f* sweet potato

batería *f* battery (*for car*)

batido *m* batter; **el batido de leche** milkshake

batidora *f* mixer

batir to beat

baúl *m* trunk

bautismo *m* baptism

bayeta *f* dishcloth

bebé *m* baby

beber to drink

bebida *f* drink; **las bebidas alcohólicas** liquor; **la bebida no alcohólica** soft drink

béisbol *m* baseball

belleza *f* beauty

berberecho *m* cockle

berenjena *f* aubergine

berro *m* watercress

berza *f* cabbage

besar to kiss

beso *m* kiss

besugo *m* sea bream; **el besugo a la donostiarra** grilled sea bream served with an oil, garlic and lemon juice sauce

betún *m* polish

biberón *m* baby's bottle

biblioteca *f* library

bicicleta *f* bicycle; **ir en bicicleta** to cycle

bien well; **está bien** that's all right; **muy bien** (that's) fine

bienes *mpl* property; possessions

bienvenida *f* welcome

bienvenido(a) welcome

biftec *m* steak

bifurcación *f* fork (*in road*)

bigote *m* moustache

bikini[1] *m* bikini

bikini[2] *m* toasted ham and cheese sandwich

bilingüe bilingual

billar *m* snooker

billete *m* ticket; **el billete de banco** bank note; **el billete de ida** one-way ticket; **el billete de ida y vuelta** return ticket; **un billete de segunda clase** a second-class ticket; **un billete turístico** a tourist ticket; **los billetes de cercanías** local tickets; **los billetes de largo recorrido** long distance tickets

bistec *m* steak

bisutería *f* imitation jewellery

bizcocho *m* sponge cake; **el bizcocho borracho** sponge cake filled with brandy or rum; **el bizcocho borracho de Guadalajara** sponge ring filled with brandy or rum and whipped cream; **los bizcochos de soletilla** sponge fingers

blanco(a) white; **en blanco** blank; **por favor dejar en blanco** please leave blank; **un blanco y negro** black coffee with a spoonful of ice-cream in it

blando(a) soft

bloc *m* pad (*notepaper*)

bloque *m* block (*of stone*); **el bloque de pisos** block of flats

blusa *f* blouse

bobina *f* reel

boca *f* mouth

bocacalle *f* intersection; turning; **la segunda bocacalle a la derecha** the second on the right

bocadillo *m* sandwich; **un bocadillo de jamón** a ham sandwich; **bocadillos** snacks

bocado *m* mouthful

bocina *f* horn; **tocar la bocina** to hoot

boda *f* wedding

bodega *f* off-licence

boina *f* beret

bola *f* ball

bolera *f* bowling alley

boletín *f* bulletin; **el boletín meteorológico** weather forecast

bolígrafo *m* ballpoint pen

bollería *f* bakery

bollo *m* roll; bun

bolsa *f* bag; **la bolsa de agua caliente** hot water bottle; **la bolsa de aseo** sponge-bag; **la bolsa de compras** shopping bag; **la bolsa de papel** paper bag; **la bolsa de plástico** plastic bag; **la bolsa de viaje** flight bag

bolsillo *m* pocket

bolsita *f* sachet; **la bolsita de té** teabag

bolso *m* bag (*handbag*); **el bolso de mano** handbag

bomba *f* bomb; **la bomba de la gasolina** fuel pump

bombero *m* fireman; **el cuerpo de bomberos** fire brigade; **el coche de bomberos** fire engine

bombilla f light bulb; **la bombilla de flash** flashbulb

bombona f: **bombona de gas** gas cylinder

bombonería f confectioner's

bombones mpl chocolates

bonito m striped tuna

bonito(a) lovely; pretty; nice

bono m voucher

bonobús m season ticket

boquerón m anchovy; **los boquerones en vinagre** pickled anchovies served with olive oil, garlic and parsley

boquilla f cigarette holder

bordado m embroidery

bordado(a) embroidered

borde m edge

bordo m: **ir a bordo** to go aboard; **a bordo del barco** aboard the ship

borracho(a) drunk

borrascoso(a) stormy

bosque m forest; wood

bota f boot; **la bota de esquí** ski boot

botavara f boom (sailing)

bote m dinghy; **el bote salvavidas** lifeboat

botella f bottle

botijo m jug

botiquín m first-aid kit

botón m button; knob

botones m bellboy

botulismo m food poisoning

boxeo m boxing

braga-pañales mpl all-in-one disposable nappies

bragas fpl knickers

bragueta f fly (on trousers)

brasa: **a la brasa** barbecued; **pan a la brasa** melba toast

brazo m arm; **el brazo de gitano** Swiss roll

brevas fpl early summer figs

bricolaje m do-it-yourself (shop)

brillante shiny

brillar to shine; **el sol está brillando** the sun is out

británico(a) British

brocha f brush; **la brocha de afeitar** shaving brush

broche m brooch

brocheta de ternera f beef kebabs

broma f joke

bronce m bronze

bronceado(a) suntanned

broncearse to tan

bronquitis f bronchitis

brújula f compass

brumoso(a) foggy

bucear to dive

budín m pudding

bueno(a) good; fine; **¡buenos días!** good morning!; **¡buenas tardes!** good afternoon!; good evening!; **¡buenas noches!** good night!

buey m ox

bufanda f scarf

bufet libre m set-price meal when you can eat as much as you want

bujía f sparking plug

bulevar m arcade; gallery

bulto m package; lump (on skin)

buñuelo m fritter; doughnut; **los buñuelos de viento** small light fritters filled with cream

buque m ship

burro m donkey

bus m: **sólo bus** buses only; **el bus aeropuerto** airport bus

buscar to look for; **ir a buscar** to fetch; **se busca** wanted

butaca f stalls; seat; **las butacas de platea/de patio** stalls seats

butano m Calor gas

butifarra f Catalan sausage

buzón m letter box

C

caballa f mackerel

caballero m gentleman; **Caballeros** Gentlemen, Gents

caballo m horse; **montar a caballo** to go riding

cabello m hair

caber to fit; **no cabe** it won't go in

cabeza f head

cabina f cabin; **la cabina telefónica** telephone box; **la cabina pública de télex** public telex machine

cable m wire; cable; **el cable de remolque** tow rope; **los cables para cargar la batería** jump leads

cabra f goat

cabritilla: **de cabritilla** kid (leather)

cabrito m kid (meat); **cabrito asado** roast kid

cacahuete m peanut

cacao m cocoa

cacerola f saucepan

cacharrería f pottery shop

cachemira f cashmere

cada every; each; **cada semana** weekly; **cada uno (c/u)** each (one)

cadena f chain

cadera f hip

caducado(a) out-of-date

caducidad *f* expiry; **fecha de caducidad** expiry date; best before

caer to fall

caerse to fall down

café *m* café; coffee; **el café cortado** small coffee with a dash of milk; **el café corto** a very milky small coffee; **el café descafeinado** decaffeinated coffee; **el café exprés** espresso coffee; **café en grano** coffee beans; **el café helado** iced coffee; **el café con leche** white coffee; **café molido** ground coffee; **el café solo** black coffee

cafetera *f* coffeepot

cafetería *f* snack bar

caja *f* box; cashdesk; **la caja de ahorros** savings bank; **la caja de cambios** gearbox; **la caja de cerillas** matchbox; **la caja fuerte** safe; **la caja de pinturas** paintbox; **la caja postal de ahorros** Girobank; **la caja de seguridad** safe

cajero(a) *m/f* teller; cashier; **el cajero automático** cash dispenser

cajetilla *f*: **la cajetilla de cigarrillos** packet of cigarettes

cajón *m* drawer

calabacín *m* courgette; **los calabacines rellenos** stuffed courgettes; **los calabacines glaseados** glazed courgettes

calabaza *f* small pumpkin

calamares *mpl* squid; **los calamares a la marinera** squid casserole with onion, garlic,

paprika and olive oil; **los calamares rellenos** squid stuffed with egg, ham and breadcrumbs and served with a wine sauce; **los calamares a la romana** squid fried in batter; **los calamares en su tinta** squid cooked in their ink

calambre *m* cramp

calcetín *m* sock

calculadora *f* calculator

caldereta *f*: **caldereta asturiana** fish and seafood stewed in sherry and peppers; **la caldereta de cordero** stewed lamb with onion, garlic, parsley and spearmint

caldo *m* soup; **el caldo canario** thick soup made with pork ribs, corn, pumpkin and marrow; **el caldo de cocido** thin soup made with meat, sausage, bacon and vegetables; **el caldo gallego** clear soup with vegetables, beans and pork; **el caldo de verduras** clear vegetable soup

calefacción *f* heating; **la calefacción central** central heating

calendario *m* calendar

calentador *m* heater; **el calentador de agua** water heater

calentar to heat

calentura *f* high fever

calidad *f* quality; **los artículos de calidad** quality goods

cálido(a) warm

caliente hot

callado(a) quiet

calle *f* street; **calle cortada** closed to traffic;

la calle de dirección única one-way street; **la calle mayor** high street; **la calle sin salida** cul-de-sac

callejero *m* street map

callejón *m*: **callejón sin salida** no through road; cul-de-sac

callista *m* chiropodist

callo *m* corn (*on foot*)

callos *mpl* tripe; **los callos a la madrileña** tripe in a spicy sauce with garlic and chorizo

calmado(a) calm

calmante *m* painkiller

calor *m* heat; **hace calor** it's warm today; **tengo calor** I'm warm

calvo(a) bald

calzada *f* roadway; **calzada deteriorada** uneven road surface; **calzada en mal estado** poor road surface

calzado *m* footwear; **calzados** shoe shop

calzoncillos *mpl* underpants

cama *f* bed; **la cama de campaña** camp bed; **la cama turca** campbed; **las camas gemelas** twin beds; **una cama individual** single bed; **una cama de matrimonio** double bed

cámara *f* camera; **la cámara de cine** cine camera

camarera *f* waitress

camarero *m* barman; waiter

camarón *m* shrimp

camarote *m* cabin

cambiar to change; to exchange; **cambiar de marcha** to change gear; **no se cambian los discos** records cannot be exchanged

cambio m change; gear (*of car*); exchange (*rate*); **cambio de cheques** cheques cashed; **cambio de sentido** motorway exit; **el cambio sincronizado de velocidades** synchromesh; **compruebe su cambio** check your change; **facilite el cambio** have your change ready; **traiga su cambio preparado** please have your change ready

camilla f stretcher

camino m path; road; **¿cuál es el camino para Londres?** which is the way to London?; **camino cerrado** road closed

camión m truck; lorry; **camión grúa** breakdown lorry

camionero m lorry driver

camioneta f van

camisa f shirt

camisería f shirt shop

camiseta f tee shirt; vest

camisón m nightdress

campana f bell

campeón m champion

campeona f champion

campeonato m championship

camping m camping; camp(ing) site; **hacer camping** to go camping; **el camping gas** Calor gas light

campo m field; countryside; **el campo de golf** golf course; **en el campo** in the country

canal m canal; **el Canal de la Mancha** the Channel

canapé m open sandwich

cancelar to cancel

cancha f: **cancha de tenis** tennis court

canción f song

canela f cinnamon

canelones mpl cannelloni

cangrejo m crab; **el cangrejo de río** crayfish

canguro m kangaroo; f babysitter

canoa f canoe

cansado(a) tired

cantante m/f singer

cantar to sing

cantidad f quantity

cantimplora f water bottle

cantina f buffet (*in station*)

caña f cane; glass of beer; **la caña de cerveza** glass of beer; **la caña de pesca** fishing rod

caoba f mahogany

capilla f chapel

capitán m captain

capó m bonnet (*car*)

cápsulas fpl capsules

capuchino m cappuccino coffee

cara f face

carabineros mpl customs police

caracol m snail

caramelo m sweet; caramel

caravana f caravan

carbón m coal

carbonada f minced beef stewed with tomatoes, onions, potatoes and fruit

carburador m carburettor

carburante m fuel

cárcel f prison

cardenal m bruise

carga f load; cargo

cargado(a) strong

cargar to load; **cargar en cuenta** to charge to account

cargo m charge; **los cargos por entrega** delivery charges; **los cargos por recogida** collection charges; **a cargo del cliente** at the customer's expense

cariñoso(a) affectionate

carnaval m carnival

carne f meat; flesh; **la carne de cerdo** pork; **la carne de cordero** lamb; **la carne de membrillo** quince jelly; **la carne picada** mince; **la carne de ternera** veal; **la carne de vaca** beef

carnet de conducir m driving licence

carnet de identidad m identity card

carnicería f butcher's

carnicero(a) m/f butcher

caro(a) expensive

carpa f carp

carpeta f file

carpintería f carpenter's shop

carrera f career; race; **las carreras de caballos** horse-racing

carrete m roll of film

carretera f road; highway; **la carretera de circunvalación** ring road; **la carretera comarcal** B-road; **carretera cortada/bloqueada por la nieve** road closed/blocked by snow; **la carretera de doble calzada** dual carriageway; **la carretera local** local road; **la carretera nacional** trunk road; **la carretera secundaria** minor road

carretilla f cart; wheelbarrow

carril m lane (on road); **el carril de aceleración** outside lane; **el carril de deceleración** exit lane; **el carril de la izquierda** the outside lane

carrito m trolley

carrocería f body(work)

carta f letter; playing card; menu; **la carta aérea** air mail letter; **la carta certificada** registered letter; **la carta verde** green card; **la carta de vinos** wine list

cartel m poster

cartelera f entertainments

cartera f wallet

carterista m pickpocket

cartero m postman

cartón m cardboard; **el cartón de cigarrillos** a carton of cigarettes

cartucho m cartridge

casa f home; house; household; **en casa** at home; **la casa de campo** farmhouse; **la casa de huéspedes** boarding house; **casa particular ofrece habitaciones** accommodation available; **la casa de socorro** first-aid post

casado(a) married

casarse to marry

cascada f waterfall

cáscara f peel; eggshell

casco m helmet

casero(a) home-made; **la comida casera** home cooking

caseta f beach hut

casete f cassette

casi nearly; almost

casilla f pigeon hole

casillero de consigna m locker

caso m case; **en caso de** in case of; **en caso de**

reclamaciones diríjanse a ... please address any complaints to ...

castaña f chestnut; **las castañas pilongas** dried chestnuts

castaño(a) brown

castañuelas fpl castanets

castellano(a) Castilian

castillo m castle

catalán(lana) Catalonian

catálogo m catalogue

catarro m catarrh; cold

catedral f cathedral

catorce fourteen

causa f cause; **a causa de** because of

causar to cause

cava m Catalan champagne-style sparkling wine

caza f hunting; game

cazador m hunter

cazadora f jerkin

cazuela f casserole; pan; **a la cazuela** casseroled

cebador m choke

cebolla f onion

cebolleta f spring onion

cebollino m chive

cebra f zebra

cecina f cured meat

ceder to give in; **ceder/ ceda el paso** give way

C.E.E. f EEC

ceja f eyebrow

célebre famous

celeste light blue

celofán m sellotape®

cementerio m cemetery

cemento m cement; concrete

cena f dinner; supper

cenicero m ashtray

centenario m centenary

centeno m rye

centésimo(a) hundredth

centímetro m centimetre

centollo m spider crab

central f: **la central**

telefónica telephone exchange

centralita f switchboard

centro m centre; **el centro asistencial** health centre; **el centro de la ciudad** city centre; **el centro comercial** shopping centre; **el centro urbano** city centre

cepillo m brush; **el cepillo de dientes** toothbrush; **el cepillo para el pelo** hairbrush; **el cepillo de uñas** nailbrush

cera f wax

cerámica f ceramics, pottery

cerca near; **cerca de** close to

cercanías fpl outskirts

cercano(a) close

cerdo m pig; pork; **el cerdo simple** pork steak

cereal m breakfast cereal

cerebro m brain

cereza f cherry

cerilla f match

cero m zero

cerrado(a) shut; off (water supply); **cerrado por reforma** closed for repairs; **cerrado por vacaciones** closed for holidays

cerradura f lock

cerrajería m locksmith's

cerrajero m locksmith

cerrar to close; to block; **cerrar con llave** to lock; **cerramos los sábados por la tarde** closed Saturday afternoons

cerrojo m bolt

certificado m certificate; **el certificado de seguros** insurance certificate; **certificados** registered letters

certificado(a) registered
certificar to register
cervecería f brewery; pub
cerveza f beer; lager; **la cerveza de barril** draught beer; **la cerveza negra** stout
césped m lawn
cesta f shopping basket
cestería f basketwork (shop)
chacinas fpl sausages
chacolí m sparkling, light red or white wine from the Basque Country
chal m shawl
chalé m villa
chaleco m waistcoat; **el chaleco salvavidas** life jacket
chalote m shallot
champán m champagne
champaña m champagne
champiñón m mushroom
champú m shampoo
chándal m track suit
chanfaina f stew of goat's offal with vegetables
chanquetes mpl small edible fish similar to whitebait
chapado en oro gold-plated
chaparrón m shower (rain)
chaqueta f jacket
charco m pool; puddle
charcutería f pork butcher's
charla f talk; chat
charol m patent leather
chasis m chassis
chateaubriand/ chatobrian m thick fillet steak covered with bacon rashers and lightly cooked in butter
chato de vino m a small glass of wine

cheque m cheque; **el cheque de viaje** traveller's cheque
chica f girl
chicle m chewing gum; **chicle sin azúcar** sugarfree chewing gum
chico m boy
chico(a) small
chile m chilli
chilindrón: al chilindrón pot-roasted with tomatoes, peppers, onions and garlic
chillar to scream
chimenea f fireplace; chimney
chino(a) Chinese
chipirones mpl baby squid
chiquillo(a) small; **el chiquillo** little boy
chirimoya f custard apple
chiringuito m bar
chispa f spark
chiste m joke
chistoso(a) funny
chivo m kid; goat
chocar to collide
chocolate m chocolate; **el chocolate con churros** drinking chocolate with fritters; **el chocolate con leche** milk chocolate; **el chocolate sin leche** plain chocolate; **el chocolate a la taza** drinking chocolate
chocolatería f a café where hot chocolate with "churros" is sold
chófer m driver
chopitos mpl small squid
choque m crash; **tener un choque con el coche** to crash one's car
chorizo m salami; hard pork sausage
choto m kid (animal); calf

chuleta f cutlet; **la chuleta de cerdo** pork chop; **las chuletas de cerdo empanadas** pork chops fried in breadcrumbs; **las chuletas de cordero** lamb chops; **las chuletas de cordero con bechamel** fried lamb chops served with white sauce; **las chuletas de ternera** veal cutlets; **las chuletas de ternera a la parrilla** grilled veal cutlets
chuletón m beef chop; **el chuletón de ternera con salsa Roquefort** large veal chop served with Roquefort cheese sauce
chupete m dummy
churrasco m steak
churrería f fritter shop or stand
churro m deep-fried batter stick sprinkled with sugar and eaten with drinking chocolate
cicatriz f scar
ciclismo m cycling
ciclista m/f cyclist
ciego(a) blind
cielo m sky
cien hundred; **ciento uno(a)** a hundred and one; **cien gramos de** 100 grammes of
cierre m fastener; zip
cierto(a) certain; **cierta gente** some people
ciervo m deer
cifra f figure
cigala f crayfish; **las cigalas cocidas** boiled crayfish; **las cigalas plancha** grilled crayfish
cigarrillo m cigarette
cigarro m cigarette
cima f mountain top

cinco five
cincuenta fifty
cine *m* cinema
cinta *f* tape; **la cinta adhesiva** adhesive tape; **cinta limpiadora** cleaning tape; **cinta virgen** blank tape
cintura *f* waist
cinturón *m* belt; **el cinturón de seguridad** safety belt; seat belt; **el cinturón salvavidas** lifebelt
circo *m* circus
circuito cicloturista *m* route for cyclists
circulación *f* traffic
circular to drive; to walk; **circulen por la otra acera** walk on the other side of the street; **circule a su derecha** keep right; **circula a diario** daily service including weekends
círculo *m* circle
cirio *m* candle
ciruela *f* plum; **la ciruela pasa** prune; **las ciruelas claudias** greengages
cirugía *f* surgery
cirujano *m* surgeon
cita *f* appointment
ciudad *f* city; town
ciudadano *m* citizen
clarete *m* light, red wine
claro(a) light (*bright, pale*); clear
clase *f* class
clásico(a) classical
**clasificado(a):
clasificada S** adults only
clavel *m* carnation
clavo *m* nail
claxon *m* horn
cliente *m/f* customer; client
clima *m* climate
climatizado(a) air-conditioned

clínica *f* clinic; nursing home; **la clínica dental** dental surgery
clip *m* paperclip
club nocturno *m* night club
cobertor *m* blanket
cobrador *m* conductor
cobrar to charge; to cash
cobre *m* copper
cobro *m* payment; **cobros** withdrawals
cocer to cook
coche *m* car; **el coche de alquiler** hired car; **el coche será devuelto en ... car to be returned to ...
coche-cama *m* sleeping car
cochecito de niño *m* pram
coche-comedor *m* dining car
coche patrulla *m* police car
cochinillo *m* piglet
cocido *m* chick-pea, meat and vegetable stew
cocido(a) cooked; **insuficientemente cocido(a)** undercooked
cocina *f* kitchen; stove; **la cocina española** Spanish cooking; **la cocina eléctrica** electric cooker; **la cocina de gas** gas cooker
cocinar to cook
cocinero(a) *m/f* cook
coco *m* coconut
cóctel *m* cocktail
código *m* code; **el código de la circulación** Highway Code; **el código postal** post-code
codo *m* elbow
codorniz *f* quail; **las codornices asadas** roast quail
coger to catch; to get;

cogimos el tren we took the train
cojinetes *mpl* bearings (*in car*)
col *f* cabbage; **las coles de Bruselas** Brussels sprouts
cola *f* glue; queue
colador *m* sieve
colchón *m* mattress; **el colchón inflable** air bed; **el colchón neumático** air bed
coleccionar to collect
colegio *m* college; school
cólera *f* anger
colgar to hang (up)
coliflor *f* cauliflower; **la coliflor al ajo arriero** boiled cauliflower served with a garlic, parsley, paprika and vinegar sauce; **la coliflor en bechamel** cauliflower in a white sauce
colilla *f*: **no tire colillas** do not drop cigarette ends
colina *f* hill
colirio *m* eye-drops
collar *m* necklace
colmado *m* grocer's
colmado(a) full
colonia *f* eau-de-Cologne
color *m* colour; **color limón** lemon
colorete *m* blusher
columna *f* column; **la columna de dirección** steering column; **la columna vertebral** spine
combustible *m* fuel
comedia *f* comedy
comedor *m* dining room
comenzar to begin
comer to eat
comercial commercial; business
comerciante *m* merchant
comercio *m* trade;

business; shop

comestibles *mpl* groceries

cometa *f* kite

cómico *m* comedian

comida *f* meal; food; lunch; **la comida para niños** baby food; **se sirven comidas** meals served; **comidas caseras** home cooking

comienzo *m* beginning

comisaría *f* police station

como like

cómo how; **¿cómo?** pardon?; **¿cómo está?** how are you?; **¿cómo se llama?** what is your name?

comodidad *f* comfort; **las comodidades** amenities

cómodo(a) comfortable

compañía *f* firm; **la compañía de seguros** insurance company

compartim(i)ento *m* compartment

compartir to share

completo(a) inclusive; **completo** no vacancies

comportarse to behave; **compórtese con el debido respeto** please respect this place of worship

composición *f*: **composición de trenes** list of train carriages

compota *f* preserve; **la compota de frutas** stewed fruit

compra *f* purchase; **compras** shopping; **ir de compras** to go shopping

comprar to buy; **se compra oro/plata** gold/ silver bought

compraventa we buy and sell anything

comprender to

understand

compresas *fpl* sanitary towels

comprobante *m* receipt; voucher

comprobar to check; **compruebe su cambio** please check your change

compromiso *m* engagement; appointment; **sin compromiso** without obligation

común common

comunicar to communicate; **estar comunicando** to be engaged

con with

concesionario *m* agent

concha *f* sea-shell; **la concha de ensaladilla** a small portion of Russian salad, served as a snack

concierto *m* concert

concurrido(a) busy

concurso *m* competition

condición *f* condition; **las condiciones de circulación** road conditions

condimento *m* seasoning

conducción *f* driving

conducir to drive; **conducir por la derecha** drive on the right; **conducir por la izquierda** drive on the left; **conducir con cuidado** drive carefully

conductor(a) *m/f* driver

conectar to connect; to plug in

conejo *m* rabbit; **el conejo a la cazadora** wild rabbit casseroled with ham, bacon, onion, garlic, brandy and thyme; **el conejo con caracoles** wild rabbit stewed with snails; **el conejo guisado**

rabbit stew

confección *f*: **de confección** ready-to-wear; **confecciones caballero** menswear; **confecciones niño** childrenswear; **confecciones señora** ladieswear

conferencia *f* conference; **la conferencia a cobro revertido** reversed charge call; **la conferencia interurbana/a larga distancia** long-distance call

confianza *f* confidence

confirmar to confirm

confitería *f* confectioner's

confitura *f* jam

confundir to mix up

congelado(a) frozen

congelador *m* freezer

congrio *m* conger eel; **el congrio asado** conger eel baked with onions and flavoured with cloves; **el congrio en cazuela** conger eel casseroled with carrots, onions, tomatoes, wine, garlic and parsley

conjunto *m* group; outfit (*clothes*)

conmigo with me

conocer to know (*person*); to meet

conocido(a) *m/f* acquaintance

conseguir to obtain; **conseguir comunicar** to get through

consejo *m* advice

conserje *m* caretaker

conservar to keep; **consérvese en lugar fresco y seco** keep in a cool, dry place; **conserve**

su billete please keep your ticket
conservas *fpl* tinned foods
consigna *f* left-luggage office
consomé *m* consommé; **el consomé de ave** chicken consommé; **el consomé de gallina** chicken consommé; **el consomé al jerez** consommé with sherry; **el consomé madrileño** onion soup
constipado *m* cold; **estoy constipado(a)** I've got a cold
construcción *f* building
cónsul *m* consul
consulado *m* consulate
consultar to consult
consultorio *m* surgery; doctor's office
consumidor *m* consumer
consumir to eat; to use; **consumir preferentemente antes de** best before
contacto *m* contact
contado *m*: **al contado** cash down
contador *m* meter
contagiarse de to catch (*illness*)
contagioso(a) contagious
contaminación *f* pollution
contar to tell; to count
contener to hold; to contain
contenido *m* contents
contento(a) pleased
contestar to answer; **contestar el teléfono** to answer the phone
continuar to continue
continuo(a) continuous
contra against; **contra reembolso** cash on delivery

contrabando *m* smuggling
contrario *m* opposite; **al contrario** on the contrary
contrato *m* contract
contraventana *f* shutter
control *m* inspection; check; **el control de pasaportes** passport control; **control de la policía** police checkpoint; **control de seguridad** security check
controlar to check
conveniente suitable
convenir to be suitable; to be convenient
convento *m* convent
conversación *f* conversation
coñac *m* cognac; brandy
copa *f* cup; **la copa de helado** mixed ice-cream; **la copa de vino** wineglass
copia *f* copy; print
coquinas *fpl* small cockles
corail *m* intercity train
corazón *m* heart
corbata *f* tie
corcho *m* cork
cordero *m* lamb; mutton; **la pierna de cordero** leg of lamb; **el cordero asado** roast leg of lamb; **el cordero en chilindrón** roast lamb with tomato, onion, pepper, garlic, parsley and paprika sauce
cordillera *f* mountain range
cordón *m* shoelace
corona *f* crown
correa *f* leash; strap; **la correa del ventilador** fanbelt
correcto(a) proper; right
correo *m* mail; **por**

correo by post; **mandar por correo** to post; **por correo aéreo** by air mail
correos *m* post office
correr to run
correspondencia *f* mail
corrida de toros *f* bullfight
corriente *f* power; current; **la corriente de aire** draught
corsetería *f* corsetry; lingerie
cortado(a) off (*milk*); sour
cortar to cut; to turn off
cortarse to cut oneself; **cortarse el pelo** to have a haircut
corte *m* cut; **el corte de helado** ice-cream wafer; **el corte de pelo** haircut
cortina *f* curtain
corto(a) short
cosa *f* thing; **las cosas** stuff
cosecha *f* harvest; vintage
coser to sew
cosméticos *mpl* cosmetics
costa *f* coast
costar to cost
costilla *f* rib; **la costilla de cerdo** pork chop
costo *m* cost; expense
costura *f* sewing; seam
cotizaciones *fpl* exchange rate
coto *m*: **coto de caza** hunting by licence; **coto de pescado** fishing by licence
crecer to grow
crecimiento *m* growth
crédito *m* credit; **a crédito** on credit
creer to believe; **creo que sí** I think so
crema *f* cream; **la crema de afeitar** shaving cream; **la crema bronceadora**

suntan lotion; **la crema catalana** caramel custard; **la crema de champiñones/espárragos** cream of mushroom/asparagus soup; **la crema dental** toothpaste; **la crema labial** lip salve; **la crema limpiadora** cleansing cream; **la crema para las manos** hand cream; **la crema de menta** crème de menthe; **la crema nutritiva** nourishing cream; **la crema para el pelo** conditioner

cremallera f zip
crepé m pancake
crimen m crime
crisis f crisis
cristal m glass; window pane; crystal
cristalería f glassware (*shop*); glazier's
croqueta f croquette; **las croquetas de camarones** shrimp croquettes
cruce m intersection; crossroads; **un cruce de línea** crossed line
cruce giratorio m roundabout
crucero m cruise; **hacer un crucero** to go on a cruise
crucigrama m crossword puzzle
crudo(a) raw
cruz f cross
cruzar to cross; **prohibido cruzar las vías** do not cross the railway line
cuaderno m exercise book
cuadrado(a) square
cuadro m picture; painting; **a cuadros**

check; **el cuadro de servicios** timetable
cuajada f curd; **la cuajada con miel** curd with honey
cuál which one
cualquier whichever
cualquiera anybody at all
cuando when; **¿cuándo? when?**
cuánto(a) how much; **¿cuánto tiempo?** how long?; **¿cuántos(as)?** how many?
cuarenta forty
cuarentena f quarantine
cuarta (gear)
cuarto m room; quarter; **el cuarto de baño** bathroom; **el cuarto de estar** living room; **un cuarto de hora** a quarter of an hour; **las 6 menos cuarto** a quarter to 6; **las 6 y cuarto** a quarter past 6
cuarto(a) fourth
cuatro four
cubalibre m rum and coke
cubertería f cutlery
cubierta f deck
cubierto(a) covered; indoor; **los cubiertos** cutlery; **cubierto no. 3** menu no. 3
cubo m bucket; pail; **el cubo de la basura** dustbin; **el cubo de flash** flashcube
cubrecama m bedspread
cubrir to cover
cuchara f spoon; tablespoon
cucharada f spoonful
cucharilla f teaspoon
cuchillo m knife
cucurucho m ice-cream cornet
cuello m neck; collar
cuenta f bill; account (*at*

bank, shop); **la cuenta bancaria** bank account; **la cuenta de gastos** expense account; **cuentas corrientes** current accounts; **pagar la cuenta** to check out
cuentakilómetros m milometer
cuento m story
cuerda f string; rope
cuero m leather
cuerpo m body
cuesta f hill; **cuesta arriba/abajo** uphill/downhill
cuestión f issue
cueva f cave
cuidado m care; **¡cuidado!** look out!; **al cuidado de (a/c)** care of, c/o; **cuidado con el perro** beware of the dog
cuidar to look after; **cuidar niños** to babysit; **cuide la compostura** please respect this place of worship
culo m bottom, backside
culpa f fault; **yo no tengo la culpa** it's not my fault
cultivar to grow
cumbre f summit
cumpleaños m birthday; **¡feliz cumpleaños!** happy birthday!
cumplido m compliment
cumplir to obey; **hoy cumple 20 años** it's his 20th birthday today
cuna f cradle; cot
cuneta f roadside
cuñada f sister-in-law
cuñado m brother-in-law
cupón m coupon
cupón-respuesta m reply coupon
cura m priest
curarse to heal
curva f bend; curve; **la**

D

curva muy cerrada hairpin bend; **curvas peligrosas en 2 km** dangerous bends in 2 kilometres

damas *fpl* draughts
damasquinado(a) inlaid
dañar to damage
dañino(a) harmful
daño *m* damage
dar to give; **dar algo a alguien** to give someone something
dársena *f* dock
dátil *m* date (*fruit*)
datos *mpl* data
de of; from; **1,000 pesetas de gasolina** 1,000 pesetas worth of petrol
debajo under; underneath
deber to owe; **¿cuándo debe llegar?** when is it due to arrive?
debido(a) due
débil weak (*person*)
decidido(a) determined
decidir to decide
décimo(a) tenth
decir to say; to tell
declaración *f* statement
declarar to declare; **nada que declarar** nothing to declare; **¿algo que declarar?** anything to declare?
declive *m* slope; **fuerte declive** steep hill
decoración *f* decoration; home furnishings
dedo *m* finger; **el dedo del pie** toe
defecto *m* fault; defect
defectuoso(a) faulty
defensa *f* defence
deformar to change

shape; to warp; **no deforma** will not lose its shape
defunción *f* funeral
degustación *f* sampling; **degustación de vinos** wine-tasting
dejar to let; **dejar de hacer algo** to stop doing something: **dejen libre el portón** keep clear; **dejar caer** to drop; **dejen las bolsas a la entrada** please leave your shopping bags at the entrance
del = de + el
delante de in front of
delantero(a) front
delgado(a) slim; thin
delicado(a) delicate
delicioso(a) delicious
demás rest; **todos(as) los/las demás** all the rest
demasiado(a) too much; **es demasiado grande** he's too big
demorar to delay
demostrar to show
denominación *f*: **denominación de origen** label guaranteeing the quality of wine
dentadura postiza *f* dentures
dentífrico(a) tooth; **el dentífrico** toothpaste
dentista *m/f* dentist
dentro (de) inside; **dentro de un mes** in a month's time
departamento *m* compartment; **departamento extranjero** foreign department
depender de to depend on
dependiente(a) *m/f* sales assistant

deporte *m* sport
deportista *m/f* sportsman/sportswoman
deportivo(a) sporty; sports
depósito *m* deposit; **el depósito de gasolina** petrol tank
depreciarse to lose value; to depreciate
deprimido(a) depressed
depuradora de agua *f* water purifier
derecha *f* right(-hand side); **a la derecha** on/to the right
derecho *m* right; **el derecho a** the right to: **los derechos de aduana** customs duty; **libre de derechos de aduana** duty-free
derecho(a) right; straight; **derecho a casa** straight home
derramar to spill
derretirse to melt
derribar to knock over
derrumbamiento *m* landslide
desabrochar to unfasten
desacuerdo *m* disagreement
desafilado(a) blunt
desagradable unpleasant
desaguadero *m* drain
desagüe *m* drainpipe
desanimado(a) discouraged
desaparecer to disappear
desarrollar to develop
desastre *m* disaster
desayuno *m* breakfast
descafeinado(a) decaffeinated
descalzo(a) barefoot
descansar to rest
descanso *m* rest; half-time
descarga *f* shock (*electric*)

descargado(a) flat

descenso m descent; **descenso peligroso** steep hill

descolgar to pick up; to lift

desconcertado(a) embarrassed

descondensador m demister

desconectar to switch off

descongelar to defrost; to thaw; to de-ice

desconocido(a) unknown; strange

describir to describe

descubierto(a) bare

descubrir to discover; to find out

descuento m discount; **con descuento** at a discount; **por favor, no pidan descuento** no discounts given

desde since; from; **desde ayer** since yesterday; **desde que** ever since

desdichado(a) unhappy

desear to want; to desire

desechos mpl refuse

desembarcadero m quay

desembarcar to land; to disembark

desembocadura f: **desembocadura de una calle** road junction

desenchufado(a) off; disconnected

deseo m desire; wish

desesperado(a) desperate

desfile m parade

desgastar to wear out

desgaste m wear and tear

desgracia f misfortune; accident; **por desgracia** unfortunately

desgraciado(a) unlucky

deshacer to undo; **deshacer las maletas** to unpack

desierto(a) deserted

desinfectante m disinfectant

desinfectar to disinfect

desinflado(a) flat (*deflated*)

deslizarse to glide

desmaquillador m make-up remover

desmayarse to faint

desnatado(a) skimmed

desnivel m unevenness

desnudar to undress

desnudarse to get undressed

desnudo(a) naked; nude

desobedecer to disobey

desobediente disobedient

desocupado(a) free

desocupar to vacate

desodorante m deodorant; **el desodorante en barra** stick deodorant; **el desodorante líquido** roll-on deodorant

desorden m mess

desordenar to make a mess of

despacho m office; **el despacho de billetes** ticket office; **el despacho de pan** bakery

despacio slowly; **cierren despacio** close gently

despedida f farewell

despedir: despedir a alguien en la estación to see someone off at the station

despedirse to say goodbye

despegue m takeoff (*of plane*)

despejado(a) clear; cloudless

despensa f larder

desperfecto m fault; **desperfectos** damage

despertador m alarm (clock)

despertarse to wake up

despierto(a) awake

después after; afterward(s)

destapar to uncover; to uncork

desteñir: no destiñe fast colours

destilería f distillery

destinatario m addressee

destino m destination

destornillador m screwdriver

destornillar to unscrew

destruir to destroy

desván m attic

desventaja f disadvantage; handicap

desvestirse to undress

desviación f diversion

desviar to divert

desvío m detour; **hacer un desvío** to make a detour; **desvío provisional** temporary detour

detallado(a) itemized; detailed

detalle m detail; **en detalle** in detail; **al detalle** retail

detención f arrest

detener to arrest

detenerse to pause

detergente m detergent; washing-up liquid

deteriorado(a) shop-soiled

detrás (de) behind

deuda f debt

devaluación f devaluation

devolución f repayment; refund; **no se admiten devoluciones** no refunds will be given

devolver to give back; to

put back; **devolver el dinero** to repay; **este teléfono no devuelve cambio** this phone does not give change

día *m* day; **todo el día** all day; **el día comercial** weekday; **el día festivo** bank holiday; **el día de fiesta** public holiday; **el día laborable** working day; **el día de mercado** market-day; **el día de semana** weekday; **el día de trabajo** working day

diabético(a) *m/f* diabetic

diagnóstico *m* diagnosis

diagrama *m* diagram

dialecto *m* dialect

diamante *m* diamond

diapositiva *f* slide (*photo*)

diario *m* newspaper

diario(a) daily

diarrea *f* diarrhoea

dibujo *m* picture; drawing; **dibujo animado** cartoon

diciembre *m* December

diecinueve nineteen

dieciocho eighteen

dieciséis sixteen

diecisiete seventeen

diente *m* tooth; **los dientes postizos** false teeth

diez ten

diferencia *f* difference

diferente different

difícil difficult

dificultad *f* difficulty

dínamo *f* dynamo

dinero *m* money; **el dinero (contante)** cash; **el dinero suelto** small change

dios *m* god

diplomático *m* diplomat

dirección *f* direction; address; steering; **la dirección local** local address; **la dirección**

particular home address; **la dirección permanente** permanent address; **dirección prohibida** one-way; **dirección única** one-way

directo(a) direct; **el tren directo** through train

director *m* director; president (*of company*); **el director de banco** bank manager; **el director gerente** managing director; **el director de hotel** hotel manager

directora *f* headmistress; manageress

dirigirse a to go towards; to speak to

disco *m* record; disc; **el disco dislocado** slipped disc; **el disco de estacionamiento** parking disc

discoteca *f* disco

discrecional optional

disculpa *f* excuse

disculparse to apologize

discusión *f* argument

discutir to discuss; to argue

diseño *m* pattern; design; **diseños exclusivos** exclusive designs

disfraz *m* mask; fancy dress

dislocar to dislocate

disminución *f* decrease

disminuir to decrease; **disminuir la marcha** to reduce speed

disolver to dissolve

disparador *m* trigger; shutter release

disparar to shoot

disponible available

dispositivo *m* gadget; **dispositivo interuterino (D.I.U.)** I.U.D.

dispuesto(a) ready; arranged

disputa *f* quarrel; dispute

distancia *f* distance; **a corta distancia del mar** within easy reach of the sea

distinguir to distinguish

distinto(a) different

distribuidor *m* distributor; **el distribuidor automático** vending machine

distrito *m* district; **el distrito postal** postal district

D.I.U. see **dispositivo**

diversión *f* fun

diverso(a) various

divertido(a) amusing

divertirse to enjoy oneself

dividir to divide

divieso *m* boil (*on skin*)

divisa *f* foreign currency

divorciado(a) divorced

divorcio *m* divorce

doblado(a) dubbed; bent

doblar to turn; to bend

doble double; **un whisky doble** a double whisky

doce twelve

docena *f* dozen

doctor(a) *m/f* doctor

documentación *f* papers; **la documentación (del coche)** car logbook

documental *m* documentary

documento *m* document

dólar *m* dollar

doler to hurt; to ache

dolor *m* ache; pain; **el dolor de barriga** stomach ache; **el dolor de cabeza** headache; **el dolor de espalda** backache; **el dolor de garganta** sore throat; **el dolor de muelas** toothache; **el dolor de oídos** earache

doloroso(a) painful
domicilio m home address
dominar to control
domingo m Sunday
don m Mister
donación f donation
donde where; **¿de dónde eres?** where are you from?; **¿dónde va?** where are you going?
dorada f sea bream
dormido(a) asleep
dormir to sleep
dormitorio m bedroom
dorso m back; **véase al dorso** P.T.O.
dos two; **dos veces** twice
dosis f dose; dosage
dossier m file
droga f drug
drogadicto(a) m/f drug addict
droguería f shop selling household cleaning articles, cosmetics *etc*; drugstore
ducha f shower; **tomar una ducha** to have a shower; **con ducha** with shower
duda f doubt
dudar to doubt
dueño m owner
dulce sweet; **el dulce** sweet
duodécimo(a) twelfth
duque m duke
duración f: **de larga duración** long-life
durante during; **durante la noche** overnight
durar to last; **¿cuánto tiempo dura el programa?** how long is the programme?
duro(a) tough; hard

E

echado(a) lying (*state*)
echar to pour; to throw
echarse to lie down; **echarse a perder** to go bad
economía f economy
económico(a) economic; economical
edad f age (*of person*); **la edad mínima** age limit
edición f edition
edificio m building
edredón m eiderdown; quilt
educación f education
educado(a) polite
efectivo m: **pagar en efectivo** to pay cash
efecto m effect; **los efectos personales** belongings
eficaz effective
eje m axle
ejecutivo(a) m/f executive
ejemplar m copy (*of book*)
ejemplo m example; **por ejemplo (p. ej.)** for example
ejercicio m exercise
ejército m army
el the
él he; him
elástico m elastic
elección f election; choice
electricidad f electricity; electrical appliances shop
electricista m electrician
eléctrico(a) electric(al)
electrodomésticos mpl electrical appliances
elefante m elephant
elegante smart; stylish
elegir to choose

elenco m list; table
elepé m L.P.
elevado(a) high
elevador m elevator
ella she; her
ellas they
ello it
ellos they
embajada f embassy
embajador m ambassador
embalar to pack
embalse m reservoir
embarazada pregnant
embarcadero m jetty
embarcarse to embark; to board
embargo m embargo
embarque m boarding
emboquillado(a) tipped
emborracharse to get drunk
embotellamiento m traffic jam; hold-up
embrague m clutch (*of car*)
embutidos mpl sausages
emergencia f emergency
emisora f radio station
emitido: emitido por issued by
empanada f Cornish pasty; **las empanadas de carne** small meat and vegetable pies eaten hot or cold
empanadilla f pasty with savoury filling; **empanadilla de salchicha** sausage roll
empanado(a) fried in breadcrumbs
empaquetar to package
emparedado m open sandwich
emparrillado(a) grilled
empaste m filling
empezar to begin
emplasto m plaster
empleado(a) m/f employee

emplear to use; to spend

empleo *m* employment; use

empresa *f* enterprise; project; firm; company

empujar to push; **empuje** push

en in; into; on; **en avión/tren/coche** by air/train/car

enaguas *fpl* petticoat

enamorado(a) in love

encaje *m* lace

encantado(a) delighted

encantador(a) charming

encargado de in charge of

encargar to order

encargo *m*: **encargos para casa** special orders accepted

encendedor *m* cigarette lighter

encender to switch on; to light; **encender una cerilla** to strike a match; **encender las luces** switch on headlights

encendido *m* ignition

encendido(a) on

enchufar to plug in

enchufe *m* plug; point; socket; **el enchufe múltiple** adaptor

encía *f* gum

encima de onto; on top of; **por encima de** beyond

encogerse to shrink; **no encoge** will not shrink

encontrar to find

encontrarse to meet

encrucijada *f* crossroads

encuentro *m* meeting

encurtidos *mpl* pickles

endeudarse to get into debt

endibias *fpl* endives

enemigo *m* enemy

energía *f* energy

enero *m* January

enfadado(a) angry

enfadarse to lose one's temper

éfasis *m* emphasis; stress

enfermedad *f* disease; illness

enfermera *f* nurse

enfermería *f* infirmary; first-aid post

enfermo(a) sick; ill

enfrente de opposite

enfriamiento *m* chill

enfriar to chill

engordar to get fat

engranado(a) in gear

engrasar to lubricate

engrase *m* lubrication

¡enhorabuena! congratulations!

enjuague *m* rinse

enlace *m* connection; **coger el enlace** to make a connection; **el enlace de la autopista** motorway junction

enlazar to connect; **este tren enlaza con el tren de las 16.45** this train connects with the 16.45

enmarcar to frame

enojado(a) angry

enorme enormous

ensaimada *f* sweet bun

ensalada *f* salad; **la ensalada de aguacates** avocado salad; **la ensalada de anchoas** anchovy, boiled eggs and vinaigrette salad; **la ensalada de endibias** endive salad with Roquefort cheese dressing; **la ensalada de frutas** fruit salad; **la ensalada de lechuga y tomate** green salad; **la ensalada mixta** mixed salad; **la ensalada verde** green salad

ensaladilla *f*: **la**

ensaladilla rusa diced vegetable salad

enseñanza *f* teaching; education

enseñar to teach; to show; **por favor, enseñen los bolsos a la salida** please show your bag when leaving

entender to understand

entero(a) whole

entierro *m* funeral

entonces then

entrada *f* entrance; ticket; admission; **el precio de entrada** admission fee; **entrada libre** admission free; **entrada prohibida** no entry; **entrada por delante** entrance at the front; **entradas** starters

entrantes *mpl* starters

entrar to go in; to come in; **entrar en** to enter; **antes de entrar, dejen salir** let passengers off first

entre among; between

entreacto *m* interval

entrecot *m* rib steak; **el entrecot grillé** grilled rib steak

entrega *f* delivery; **la entrega de equipajes** baggage reclaim; **la entrega de lista** poste restante; **entrega en el acto** while-you-wait; **entrega de paquetes** parcels to be collected here

entregar to deliver

entremeses *mpl* hors d'œuvres; **los entremeses de jamón en tacos** diced Spanish ham; **los entremeses variados** assorted hors d'œuvres

entresuelo *m* mezzanine

entretener to amuse; to entertain

entretenido(a) amusing

entusiasmado(a) excited

entusiasmo m enthusiasm

envase m container; **envase no retornable** non-returnable bottle

envenenamiento m: **envenenamiento de la sangre** blood poisoning

enviar to send

envidioso(a) jealous; envious

envío m shipment; dispatch

envoltura f wrapping

envolver to wrap

epidemia f epidemic

epilepsia f epilepsy

equilibrio m balance; **perder el equilibrio** to lose one's balance

equipaje m luggage; baggage; **la reclamación de equipajes** baggage claim; **el equipaje de mano** hand-luggage; **el equipaje permitido** luggage allowance

equipo m team; equipment; kit (sports)

equitación f horseriding

equivocación f mistake

equivocado(a) wrong; mistaken

eres you are

erizo de mar m sea urchin

error m error; mistake

es he/she/it is; you are

esa that (feminine); **ésa** that one

esas those (feminine); **ésas** those ones

esbelto(a) slim

escabechado(a) pickled

escabeche m spicy marinade; **en escabeche** pickled; in a marinade; **el escabeche de pescado** marinated fish

escala f stopover

escalar to climb

escaldar to scald; to poach (eggs)

escalera f flight of steps; stairs; ladder; **la escalera de incendios** fire escape; **la escalera mecánica** escalator; **la escalera de tijera** stepladder

escalón m step (stair); **el escalón central** ramp; **escalón lateral** steep verge

escalope m escalope; **los escalopes de ternera** veal escalopes

escama f flake; scale (of fish); **las escamas de jabón** soap-flakes

escanciador m wine waiter

escapar(se) to escape

escaparate m shop window

escape m exhaust

escarabajo m beetle

escarcha f frost

escarchado(a) glacé

escarlata scarlet

escarpado(a) abrupt; steep

escayola f plaster

escayolar to put in plaster

escenario m stage

esclava f name bracelet

escoba f broom

escobilla (para pipas) f pipe cleaner

escocés(esa) Scottish

Escocia f Scotland

escoger to choose

escombro m mackerel

escombros mpl rubbish

esconder to hide

escota f sheet (sailing)

escribir to write

escrito: por escrito in writing

escritor m writer

escritura f writing

escuchar to listen; to listen to

escuela (primaria) f primary school

escupir: prohibido escupir en el suelo no spitting on the floor

escurrir to wring

ese that (masculine); **ése** that one

esencial essential

esfuerzo m effort

esmalte m enamel; **el esmalte para las uñas** nail polish

esmeralda f emerald

eso that

esos those; **ésos** those ones

espacio m space

espaguetis mpl spaghetti; **los espaguetis boloñesa** spaghetti bolognese

espalda f back

España f Spain

español(a) Spanish

espantoso(a) dreadful

esparadrapo m sticking plaster

espárrago m asparagus; **los espárragos gigantes** large asparagus; **los espárragos trigueros** wild asparagus

espátula f spatula

especial special; particular

especialidad f speciality

especialista m consultant

especias fpl spices

especie f kind; **una especie de judía** a kind of bean

espécimen m specimen

espectáculo m entertainment; show; **el espectáculo de variedades** variety show

espectador(a) *m/f* spectator

espejo *m* mirror; **el espejo retrovisor** rear-view mirror

espera *f* wait

esperanza *f* hope

esperar to hope; to wait (for); **espero que sí/no** I hope so/not

espeso(a) thick

espetos *mpl* barbecued sardines

espina *f* fishbone; spine; thorn (*of flowers*)

espinaca *f* spinach; **las espinacas con pasas y piñones** spinach with raisins and pine kernels

espinazo *m* spine

espinilla *f* shin; spot

esponja *f* sponge

esposa *f* wife

esposo *m* husband

espray *m* spray

espuma *f* foam; **la espuma de afeitar** shaving foam

espumadera *f* spatula (*for cooking*)

espumoso(a) frothy; sparkling; **el espumoso** sparkling wine

esq. see **esquina**

esquí *m* skiing; ski; **el esquí acuático** water-skiing; **hacer esquí acuático** to go water-skiing

esquiador(a) *m/f* skier

esquiar to ski

esquina *f* street corner; **esquina (esq.) Goya y Corrientes** on the corner of Goya St. and Corrientes St.

esta this; **ésta** this one

establecimiento *m* shop

estación *f* (railway) station; season; stop; bus station; **la estación de** autobuses terminal (*buses*); **la estación de servicio** petrol station; **la estación de metro** underground station; **la estación marítima** port

estacionado(a) parked

estacionamiento *m* parking

estacionar to park

estadio *m* stadium; football ground

estado *m* state; **el estado del tiempo** weather conditions

Estados Unidos (EE.UU.) *mpl* United States

estampilla *f* postage stamp

estancia *f* stay

estanco *m* tobacconist's (*shop*)

estanquero(a) *m/f* tobacconist

estaquilla *f* tent peg

estar to be (*temporary state*); **está Ud en lugar sagrado** this is a place of worship

estas these; **éstas** these ones

estatua *f* statue

este¹ this; **éste** this one

este² *m* east

esterilizar to sterilize

estilo *m* style

estilográfica *f* fountain pen

estimado(a): estimada Señora Dear Madam; **estimado Señor Smith** Dear Mr Smith

esto this

estofado *m* stew; **el estofado de vaca con patatas** beef stew with potatoes

estómago *m* stomach

estorbar to get/be in the way (of)

estornudar to sneeze

estornudo *m* sneeze

estos(as) these

estrangulador *m* choke (*of car*)

estrecho(a) narrow

estrella *f* star

estreno *m* première; new release; **el estreno de gala** grand première

estreñido(a) constipated

estreñimiento *m* constipation

estropeado(a) out of order

estructura *f* structure

estudiante *m/f* student

estudiar to study

estudio *m* studio

estufa *f* stove

estúpido(a) stupid

etapa *f* stage; phase

etiqueta *f* label; ticket; tag; **de etiqueta** formal

Europa *f* Europe

europeo(a) European

evidente obvious

evitar to avoid

exacto(a) accurate; exact; precise

examen *m* examination; **el examen de conducir** driving test

examinar to examine

excelente excellent

excepción *f* exception

excepto except (for); excepting

excesivo(a) unreasonable

exceso *m* excess; **el exceso de equipaje** excess baggage; **el exceso de velocidad** speeding

exclusivo(a) exclusive

excursión *f* tour; excursion; outing; **la excursión en autocar** coach trip; **la excursión a pie** hike

excursionismo *m* hiking

exigir to demand

existir to exist
éxito m success
expedición f expedition
expedido(a) issued
expedidor m: **el expedidor del telegrama** the sender of the telegram
expedir to send
experiencia f experience
experimentado(a) experienced
experto m expert
explicación f explanation
explicar to explain
exponer: no exponer a los rayos solares do not expose to sunlight; **no exponer a temperaturas superiores a ...** do not expose to temperatures above ...
exportación f export
exportar to export
exposición f exhibition; show
exposímetro m exposure meter
expreso m express train
exprimidor m lemon-squeezer
exquisito(a) delicious
extender to stretch; to extend; to spread
extensión f extension
exterior outside
externo(a) outside; external
extintor m fire extinguisher
extranjero(a) foreign; m/f foreigner; **en el extranjero** abroad
extraño(a) peculiar; odd; strange
extremidad f limb
extremo m end

F

fabada f Asturian dish made of beans, pork sausage and bacon
fábrica f factory; **la fábrica de cerveza** brewery
fabricación f manufacturing; **la fabricación en serie** mass production
fabricante m manufacturer
fácil easy
facilidades fpl easy terms
facilitar to make easy; to supply; **facilite el cambio** please have your change ready
factor m guard
factura f receipt; bill; **la factura desglosada** itemized bill
facturación f: **la facturación de equipajes** luggage check-in
faisán m pheasant
falda f skirt; **la falda ecocesa** kilt; **la falda pantalón** culottes; **la falda plisada** pleated skirt
fallar to go wrong; to fail
fallo m failure
falso(a) false
falta f defect; shortage
faltar to be missing
fama f reputation
familia f family
famoso(a) famous
farmacéutico(a) m/f chemist
farmacia f chemist's shop; **la farmacia de guardia** duty chemist
faro m headlamp; headlight; lighthouse; **el faro antiniebla** fog-lamp
farol m lamppost
favor m favour; **por favor** please
f.c. see **ferrocarril**
febrero m February
fecha f date; **fecha de caducidad** valid until; best before; **fecha de expedición** date of issue
felicidad f happiness; **felicidades** fpl congratulations
felicitaciones fpl congratulations
feliz happy
felpudo m doormat
femenino(a) feminine
feo(a) ugly
feria f trade fair; fun fair
feroz fierce
ferretería f hardware store
ferretero m ironmonger
ferrobús m local train
ferrocarril (f.c.) m railway; **por ferrocarril** by rail
festín m feast
festivos mpl public holidays
fiambre m cold meat; **el fiambre variado** slices of assorted cold meats
fianza f security
fiar: no se fía no credit given
fibra f fibre; **la fibra de vidrio** fibre-glass
ficha f chip (in gambling); token; counter
fideos mpl spaghetti; noodles; **fideos a la catalana** thick soup with pork rib, bacon, onion, tomato, garlic and noodles
fiebre f fever; **tener fiebre** to have a temperature; **la fiebre**

del heno hay fever
fiesta f party; public holiday
figón m bar; economical restaurant
fijador m styling gel
fijar to fix; to fasten
fijo(a) fixed; firm; set
fila f row
filatelia f stamp collectors' shop; stamp collecting
filete m fillet; **el filete de lomo (de vaca)** rump steak; **los filetes de lenguado** rolled sole baked with wine, mushrooms and butter
filial f branch
film(e) m film
filtro m filter; **el filtro de aceite** oil filter; **el filtro de aire** air filter; **con filtro** filter-tipped; **sin filtro** plain
fin m end; **el fin de semana** weekend; **por fin** at last
final final; **el final** end
financiero(a) financial
finca f farm; property
fino m light dry, very pale sherry
fino(a) fine; thin
firma f signature
firmar to sign
firme firm; **firme en mal estado** poor road surface; **firme deslizante** slippery surface
flaco(a) thin
flan m cream caramel; **el flan de la casa** homemade cream caramel; **el flan con guindas** cream caramel with black cherries; **el flan con nata** cream caramel with whipped cream
flash m flashlight

flatulencia f wind
flequillo m fringe
flete m freight; **el flete por avión** air freight
flojo(a) slack; weak (*tea*); mild
flor f flower
florero m vase
florista m/f florist
floristería f florist's
flotador m rubber ring (*for swimming*)
flotar to float
flúor m fluoride
foco m spotlight
foie-gras m liver pâté
folleto m brochure
fonda f inn; tavern; small restaurant
Fondillón m dark red wine from Alicante
fondo m bottom; background; back (*of hall, room*)
fontanería f plumbing
fontanero m plumber
footing m jogging
forastero m stranger
forfait m lift pass
forma f form; shape
formulario m form
forro m lining
fortaleza f fortress
fortuito(a) accidental
fósforo m match
foto f picture; photo
fotocopia f photocopy; **se hacen fotocopias en el acto** photocopies while you wait
fotografía f photography; photograph
fotógrafo m photographer
fotómetro m light meter
fractura f fracture
frágil fragile; handle with care
frambuesa f raspberry
francés(esa) French
Francia f France

franela f flannel
franqueo m postage
frasco m flask
frazada f blanket
fregadero m sink
fregar to mop; **fregar los platos** to wash up
freiduría f fried-fish restaurant
freír to fry
frenar to put on the brakes; to brake
freno m brake; **el líquido de frenos** brake fluid; **el freno de pie** foot-brake; **el freno de mano** hand-brake; **los frenos de disco** disc brakes
frente¹ f forehead
frente²: en frente opposite; **frente a** facing; **de frente** head-on
fresa f strawberry; **las fresas con nata** strawberries with cream
fresco(a) fresh; crisp; cool
fresón m large strawberry
frigorífico m refrigerator
frío(a) cold; **sírvase frío** serve chilled; **tengo frío** I'm cold
fritada f: **la fritada de pimientos y tomates** fried green peppers, tomatoes, onion and garlic
frito(a) fried; **un huevo frito** a fried egg
fritura f mixed fried fish or meat
frontera f border; frontier
frotar to rub
fruta f fruit; **la fruta escarchada** candied fruit; **la fruta del tiempo** fresh fruit of the season
frutería f fruit shop
frutos secos dried fruit

and nuts

fuego *m* fire; **fuegos artificiales** fireworks; **¿tiene fuego?** have you got a light?; **prohibido hacer fuego** it is forbidden to light fires

fuente *f* fountain

fuera outdoors; out; **está fuera** he's out

fuera-borda *f* speedboat

fuerte strong; loud

fuerza *f* force; strength

fuga *f* leak (*gas*)

fumador(a) *m/f* smoker; **no fumadores** non-smokers

fumar to smoke; **prohibido fumar** no smoking; **no fumar** no smoking

funcionar to run; to work; **no funciona** out of order

furgón de equipajes *m* baggage car

furgoneta *f* van

fusible *m* fuse

fútbol *m* football

G

gachas *fpl* creamed cabbage and potatoes

gafas *fpl* glasses; **las gafas de bucear** goggles; **las gafas de esquí** ski goggles; **las gafas de sol** sunglasses

galería de arte *f* art gallery

Gales *m* Wales

galés(esa) Welsh

gallego(a) Galician

galleta *f* biscuit; **las galletas saladas** savoury biscuits

gallina *f* hen

gallo *m* cock(erel)

galón *m* gallon

gamba *f* prawn; **las gambas al ajillo** garlic-fried prawns; **las gambas con gabardina** prawns fried with batter; **las gambas al pil-pil** prawns cooked with garlic, oil and red pepper; **las gambas a la plancha** grilled prawns

gamuza *f* chamois (leather)

ganado *m* cattle

ganador(a) *m/f* winner

ganar to win; to earn

ganas *fpl*: **tener ganas de hacer algo** to feel like doing something

ganga *f* bargain

ganso *m* goose

garaje *m* garage

garantía *f* guarantee

garantizado guaranteed

garantizar to guarantee

garbanzo *m* chickpea

garganta *f* throat

gargantilla *f* choker

garrafa *f* decanter

gas *m* gas; **el gas butano** Calor gas; **con gas** fizzy; **sin gas** non-fizzy

gasa *f* gauze; nappy

gaseosa *f* lemonade; fizzy drink

gasfitero *m* plumber

gasoil *m* diesel fuel

gasóleo *m* diesel oil

gasolina *f* petrol; **gasolina normal** 3-star petrol; **gasolina super** 4-star petrol

gasolinera *f* petrol station

gastar to spend; to use

gasto *m* expense; **los gastos** expenditure

gastrónomo *m* gourmet

gato *m* cat; jack (*for car*)

gaviota *f* seagull

gazpacho *m* cold soup

made with tomatoes, onion, cucumber, green peppers and garlic

generación *f* generation

género *m* type; material; **los géneros de punto** knitwear

generoso(a) generous

gente *f* people

gerente *m/f* manager/manageress

gesto *m* gesture

gimnasio *m* gym(nasium)

ginebra *f* gin

ginecólogo(a) *m/f* gynaecologist

girar to turn; to twist

giro *m*: **giros y transferencias** drafts and transfers; **el giro postal** money order; postal order

gitano(a) *m/f* gypsy

glándula *f* gland

globo *m* balloon

glorias *fpl* pastries with an almond and sweet potato filling

glorieta *f* roundabout

gobernador *m* governor

gobernadora *f* governess

gobierno *m* government

gol *m* goal

golf *m* golf

golpe *m* blow; stroke

golpear to hit; to beat; to bump; **golpearse la cabeza** to bang one's head

goma *f* rubber; gum; **la goma de borrar** rubber; **la goma de mascar** chewing gum

goma-espuma *f* foam rubber

gordo(a) fat

gorro de baño *m* bathing cap

gota *f* drop; **las gotas nasales** nose drops

gotear to leak; to drip

grabado *m* print; engraving
gracias thank you
gracioso(a) funny
grada *f* tier; **gradas** terraces
gradería *f* terrace
grado *m* degree; grade
gramática *f* grammar
gran see **grande**
granada *f* pomegranate
Gran Bretaña *f* Great Britain
grande large; great; tall; wide
grandes almacenes *mpl* department stores
granero *m* barn
granizo *m* hail
granja *f* farm; milk bar
grano *m* spot; pimple
grapa *f* staple
grapadora *f* stapler
grasa *f* fat; grease; lubricant
gratén: al gratén with a cheese and browned breadcrumb topping
gratinado(a) au gratin
gratis free of charge
grave serious; deep
gravilla suelta *f* loose chippings
grelo *m* young turnip
grieta *f* crack
grifo *m* tap
gripe *f* flu
gris grey; dull
gritar to scream
grito *m* shout; cry
grosella *f* red currant; **grosella espinosa** gooseberry; **la grosella negra** blackcurrant
grosero(a) rude
grúa *f* crane; breakdown van
grueso(a) thick
grupo *m* party; group; **el grupo sanguíneo** blood group

gruta *f* grotto; cave
guante *m* glove
guantera *f* glove compartment
guapo(a) handsome; pretty
guardabarros *m* mudguard
guardacostas *m* coastguard
guardar to put away
guardarropa *m* cloakroom
guardería *f* nursery
guardia *f* guard; **el Guardia Civil** Civil Guard; **Guardia Civil de Carreteras** traffic police; **el guardia de tráfico** traffic warden
guarnición *f*: **la guarnición de legumbres** garnish of vegetables
guerra *f* war
guía *m/f* courier; guide; **la guía telefónica** telephone directory
guinda *f* black cherry
guisantes *mpl* peas
guiso *m* stew
guitarra *f* guitar
gustar to enjoy; **¿le gustaría una taza de café?** would you like a cup of coffee?; **me gusta bailar** I like dancing
gusto *m* taste; pleasure

H

haba *f* broad bean; **las habas a la catalana** broad beans with ham, onions and tomatoes stewed in white wine; **las habas con jamón** broad beans sautéed with diced ham; **las habas a la**

rondeña broad beans fried with red peppers, tomatoes, onions and ham
habano *m* cigar
habichuelas *fpl* haricot beans
hábil skilful
habitación *f* room; **la habitación doble** double room; **una habitación individual** a single room
habitante *m* inhabitant
habitar to live (in)
hablar to speak; to talk; **¿habla Ud inglés?** do you speak English?; **se habla inglés** English spoken
hacer to do; to make; **hace calor** it is hot; **hace frío** it's cold; **hacer una foto** to take a photo; **hace sol** it's sunny; **se hacen trajes a medida** suits made to measure; **hacer noche** to stay overnight; **hace una semana** one week ago
hacia toward(s); **hacia adelante** forwards; **hacia atrás** backwards; **conducir hacia atrás** to reverse
hacienda *f* farm; ranch; **Hacienda** Tax Department
hallar to find
hamaca *f* hammock
hambre *f* hunger; **morirse de hambre** to starve; **tengo hambre** I am hungry
hamburguesa *f* hamburger; **la hamburguesa con guarnición** a hamburger served with chips or vegetables
hamburguesería *f*

hamburger restaurant

harina f flour

hasta until; till; **¡hasta luego!** see you soon!

hay there is/there are

hecho(a) finished; done; ripe (*cheese*); **hecho a mano** handmade; **poco hecho** underdone; rare; **hecho a la medida** made to measure; **muy hecho** well done

helada f frost; **peligro – en heladas** danger – ice on road

heladería f ice-cream parlour

helado m ice-cream; **el helado de mantecado** vanilla ice-cream; **el helado de nata** plain ice-cream; **el helado de turrón** nougat ice-cream; **el helado de tutti-frutti** assorted fruit ice-cream; **el helado de vainilla** vanilla ice-cream

helar to freeze

hélice f propeller

helicóptero m helicopter

hemorragia f haemorrhage

hemorroides fpl haemorrhoids

heno m hay

herbolario m health food shop

herida f injury; wound

herido(a) injured

hermana f sister

hermanastra f stepsister

hermanastro m stepbrother

hermano m brother

hermético(a) air-tight

hermoso(a) beautiful

herpes fpl shingles

herramienta f tool

hervido(a) boiled

hervidor m kettle

hervir to boil

hidropedal m pedal boat

hielo m ice; **con hielo** on the rocks

hierba f grass; herb

hierbabuena f mint

hierro m iron

hígado m liver; **el hígado con cebolla** fried calf's liver with onions; **el hígado de ternera salteado** sautéed calf's liver served with a wine, parsley, butter and garlic sauce

higiénico(a) hygienic; **papel higiénico** toilet paper

higo m fig; **los higos chumbos** prickly pears; **los higos pasos** dried figs

hija f daughter

hijastra f stepdaughter

hijastro m stepson

hijo m son

hilas fpl lint

hilo m thread; linen

hincha m fan

hinchazón f swelling

hipermercado m superstore

hípica f showjumping

hipo m hiccups

hipódromo m racecourse

historia f story; history

hogar m fireplace; home; household goods

hoja f leaf; blade; sheet of paper; **la hoja de afeitar** razor blade

hojaldre m puff pastry

hola hullo; hello

hombre m man; **el hombre de negocios** businessman

hombro m shoulder

hondo(a) deep

honrado(a) honest

hora f hour; **¿qué hora es?** what's the time?; **las**

horas de oficina opening hours; **hora prescrita de llegada** time due; **hora prevista de llegada** expected arrival time; **las horas puntas** rush hour; **las horas de recogida** times of collection

horario m timetable; **el horario de salidas** departure board; **el horario de caja** opening hours; **el horario atención al público** opening hours

horario(a) hourly

horchata de chufa f cold drink made from almonds

horizonte m horizon

hormiga f ant

hormigón m concrete

hornillo m: **el hornillo de camping gas** camping stove

horno m oven; **al horno** baked; roasted

horquilla f hairpin

hortalizas fpl vegetables

hospedaje m hostel

hospedería f hostel

hospital m hospital

hostal m bed and breakfast

hotel m hotel

hoy today

hueco(a) hollow

huelga f strike

huérfano(a) m/f orphan

huerta f orchard

hueso m bone; stone (*in fruit*)

huésped m host; guest

huéspedes mpl guest house

huevas fpl roe; **las huevas de bacalao** cod roe; **las huevas de merluza** hard hake roe

huevería f poultry shop

huevo m egg; **el huevo**

hilado garnish made with egg yolk and sugar; **el huevo pasado por agua** soft-boiled egg; **los huevos de aldea** free-range eggs; **los huevos con chorizo** baked eggs with Spanish sausage; **los huevos duros** hard-boiled eggs; **los huevos escalfados** poached eggs; **los huevos a la española** stuffed eggs with a cheese sauce; **los huevos a la flamenca** baked eggs with ham and peas; **los huevos fritos** fried eggs; **los huevos fritos al nido** eggs fried in thick slices of bread; **los huevos con migas** fried eggs with fried breadcrumbs; **los huevos con patatas** fried eggs and chips; **los huevos al plato** baked eggs; **los huevos revueltos** scrambled eggs
humedad f moisture
húmedo(a) wet; damp
humo m smoke
humor m mood; **de mal humor** in a bad temper; **de buen humor** in a good mood
hundirse to sink
huracán m hurricane

I

ida f departure; **de ida y vuelta** return
idea f idea
identificar to identify
idioma m language
iglesia f church
igual even; equal; **me da igual** I don't care
ileso(a) unhurt

ilimitado(a) unlimited
iluminación f lighting
imán m magnet
impaciente impatient; eager
impar odd; **impares** parking allowed on odd days of month
impedir to prevent
imperdible m safety pin
impermeable waterproof; **el impermeable** raincoat
importación f import
importante important
importar: no importa it doesn't matter
importe m amount; **el importe exacto** exact amount; **el importe final** final total; **el importe de la factura** the amount of the bill
imposible impossible
imprescindible vital
impresionante amazing; impressive
impreso m form
impresos mpl printed matter; **impresos certificados** registered printed matter
imprevisto(a) unexpected
impuesto m tax; **el impuesto sobre la renta** income tax; **el impuesto al valor añadido (I.V.A.)** VAT
incapacitado(a) disabled
incendio m fire (*accident*); **en caso de incendio rompan el cristal** break glass in case of fire
inclinar to tip (*tilt*)
inclinarse to lean
incluido(a) included; including
incluir to include
incluso(a) included; including

incómodo(a) uncomfortable
inconsciente unconscious
inconveniente m trouble; problem
incumplimiento m: **el incumplimiento de contrato** breach of contract
indemnización f compensation
independiente independent; self-contained
indicaciones fpl directions
indicador m gauge; **el indicador de dirección** indicator
indicativo m dialling code; **el indicativo de la población** dialling code of the town
índice m index; index finger
individual individual; single
industria f industry
infarto m heart attack
infección f infection
infeccioso(a) infectious
inferior inferior; lower
inflable inflatable
inflador m air bed pump
inflamable inflammable
inflamación f inflammation
inflamado(a) inflamed
inflar to inflate
información f information (office)
informaciones fpl information desk
infracción f offence; **la infracción de tráfico** traffic offence
ingeniero m engineer
ingenioso(a) clever
Inglaterra f England
inglés(esa) English; **en**

inglés in English; **se habla inglés** English spoken

ingreso m entrance; **ingresos** deposits; income

inmediatamente at once; immediately

inmobiliaria f estate agent's

inmueble m property

innecesario(a) unnecessary

inocente innocent

inoculación f inoculation

inodoro m toilet

inoportuno(a) inconvenient

inoxidable stainless; rustproof

inquieto(a) worried; restless; fidgety

inquilino m tenant

inscribirse to check in

insecticida m insecticide

insecto m insect

insistir to insist

insolación f sunstroke

insólito(a) unusual

insoportable unbearable

inspección f inspection; survey

instalación f: **la instalación sanitaria** plumbing; **las instalaciones deportivas** sports facilities

instalarse to move in; to settle in

instante m moment; **al instante** right away

instituto m institute; **el instituto de belleza** beauty salon; **el instituto de segunda enseñanza** secondary school

instrucciones fpl directions; instructions

instrumento m instrument

insulina f insulin

insulto m insult

integral: pan integral wholemeal bread

íntegro(a) complete

inteligencia f intelligence

intención f intention; **tener la intención de hacer algo** to intend to do something

intentar to attempt

interés m interest

interesante interesting

interior inside

intermedio m interval

intermitente m indicator; **el intermitente de emergencia** hazard lights

internacional international

intérprete m/f interpreter

interrumpir to disturb; to interrupt

interruptor m switch

interurbano(a) long-distance

intoxicación f: **la intoxicación por alimentos** food poisoning

intransitable blocked; closed to traffic

introducir to introduce; to insert; **introduzca monedas** insert coins

inundación f flood

inútil useless

inválido m invalid

inventario m stocktaking; inventory

invernadero m greenhouse

invertir to invest

investigación f research

invierno m winter; **los deportes de invierno** winter sports

invitación f invitation

invitado(a) m/f guest

invitar to invite

inyección f injection

inyectar to inject

ir to go

Irlanda f Ireland

irlandés(esa) Irish

irrompible unbreakable

irse to go away; to leave

isla f island

itinerario m route; schedule

I.V.A. see **impuesto**; **I.V.A. incluido** VAT included

izquierda f left; **torcer hacia la izquierda** to turn left

izquierdo(a) left; **el lado izquierdo** the left side

J

jabalí m wild boar

jabón m soap; **el jabón líquido** liquid soap; **el jabón en polvo** washing powder; soap powder; **el jabón de tocador** beauty soap

jacinto m hyacinth

jamás never

jamón m ham; **el jamón de Jabugo** Andalucian cured ham; **el jamón serrano** cured ham; **el jamón de Trevélez** a mild cured ham from Granada; **el jamón de pata negra** best quality (Parma) ham

jaqueca f migraine

jarabe m syrup; **el jarabe para la tos** cough syrup

jardín m garden; **el jardín botánico** botanical gardens; **jardín zoológico** zoo

jardinero(a) m/f gardener

jarra f jug; **la jarra de**

cerveza glass of beer
jaula *f* cage
jefe(a) *m/f* chief; head; boss; **el jefe de cocina** chef; **el jefe de estación** station master; **el jefe de tren** guard
jengibre *m* ginger
jerez *m* sherry
jeringa *f* syringe
jersey *m* sweater; pullover
jornada *f* day
joven young
joya *f* jewel; **las joyas** jewellery; **las joyas de fantasía** costume jewellery
joyería *f* jeweller's
joyero *m* jeweller; jewel box
jubilado(a) *m/f* pensioner
judías *fpl* beans; **las judías blancas** white haricot beans; **las judías con chorizo** white haricot beans cooked with sausage, potatoes and onion; **las judías encarnadas a la madrileña** red haricot beans with bacon, garlic, onion and sausage; **las judías salteadas con gambas** sautéed beans with prawns; **las judías salteadas con jamón** sautéed beans with ham; **las judías verdes** French beans; **las judías verdes a la riojana** boiled green beans with sausage, bacon, onion and fried pork chops
judío(a) Jewish
juego *m* game; **el juego de cartas** card game; **un juego de tenis** a game of tennis; **prohibidos los juegos de pelota** ball games prohibited

juerga *f* party
jueves *m* Thursday
juez *m* judge
jugador(a) *m/f* player; **el jugador de golf** golfer
jugar to play; to gamble; **jugar bien al golf** to be good at golf
jugo *m* juice
juguete *m* toy
juguetería *f* toy shop
julio *m* July
jumbo *m* jumbo jet
Jumilla *m* dry red wine from Murcia
junio *m* June
juntarse to gather
junto(a) together; **¿están juntos?** are you together?
jurar to swear
justicia *f* justice
justo(a) fair
juvenil junior
juventud *f* youth
juzgar to judge

K

kilo *m* kilo; **un kilo de** a kilo of
kilogramo *m* kilogramme
kilometraje *m* = mileage; **kilometraje ilimitado** unlimited mileage
kilómetro *m* kilometre
kilovatio *m* kilowatt

L

la the; her; it
labio *m* lip
laborable working (*day*); **laborables** weekdays; **laborables de 9 a 20 h** in force weekdays from

9am to 8pm
laboratorio *m* laboratory
labrador *m* farmer
laca *f* hair spray
lado *m* side; **al lado de** beside
ladrón *m* thief; burglar
lago *m* lake
lágrima *f* tear
lampa *f* spade
lámpara *f* lamp; **la lámpara indicadora** pilot light; **la lámpara fluorescente** fluorescent light
lampistería *f* electrical repairs
lana *f* wool; **de lana** woollen; **pura lana virgen** pure new wool; **lanas** wool shop
lancha *f* launch; **la lancha motora** speedboat; motorboat; **la lancha de socorro** lifeboat
langosta *f* lobster
langostino *m* large prawn
lanolina *f* lanolin
lápiz *m* pencil; **el lápiz de color** crayon; **el lápiz de labios** lipstick; **el lápiz de ojos** eyeliner/eye pencil; **el lápiz para cejas** eyebrow pencil
largo(a) long; **a largo plazo** long-term
largometraje *m* feature film
laringitis *f* laryngitis
las them; the
lasaña *f* lasagna
lástima *f*: **¡qué látima!** what a pity!
lastimar to hurt
lastimarse to be injured; to hurt oneself
lata *f* can (*container*); tin; **en lata** tinned; canned
lateral side

Latinoamérica f Latin America

latinoamericano(a) Latin American

lavable washable

lavabo m lavatory; washbasin

lavadero m laundry room

lavado m: **lavado en seco** dry-cleaning; **lavado y engrase** car wash and oil put in; **lavado y marcado** shampoo and set

lavado(a): lavado(a) a la piedra stonewashed

lavadora f washing machine

lavandería f laundry; **la lavandería automática** launderette; laundry

lavaplatos m dishwasher

lavar to wash

lavarse to wash oneself

laxante m laxative

le him; you; to him/her/it/you

leche f milk; **con leche** white (*coffee*); **la leche condensada** condensed milk; **la leche desnatada** skimmed milk; **la leche entera** full cream milk; **la leche evaporada** evaporated milk; **la leche fresca** fresh milk; **la leche frita** thick slices of custard fried in breadcrumbs: **la leche hidratante** moisturizer; **la leche de larga duración/uperisada** long-life milk; **la leche merengada** milk and egg sorbet; **la leche en polvo** dried milk

lechería f dairy

lechero m milkman

lechón m sucking pig

lechuga f lettuce

leer to read

legumbres fpl vegetables; pulses

lejano(a) distant

lejía f bleach

lejos far

lencería f lingerie; linen; draper's

lengua f language; tongue; **la lengua en salsa de nueces** tongue with a walnut and wine sauce; **la lengua de ternera en salsa picante** cooked veal tongue oven-baked and with a butter, onion, gherkin and caper sauce; **las lenguas de gato** sponge fingers

lenguado m sole; lemon sole; **el lenguado meunière** fried sole baked in the oven with butter and lemon sauce; **el lenguado a la plancha** grilled lemon sole; **los lenguados rellenos** fillet of sole stuffed with shrimps or prawns

lente f lens; **las lentes de contacto** contact lenses

lentejas fpl lentils

lento(a) slow

leña f firewood

León m light dry wine from Northern Spain

león m lion

leotardos mpl tights

les them; you; to them/you

letra f letter (*of alphabet*)

letrero m notice

levantar to lift

levantarse to get up; to rise

ley f law

libertad f freedom

libra f pound (*currency, weight*); **la libra esterlina** sterling

libre free; vacant; for hire (*taxi*); **libre de impuestos** tax-free; **dejen libre el portón** keep clear

librería f bookshop

librito m: **el librito de papel de fumar** packet of cigarette papers

libro m book; **el libro de bolsillo** paperback; **existe libro de reclamaciones** a complaints book is provided

licencia f licence; degree; **la licencia de conducir** driving licence

licor m liqueur; **los licores** spirits

liebre f hare; **la liebre estofada con judías** hare stew with French beans

ligero(a) light (*not heavy*)

lima f file; lime; **el zumo de lima** lime juice; **la lima de uñas** nailfile

límite m limit; boundary; **el límite de velocidad** speed limit

limón m lemon

limonada f lemon drink

limpiador(a) cleaning; cleansing; m/f cleaner

limpiaparabrisas m windscreen wiper

limpiar to clean; to polish; **limpiar en seco** to dry-clean

limpieza en seco f dry cleaning

limpio(a) clean

línea f line; **la línea está cortada** the line is dead; **las líneas aéreas** airlines

lino m linen

linterna f torch

lío m fuss; **armar un lío** to make a fuss

liquidación f liquidation;

liquidación total clearance sale; closing down sale

líquido *m* liquid; **el líquido de frenos** brake fluid

lisa *f* grey mullet

liso(a) plain

lista *f* list; **la lista de correos** poste restante; **la lista de espera** waiting list; **la lista de precios** price list; **la lista de vinos** wine list

listo(a) ready; clever; **listo(a) para comer** ready-cooked

litera *f* bunk; berth; couchette; **litera reservada** reserved berth; **literas** bunk beds

litoral *m* coast

litro *m* litre

llama *f* flame

llamada *f* call; **la llamada automática** direct-dialled call; **la llamada interurbana** long-distance call; **la llamada telefónica** telephone call; **la llamada a través de la operadora** operator-dialled call; **la llamada urbana** local call

llamar to call; **llamar por teléfono** to telephone

llamarse to be called; **me llamo Paul** my name is Paul

llano(a) flat; even

llanta *f* tyre

llave *f* key; **la llave de contacto** ignition key; **la llave inglesa** spanner; **la llave maestra** master key; **la llave de socorro** emergency handle; **se hacen llaves en el acto** keys made while you wait

llavero *m* key ring

Lleg. see **llegada**

llegada *f* arrival; **llegadas (Lleg.)** arrivals; **llegadas nacionales** domestic flights (arrival)

llegar to arrive; to come

llenar to fill; to fill in/out

lleno(a) full; **lleno de** full of

llevar to bring; to wear; to carry; to take; **para llevar** to take away

llorar to cry

llover to rain

llovizna *f* drizzle

llueve it's raining

lluvia *f* rain

lluvioso(a) rainy; wet

lo it; him

lobo *m* wolf

local *m*: **el local** premises; bar; **local climatizado** air-conditioned premises

localidad *f* place; **las localidades** tickets

loción *f* lotion; **la loción contra los insectos** insect repellent; **la loción para después del afeitado** aftershave (lotion); **la loción desmaquillante** make-up removal lotion

loco(a) mad; crazy

lograr to get; to manage; to achieve

lombarda *f* red cabbage

lomo *m*: **el lomo de cerdo** loin of pork; **el lomo relleno** stuffed loin of pork

lona *f* canvas

loncha *f* slice; **en lonchas** sliced

Londres *m* London

longaniza *f* red sausage

longitud *f* length

loro *m* parrot

los them; the

loza *f* crockery

lubina *f* bass; **la lubina cocida** boiled bass; **lubina a la flor de tomillo** bass seasoned with thyme

lubricantes *mpl* lubricants

luces see **luz**

lucio *m* pike

lugar *m* place; **el lugar de nacimiento** place of birth; **el lugar de expedición** issued in; **en lugar de** instead of

lujo *m* luxury; **de lujo** de luxe

lujoso(a) luxurious

luna *f* moon; **la luna de miel** honeymoon

lunes *m* Monday

lustrar to polish

luz *f* light; **apagar la luz** to put out the light; **encender la luz** to put on the light; **las luces de detención** brake lights; **las luces de estacionamiento** parking lights; **las luces laterales/de posición** side lights; **la luz de marcha atrás** reversing light; **la luz roja** red light; **la luz trasera** rear light

M

macarrones *mpl* macaroni; **los macarrones al gratén** macaroni in cheese browned in the oven; **los macarrones con tomate** macaroni with tomato sauce

macedonia (de frutas) *f*

fresh fruit salad
maceta *f* flowerpot
madera *f* wood; **de madera** made out of wood; wooden
madrastra *f* stepmother
madre *f* mother
madrugada *f* dawn; early morning
maduro(a) ripe; mature
maestro(a) *m/f* primary schoolteacher
magnetófono *m* tape recorder
magnífico(a) magnificent; great
mahonesa *f* mayonnaise
maicena *f* cornflour
maíz *m* maize; **el maíz en la mazorca** corn-on-the-cob
mal¹ *m* evil; **el mal de alturas** mountain/air sickness
mal² see **malo**
Málaga *f* Malaga; *m* sweet, dark dessert wine
mala hierba *f* weed
malestar *m* discomfort; annoyance
maleta *f* case; suitcase
maletero *m* boot (*of car*)
Mallorca *f* Majorca
malo(a) bad
Malta *f* Malta
malva mauve
mamá *f* mum(my)
mancha *f* stain; mark
Mancha *f* the English Channel; **La Mancha** La Mancha
mandar to send; **mandar por correo** to post
mandarina *f* tangerine
mandíbula *f* jaw
mandos *mpl* controls
manejar to drive
manera *f* manner; way
manga *f* sleeve
mango *m* handle; mango

manguera *f* hose
manicura *f* manicure
manitas *fpl*: **las manitas de cerdo** pig's trotters
mano *f* hand; **a mano** by hand; **de segunda mano** used; **las manos de cerdo** pig's trotters; **una mano de pintura** a coat of paint
manopla *f* facecloth
manso(a) tame
manta *f* blanket; **la manta eléctrica** electric blanket; **la manta de viaje** travelling rug
mantel *m* tablecloth
mantelería *f* table linen
mantener to support; to maintain; **por favor mantengan las puertas despejadas** please do not block the doors; **manténgase en posición vertical** this way up; keep upright; **manténgase fuera del alcance de los niños** keep out of reach of children; **mantenga limpia la ciudad** keep your city tidy
mantequería *f* grocer's
mantequilla *f* butter
manual *m* handbook
manzana¹ *f* apple; **las manzanas al horno** baked apples; **las manzanas rellenas** stuffed apples
manzana² *f* block (*area, distance*)
manzanilla *f* camomile tea; dry, sherry-type wine
mañana tomorrow; **la mañana** morning; **mañana por la mañana** tomorrow morning
mapa *m* map; **el mapa de carreteras** road map

maquillaje *m* make-up
máquina *f* machine; **la máquina de coser** sewing machine; **la máquina de afeitar** electric razor; **la máquina de escribir** typewriter; **la máquina de fotos** camera; **máquina tragaperras** fruit machine
maquinaria *f* machinery; **maquinaria pesada en movimiento** heavy machinery on the move
maquinilla de afeitar *f* razor
maquinista *m* engine driver
mar *m* sea
maravilloso(a) wonderful; marvellous
marca *f* make; brand
marcar to dial; to mark
marcha *f* march
marcha atrás *f* reverse gear; **en marcha atrás** in reverse (gear)
marcharse to leave
marco *m* frame
marea *f* tide; **la marea baja** low tide; **la marea alta** high tide
mareado(a) dizzy; **estar mareado** to be seasick
mareo *m* seasickness; giddiness
marfil *m* ivory
margarina *f* margarine
margarita *f* daisy
marido *m* husband
marina *f* navy
marinera: a la marinera in a fish or seafood sauce
marinero *m* sailor
mariposa *f* butterfly
mariscos *mpl* seafood; shellfish
marisquería *f* seafood restaurant

mármol *m* marble
marrón brown
marroquí Moroccan
marroquinería *f* leather goods; leather goods shop
Marruecos *m* Morocco
martes *m* Tuesday; **el martes de carnaval** Shrove Tuesday
martillo *m* hammer
marzo *m* March
más more; plus; **más allá de** beyond
masaje *m* massage
masajista *m/f* masseur/ masseuse
masculino(a) masculine
mástil *m* mast
matador *m* bullfighter
matar to kill
materia *f* material; subject
material *m* material; **de material** leather
Maternidad *f* Maternity Hospital
matinal morning
matrícula *f* registration number
matrimonio *m* marriage; married couple
matrona *f* midwife
máximo *m* maximum
mayo *m* May
mayonesa *f* mayonnaise
mayor senior; elder; **mayores de 18 años** over-18s
mayoría *f* majority; **la mayoría de la gente** most people
mayorista *m* wholesaler
mayúscula *f* capital letter
mazapán *m* marzipan
mazo *m* mallet
me me; to me
mecánico *m* mechanic
mecha *f* wick; **ponerse mechas** to have one's hair streaked

mechero *m* lighter
medallones *mpl*: **los medallones de ternera** small sirloin of veal steaks
media *f* stocking
mediano(a) medium; middling
medianoche *f* midnight; **a medianoche** at midnight; **las medianoches** small slightly sweet buns
mediante by means of
medicina *f* medicine; drug
médico *m* doctor; **el médico odontólogo** dentist
medida *f* measurement; size; **a la medida** made-to-measure
medio(a) half; **el medio** the middle; **el medio ambiente** the environment; **a medio camino** halfway; **la media hora** half an hour
mediodía *m* midday; noon; **a mediodía** at midday
medios *mpl* means
medir to measure; **¿cuánto mide?** how tall are you?
Mediterráneo *m*: **el Mediterráneo** the Mediterranean (Sea)
medusa *f* jellyfish
mejilla *f* cheek
mejillón *m* mussel; **los mejillones en escabeche** tinned mussels in a spicy sauce; **los mejillones a la marinera** mussels in white wine; **los mejillones al vapor** steamed mussels; **los mejillones vinagreta** mussels in vinaigrette sauce

mejor better; best
mejora *f* improvement
mejorana *f* marjoram
mejorar to improve; to get better
melaza *f* molasses; treacle
melocotón *m* peach; **los melocotones en almíbar** tinned peaches; **los melocotones naturales** fresh peaches
melón *m* melon; **el melón con jamón** melon with cured ham
membrillo *m* quince
memoria *f* memory
menaje *m* kitchen utensils; **el menaje de cocina** kitchenware; **el menaje de hogar** household goods
mendigo *m* beggar
menestra *f* vegetable stew
menor least; **menores** all ages (*at cinema*)
Menorca *f* Minorca
menos minus; less; except; **niños de menos de 10 años** children under 10
mensaje *m* message
mensajero *m* messenger; courier
mensual monthly
menta *f* mint; peppermint
mente *f* mind
mentir to tell a lie
mentira *f* lie
mentolado(a) mentholated
menú *m* menu; **menú fijo** table d'hôte
menudencias *fpl* offal; giblets
menudillos *mpl* giblets
menudo(a) small; **a menudo** often
mercado *m* market; **el**

mercado de divisas foreign exchange market

Mercado Común m Common Market

mercancías fpl goods; **mercancías peligrosas** dangerous goods

mercería f haberdasher's

merendar to have a snack

merendero m open-air snack bar

merengue m meringue

meridional southern

merienda f tea (meal); picnic

merluza f hake; **la merluza cocida con vinagreta** hake boiled and served with vinaigrette sauce; **la merluza imperial** boiled hake served with vegetables and mayonnaise; **la merluza a la plancha** grilled hake; **la merluza a la romana** hake fried in batter; **la merluza en salsa verde** hake in parsley sauce; **la merluza con sidra** hake baked with clams, onions and cider; **la merluza a la vasca** hake casseroled with clams and asparagus

mermelada f jam; **la mermelada de naranjas** marmalade

mero m grouper; **el mero emparrillado** grilled grouper

mes m month

mesa f table

mesón m reasonably priced restaurant

meter to put

método m method

métrico(a) metric

metro m metre; underground

mexicano(a) Mexican

México m Mexico

mezcla f mixture; motorbike petrol

mezclarse to mix

mezquita f mosque

mi my

mí me

microbio m microbe

microbús m minibus

micrófono m microphone

miedo m fear; **tener miedo** to be scared

miel f honey

mientras while

miércoles m Wednesday

migas fpl fried breadcrumbs

migraña f migraine

mil thousand

miligramo m milligramme

mililitro m millilitre

milímetro m millimetre

militar military

milla f mile

millón m million

millonario(a) m/f millionaire

mimbre m wicker

mimbrería f wickerwork

mina f mine (for coal etc)

miniatura f miniature

mínimo m minimum

ministerio m ministry; **el Ministerio de Asuntos Exteriores** Foreign Office

ministro m minister

minusválido(a) handicapped

minuto m minute

mío(a) my; **el/la mío(a)** mine

miope short-sighted

mirada f look

mirador m viewpoint

mirar to look at

mis my (plural)

misa f mass

mismo(a) same

misterio m mystery

mitad f half; **a mitad de precio** half-price

mixto(a) mixed

mochila f rucksack

moda f fashion; **modas** clothes shop; **moda infantil** children's clothes

modales mpl manners

modelo m model; style; make; **modelo a cumplimentar para solicitar moneda extranjera** fill out this form when ordering foreign currency; **modelos exclusivos** exclusive models

modista f dressmaker

modo m way; manner; **modo de empleo** directions for use

mojado(a) wet

mojama f salted tuna

mojarse to get wet

moldeador m soft perm

molestar to bother; to annoy; **no molestar** do not disturb

molestia f bother; nuisance

molido(a) ground

molino m mill; **el molino de viento** windmill

mollejas fpl sweetbreads

momento m instant; moment

monasterio m monastery

moneda f currency; coin; **introduzca monedas** insert coins; **la moneda extranjera** foreign currency

monedero m purse

monja f nun

monje m monk

mono m monkey

mono(a) pretty

montaña f mountain

montañismo m mountaineering

montar to ride; **montar a caballo** to ride a horse; **montar en bicicleta** to ride a bicycle

montilla *m* a dry sherry

montón *m*: **un montón de** a lot of

monumento *m* monument

mora *f* mulberry; blackberry

morado(a) purple

moraga *f*: **moraga de sardinas** barbecued sardines

morcilla *f* black pudding

mordedura *f* bite

morder to bite

moreno(a) dark(-skinned)

morir to die

morros *mpl* pig's or calf's cheeks; **los morros y sesos de ternera a la vinagreta** calf's cheeks and brains cooked and served with a vinaigrette sauce and capers; **los morros de ternera a la vizcaína** calf's cheeks cooked with onions, red peppers and garlic

mosca *f* fly

moscarda *f* bluebottle

Moscatel *m* sweet white wine

mosquitero *m* mosquito net

mostaza *f* mustard

mosto *m* grape juice

mostrador *m* counter

mostrar to show; to demonstrate

motivo *m* reason

moto *f* bike

motocicleta *f* motorbike

motociclista *m/f* motorcyclist

motoneta *f* motor scooter

motor *m* engine; motor

mousse *f* mousse; **la mousse de chocolate** chocolate mousse; **la mousse de limón** lemon mousse

mover to move

movimiento *m* motion; movement

mozo *m* porter

muchacha *f* girl; maid

muchacho *m* boy

muchedumbre *f* crowd

mucho(a) a lot (of); much; very; **me gusta mucho** I like it very much

muchos(as) many

mudar to change

mudo(a) dumb

mueble *m* piece of furniture; **los muebles** furniture (shop)

muela *f* tooth

muelle *m* quay; pier; spring

muerte *f* death

muerto(a) dead

muestra *f* exhibition; sample

mujer *f* woman; wife; **la mujer de la limpieza** cleaning lady; **la mujer de negocios** businesswoman

muleta *f* crutch

multa *f* fine

mundo *m* world

muñeca *f* wrist; doll

murciélago *m* bat (*animal*)

muro *m* wall

músculo *m* muscle

museo *m* museum

música *f* music

musical *m* musical instruments shop

músico(a) *m/f* musician

muslo *m* thigh

musulmán(ana) Muslim

muy very

N

nabo *m* turnip

nácar *m* mother-of-pearl

nacer to be born

nacimiento *m* birth

nación *f* nation

nacional national

nacionalidad *f* nationality

nada nothing; **no veo nada** I can't see anything; **de nada** don't mention it

nadador(a) *m/f* swimmer

nadar to swim

nadie no one; nobody

naipe *m* playing card

naranja[1] *f* orange

naranja[2] orange (*colour*)

naranjada *f* orangeade

narciso *m* daffodil

nariz *f* nose

nata *f* cream; **la nata batida** whipped cream

natación *f* swimming

natillas *fpl* egg custard; **las natillas de la casa** homemade egg custard

natural natural; unsweetened

naturista nudist

náusea *f* nausea

navaja *f* pocketknife; penknife

navegar to sail

Navidad *f* Christmas; **el día de Navidad** Christmas Day

neblina *f* fog

nebuloso(a) foggy

necesario(a) necessary

necesitar to need; **se necesita** needed

negar to deny

negarse to refuse

negativo *m* negative

negocios *mpl* business

negro(a) black

nervio *m* nerve

nervioso(a) tense; nervous
neumático m tyre
nevar to snow
nevera f refrigerator
ni nor; **ni ... ni** neither ... nor
nido m nest
niebla f fog; mist
nieta f granddaughter
nieto m grandson
nieve f snow
nilón m nylon
ningún, ninguno(a) none; **en ninguna parte** nowhere
niña f girl; baby girl
niño m boy; baby; **los niños** children; **los niños también pagan** children pay full price
níspero m medlar
nivel m level; standard
no no; not
no. see **número**
no alcohólico(a) non-alcoholic
noche f night; **de una noche** overnight; **esta noche** tonight
nochebuena f Christmas Eve
nochevieja f New Year's Eve
nocivo(a) harmful
no fumador m non-smoker
nombre m name; **el nombre de pila** first name
noreste m northeast
normal normal; ordinary
noroeste m northwest
norte m north
nosotros(as) we; us
nota f note; mark
notar to notice
notaría f solicitor's office
notario m notary; solicitor
noticiario m news

bulletin; newsreel
noticias fpl news
novela f novel
noveno(a) ninth
noventa ninety
novia f bride; girlfriend; fiancée
noviembre m November
novio m bridegroom; boyfriend; fiancé
nube f cloud
nublado(a) cloudy
nudillo m knuckle
nudo m knot
nuera f daughter-in-law
nuestro(a) our
nueve nine
nuevo(a) new
nuez f nut; walnut; **la nuez moscada** nutmeg; **las nueces con nata y miel** walnuts with cream and honey
núm see **número**
numerado(a) numbered
número m number; size; issue; **el número del abonado** the subscriber's telephone number; **el número de matrícula** registration number; **el número de teléfono** telephone number; **coja su número** take a number
nunca never
nutrir to feed

O

o or; **o ... o ...** either ... or ...
obedecer to obey
obispo m bishop
objetivo m camera lens; **el objetivo granangular** wide-angle lens; **el objetivo zoom** zoom lens

objeto m object; **los objetos de valor** valuables; **los objetos de regalo** gifts
oblongo(a) oblong
obra f work; **la obra de teatro** play; **la obra de arte** work of art
obras fpl road works
obrero m workman; **obreros trabajando** men at work
observar to watch
obstáculo m obstacle
obstrucción f blockage
obstruir to block; **por favor no obstruyan las puertas** please stand clear of the doors
obtener to obtain
obturador m shutter (camera)
occidental western
océano m ocean
ochenta eighty
ocho eight
ocio m spare time
octavo(a) eighth
octubre m October
ocupado(a) engaged; busy
ocurrir to happen
odio m hatred
oeste m west
ofensivo(a) rude
oferta f offer; special offer
oficial official
oficina f office; **la oficina de objetos perdidos** lost property office; **la oficina de turismo** tourist office
Oficina de Correos f the Post Office
oficio m church service; occupation
ofrecer to offer; **se ofrece/ofrécese** offered
oído m hearing; ear
oír to hear

ojo m eye; **¡ojo!** careful, look out; **ojo, pinta** wet paint

ola f wave

oler to smell

olla f pot; **la olla de garbanzos** chick-pea, bacon and cabbage stew; **la olla podrida** spicy hotpot; **la olla a presión** pressure cooker

olmo m elm

olor m smell

oloroso m cream sherry

olvidar to forget

ombligo m navel

ómnibus m bus; stopping train

once eleven

onda f wave; **la onda corta** short wave; **la onda larga** long wave; **la onda media** medium wave

onza f ounce

ópera f opera

operación f operation

operador(a) m/f telephone operator

opinar: opino que ... I think that ...

opinión f view; opinion

oporto m port wine

oportunidad f opportunity; **oportunidades** bargains

oprimir to press

óptica f optician's

óptico m optician

óptimo(a) excellent

opuesto(a) opposite

orden f command; **por orden de la dirección** by order of the management

oreja f ear

orfebrería f gold/silver work

organización f organization

organizado(a) organized

organizador m steward

organizar to organize

oriental eastern; oriental

orilla f shore; **la orilla del mar** seaside

orín m rust

orinal de niño m potty

ornamento m ornament

oro m gold; **de oro** gold

orquesta f orchestra

oscuro(a) dark; dim

oso m bear

ostra f oyster

otoño m autumn

otro(a) other

ovalado(a) oval

oveja f sheep

oxidado(a) rusty

P

pabellón m: **el pabellón de deportes** sports centre

paciente m/f patient

padre m father; **los padres** parents

paella f rice dish of chicken, shellfish, garlic, saffron and vegetables

pagado(a) paid; **pagado por adelantado** paid in advance

pagar to pay for; to pay; **pagar al contado** to pay cash

pagaré m I.O.U.

página f page

pago m payment; **pago(s) al contado** cash only accepted

pague: pague en caja please pay at the cashdesk

país m country

paisaje m scenery; **paisajes pintorescos** scenic route

paja f straw

pájaro m bird

pajita f drinking straw

pala f shovel; spade

palabra f word

palacio m palace

palanca f lever; **la palanca de cambio** gear lever

palco m box (in theatre)

pálido(a) pale

palillo m toothpick

palmera¹ f palm-tree

palmera² f small sweet puff pastry

palmito m palm heart

palo m stick; mast; **el palo de esquí** ski stick; **el palo de golf** golf club

paloma f pigeon; dove

palta f avocado pear

pan m bread; loaf of bread; **el pan de centeno** rye bread; **el pan de higos** dried figs with spices; **el pan integral** wholemeal bread; **el pan de molde** sliced bread; **el pan tostado** toast; **el pan de nueces** walnut and raisin cake

pana f corduroy

panache de legumbres m mixed vegetables

panadería f bakery

panadero m baker

panecillo m roll

panqueque m pancake

pantalla f screen; lampshade

pantalones mpl pair of trousers; trousers; **el pantalón de sport** casual trousers; **el pantalón vaquero** jeans; **los pantalones cortos** shorts

pantys mpl tights

pañal m nappy; **los pañales de usar y tirar** disposable nappies

paño m flannel; cloth; **el paño higiénico** sanitary towel

pañuelito m: **los pañuelitos mojados** baby wipes

pañuelo m handkerchief; **el pañuelo de papel** tissue (*handkerchief*)

papa f potato; **las papas fritas** chips; French fries

papá m dad(dy)

papel m paper; **el papel de cartas** writing pad; **el papel de envolver** wrapping paper; **el papel de escribir** stationery; **los papeles de fumar** cigarette papers; **el papel higiénico** toilet paper; **el papel pintado** wallpaper; **el papel timbrado** paper with official stamp

papelera f waste paper basket; **use las papeleras** please use the litter bins provided

papelería f stationer's

paperas fpl mumps

papilla f baby cereal

paquete m packet; parcel

paquetería f haberdasher's

par[1] m pair; **un par de** a couple of; **pares sueltos** odd pairs

par[2]: **un número par** an even number; **pares** parking allowed on even days of month

para for; towards

parabrisas m windscreen

paracaídas m parachute

parachoques m bumper

parada f stop; **la parada de autobús** bus stop; **la parada discrecional** request stop; **la parada de taxis** taxi rank

parador m: **el parador nacional** state-run inn

paragolpes m bumper

paraguas m umbrella

paraíso m gallery (*theatre*)

paralizado(a) paralysed

parar to stop

parcela f plot of land

parecer to seem; to look

parecido(a) similar

pared f wall

pareja f pair

pariente m/f relation

parlamento m parliament

párpado m eyelid

parque m park; **el parque de atracciones** amusement park; **el parque de bomberos** fire station; **el parque infantil** children's playground

parquímetro m parking meter

parra f vine

parrilla f grill; **a la parrilla** grilled

parrillada f grilled meat or fish; barbecue

parroquia f parish church

parte[1] f part

parte[2] m report; **el parte meteorológico** weather forecast

particular particular; private

partida f departure

partido m political party; match (*sport*); round of golf

partir to depart

pasa f raisin; currant

pasado(a) off (*meat*); past; **pasado mañana** the day after tomorrow; **muy pasado** well done; **poco pasado** rare; **la semana pasada** last week

pasaje[1] m alleyway

pasaje[2] m ticket; fare

pasajero(a) m/f passenger

pasamano m handrail

pasaporte m passport; **el pasaporte familiar** joint passport

pasar to pass; to spend (*time*); **pasarlo bien** to have a good time; **pase sin llamar** enter without knocking

pasarela f gangplank; catwalk

pasatiempo m hobby

Pascua f Easter

pase m: **los pases de favor** complimentary tickets

paseo m walk; avenue; promenade; **el Paseo Colón** Columbus Avenue; **dar un paseo** to go for a walk; **dar un paseo en coche** to go for a drive

pasillo m corridor; passage; gangway

paso m step; pace; **el paso elevado** footbridge; **el paso de ganado** cattle crossing; **el paso inferior** subway; **el paso a nivel** level crossing; **el paso de peatones** pedestrian crossing; **el paso sin guarda** open level crossing; **el paso subterráneo** subway; **los pasos de contador** telephone meter units; **prohibido el paso a personal no autorizado/a toda persona ajena** no unauthorised personnel allowed

paso(a) dried

pasta f pastry; pasta; **las pastas** pastries; spaghetti; **la pasta dentífrica** toothpaste; **la pasta de**

dientes toothpaste
pastel m cake; **los
pasteles** pastries; **el
pastel de tortilla**
omelettes of different
flavours in layers
separated by mayonnaise
pastelería f cake and
confectionery shop; cakes
and pastries
pastilla f tablet (*medicine*);
la pastilla de jabón bar
of soap; **las pastillas
para el mareo**
seasickness tablets
pastor m minister
pastor(a) m/f shepherd/
shepherdess
patada f kick
patata f potato; **las
patatas al ajillo** potatoes
fried with garlic and
parsley; **las patatas en
ajo pollo** potatoes
cooked in a sauce made
with garlic, almonds,
bread, parsley and
saffron; **las patatas
bravas** hot spicy
potatoes; **las patatas
fritas** French fries; **las
patatas fritas a la
inglesa** crisps; **las
patatas al gratén con
queso** potatoes and ham
with cheese sauce
browned under grill; **las
patatas guisadas**
potatotes cooked with
pork ribs, paprika and
onion; **las patatas a la
riojana** fried potatoes in
a spicy pepper and chilli
sauce
patinaje m skating; ice-
skating
patinazo m skid
patines mpl roller skates
patio m patio; courtyard
pato m duck; **pato a la
naranja** duck in orange

sauce
patrón m pattern
patrulla f patrol
pavo m turkey; **el pavo
trufado** turkey with
truffle stuffing
paz f peace
P.D. P.S.
peaje m toll
peatón m pedestrian;
**peatón, en carretera
circula por tu izquierda**
pedestrians should keep
to the left
peces mpl fish
pecho m breast; chest
pechuga f breast (*poultry*);
la pechuga de pollo
chicken breast
pedazo m bit; piece
pediatra m/f paediatrician
pedicuro m chiropodist
pedido m order; request
pedir to ask for
pedregoso(a) stony
pegamento m gum
pegar to stick (on)
peinado m hair-style;
hairdo
peinar to comb
peine m comb
p.ej. see ejemplo
peladilla f sugared
almond
pelar to peel
peldaño m doorstep;
stair
pelea f fight
peletería f furrier's
película f film; **la película
de miedo** horror film
peligro m danger; **peligro
de incendio** danger of
fire; **peligro de muerte**
danger – keep out;
peligros diversos danger
peligroso(a) dangerous;
no peligroso(a) safe
pelo m hair
pelota f ball
peltre m pewter

peluca f wig
peluquería f
hairdresser's; barber's; **la
peluquería de
caballeros** barber's
peluquero(a) m/f
hairdresser
pena: ¡qué pena! what a
pity!
pendiente m earring
pene m penis
Penedés m good quality
table wine and sparkling
white wine
penicilina f penicillin
pensar to think
pensión f lodgings;
boarding house; bed and
breakfast; **la pensión
completa** full board; **la
media pensión** half
board
peor worse
pepinillo m gherkin
pepino m cucumber
pepitoria: a la pepitoria
stewed with onions,
tomatoes and green
peppers
pequeño(a) little; small;
slight
pera f pear
percebe m edible
barnacle
percha f coat hanger; peg
perder to miss (*train*); to
lose; **perder el tiempo**
to waste one's time
perderse to lose one's
way; to get lost
pérdida f loss
perdido(a) lost
perdiz f partridge; **la
perdiz a la cazadora**
partridge cooked with
shallots, mushrooms,
herbs and wine; **la
perdiz estofada**
partridge stew; **las
perdices con chocolate**
partridges in red wine

and chocolate-flavoured sauce; **las perdices escabechadas** pickled partridges

perdón m pardon; **¡perdón!** sorry!

perdonar to forgive; **perdonen las molestias** we apologise for any inconvenience

perejil m parsley

perezoso(a) lazy

perfecto(a) perfect

perforar: no perforar do not pierce

perfume m perfume

perfumería f perfume shop

periódico m newspaper

periodista m/f reporter; journalist

período m period; menstruation

perla f pearl

permanecer to stay; **permanezcan en sus asientos** please remain seated

permanencia f stay

permanente f perm

permiso m permission; pass; permit; **con permiso** excuse me; **el permiso de conducir** driving licence; **el permiso de residencia** residence permit; **el permiso de trabajo** work permit

permitido(a) permitted

permitir: no se permite llevar envases a la grada no bottles or cans may be taken onto the stand

pero but

perra f bitch

perro m dog; **el perro caliente** hot dog; **perros no** no dogs allowed

persianas fpl blinds

persona f person

personal personal; **el personal** personnel; staff

persuadir to persuade

pertenecer a to belong to

pesadilla f nightmare

pesado(a) heavy

pesar to weigh

pesca f fishing; **la pesca salada** salted fish

pescadería f fishmonger's

pescadilla f whiting; baby hake; **las pescadillas al vino** whiting cooked in wine, stock and butter and then oven-baked

pescado m fish

pescador m fisherman

peseta f peseta

pésimo(a) dreadful

peso m weight; **al peso** by weight

pesquero m fishing boat

pestaña f eyelash

pestiños mpl crisp honey-fritters

petaca f tobacco pouch

petróleo m petroleum

pez m fish; **el pez espada** swordfish

picadillo m minced beef (sometimes in a salad with bacon, garlic, egg etc)

picado(a) chopped; minced

picadura f bite (by insect); sting; cut tobacco

picante peppery; hot; spicy

picar to itch; to sting

picatostes mpl pieces of fried bread usually accompanied by hot chocolate

pichón m pigeon

pico m peak

pidan: no pidan descuento no discounts given

pie m foot

piedra f stone; **la piedra preciosa** gem; **las piedras de mechero** flints

piel f fur; skin; leather; **la piel de carnero** sheepskin

pierna f leg; **la pierna de cordero** leg of lamb

pieza f part; **la pieza de repuesto** spare part

pijama m pyjamas; fruit dessert with custard

pila f battery

píldora f pill; the pill; **tomar la píldora** to be on the pill

piloto m pilot; captain

pilotos mpl sidelights

pimentón m paprika

pimienta f pepper; **a la pimienta** au poivre

pimiento m pepper (vegetable); **el pimiento verde/rojo** green/red pepper; **el pimiento morrón** red pepper; **los pimientos fritos** fried small green peppers; **los pimientos rellenos** stuffed peppers

pinacoteca f art gallery

pinchazo m blow-out; puncture

pincho m: **el pincho morruno** shish kebab

pino m pine

pintar to paint

pintor m painter

pintura f paint; painting

pinza f clothes-peg

pinzas fpl tweezers

piña f pineapple; **la piña en almíbar** tinned pineapple; **la piña natural** fresh pineapple

piñones mpl pine kernels

piononos mpl small Swiss rolls

pipa f pipe

pipirrana f a salad of

tomatoes, peppers, cucumber, onion, tuna and boiled egg
piragua f canoe
piragüismo m canoeing
Pirineos mpl Pyrenees
pisar to step on; to tread on
piscina f swimming pool; **la piscina cubierta** indoor pool; **la piscina para niños** paddling pool
piso m floor; flat; **el primer piso** first floor; **piso deslizante** slippery road
pista f track; **la pista de aterrizaje** runway; **la pista de baile** dance floor; **la pista de esquí** ski run; **la pista de patinaje** skating rink; **la pista de tenis** tennis court
pisto m sautéed peppers, onions, aubergines, tomatoes and garlic; **el pisto manchego** sautéed tomatoes, aubergines, peppers and ham with beaten egg mixed in
pitillera f cigarette case
pitillo m cigarette
pizarra f slate; blackboard
pizca f pinch (of salt etc)
pizza f pizza
placa f number plate; plaque; **placa conmemorativa** commemorative plaque; **placa dental** (dental) plaque
placer m pleasure
plancha f iron (for clothes); **a la plancha** grilled
planeta m planet
plano m plan; town map
plano-guía m: **plano-guía de la ciudad** city plan

planta f plant; sole; **la planta baja** ground floor; **la planta sótano** basement
plástico m plastic
plata f silver; **plata de ley** sterling silver
plataforma f platform
plátano m banana
platea f stalls (theatre)
platería f jeweller's
platija f plaice
platillo m saucer
platino m platinum
platinos mpl contact points
plato m plate; dish (food); course; **el plato del día** set menu; **el plato fuerte** main course; **los platos fríos** cold starters
playa f beach; **la playa nudista** nudist beach
plaza f square; **la plaza del mercado** marketplace; **la plaza de toros** bull ring; **plazas libres** vacancies; parking space available; **plazas limitadas** limited number of seats available
plazo m period; expiry date
plazoleta f square
plazuela f square
pleamar f high tide
plegable folding
plomero m plumber
plomo m lead
pluma f feather; pen; **la pluma estilográfica** fountain pen
población f population
pobre poor
poco(a) little; **un poco** a little; **un poco de** a bit of
pocos(as) a few
poder to be able
podólogo m chiropodist
podrido(a) rotten

policía f police; **el policía** police officer; policeman
polideportivo m sports centre
polietileno m polythene
político(a) political; m/f politician
póliza f policy; **la póliza de seguros** insurance policy
pollería f poultry shop
pollo m chicken; **el pollo al ajillo** garlic-fried chicken; **el pollo asado** roast chicken; **el pollo a l'ast** spit-roasted chicken; **el pollo a la buena mujer** chicken casserole with onions, bacon, potatoes and brandy; **el pollo a la cacerola** chicken casserole; **el pollo a la catalana** sautéed chicken with mussels and prawns, covered with tomato sauce; **el pollo al chilindrón** chicken garnished with tomatoes and peppers; **el pollo estofado** casseroled chicken with potatoes, mushrooms, shallots and brandy; **el pollo en pepitoria** casseroled chicken in herbs, garlic, almonds and sherry
polvo m dust; powder; **el polvo de talco** talcum powder; **los polvos faciales** face powder
pomada f ointment
pomelo m grapefruit
ponche m punch
poner to put; to place; to switch on; **poner a media luz** to dip (headlights)
poney m pony
popa f stern
popular popular

póquer *m* poker
por for; per; through; about; **¿por qué?** why?; **100 km por hora** 100 km per hour; **20 por ciento** 20 per cent; **por supuesto** of course; **por día/semana** per day/week
porcelana *f* china; porcelain
porción *f* helping; portion
por favor please
porque because
porrón *m* glass wine jar with a long spout
porrusalda *f* cod, potato and leek soup
portaequipajes *m* luggage rack; boot
portafolio *m* briefcase
portamonedas *m* purse
portátil portable
portería *f* caretaker's office
portero(a) *m/f* caretaker; doorman/woman
portón *m* door
Portugal *m* Portugal
portugués(esa) Portuguese
posada *f* inn; lodgings
poseer to own
posible possible
posición *f* position
postal postal; **la (tarjeta) postal** postcard
poste *m* mast; post; **el poste indicador** signpost
posterior back; later
postre *m* dessert; sweet; **el postre de músico** dessert of assorted nuts and raisins
potable drinkable
potaje *m* stew; thick vegetable soup; **el potaje de garbanzos** thick chickpea soup; **el potaje de habichuelas** thick haricot bean soup; **el**

potaje de lentejas thick lentil soup
pote gallego *m* stew with potatoes, pig's trotters and ears
potente powerful
práctico(a) convenient; practical
precaución *f* caution; **precaución, obras** drive carefully, roadworks ahead
precio *m* price; **el precio del cubierto** cover charge; **el precio de entrada** entrance fee; **el precio fijo** set price; **el precio de oferta** sale price; **el precio del viaje** fare
precioso(a) precious; beautiful
precipicio *m* cliff
preciso(a) precise; necessary
preferentemente preferably
preferir to prefer
prefijo *m* dialling code; **el prefijo de acceso a internacional** international dialling code
pregunta *f* question; **hacer una pregunta** to ask a question
preguntar to ask
premio *m* prize
prenda *f* garment
prender to switch on; to turn on
prensa *f* newspaper stand; press; **hay prensa extranjera** we sell foreign newspapers
preocupado(a) worried
preparación *f* preparation
preparar to prepare; to fix
preparativos *mpl* preparations

presa *f* dam
presentar to introduce
presentarse to check in; to turn up
preservativo *m* condom
presión *f* pressure; **la presión de los neumáticos** tyre pressure
prestar to lend
presupuesto *m* estimate
prevención *f* precaution
prima *f* cousin
primario(a) primary
primavera *f* spring
primer, primero(a) first; **en primera** in first gear; **los primeros auxilios** first aid; **viajar en primera** to travel first class; **a primera vista** at first sight
primo *m* cousin
princesa *f* princess
principal main; principal
príncipe *m* prince
principiante *m/f* beginner
principio *m* beginning
prioridad de paso *f* right of way
prisa *f* rush; haste; **tener prisa** to be in a hurry
prismáticos *mpl* binoculars
privado(a) personal; private
proa *f* bow (of ship)
probable probable; **poco probable** unlikely
probadores *mpl* fitting rooms
probar to try; to sample; to taste
problema *m* problem
procedencia *f* point of departure; **procedencia Madrid** coming from Madrid
procedente de coming from
productos *mpl* produce

profesión f profession; job

profesor(a) m/f secondary school teacher

profundo(a) deep

programa m programme; schedule

prohibición f ban

prohibido(a) prohibited; **prohibido estacionarse** no waiting; **prohibido fumar** no smoking; **prohibido el paso** no entry; **prohibido acampar** no camping

prohibir to ban; to forbid; **se prohíbe fumar** no smoking

promedio m average

promesa f promise

prometer to promise

pronóstico m forecast; **el pronóstico del tiempo** weather forecast

pronto soon

propiedad f property; **propiedad privada** private

propietario(a) m/f owner

propina f tip

propio(a) own

proponer to suggest

propuesta f proposal; suggestion

prostituta f prostitute

protección f insurance cover; protection; **la protección civil** civil defence

protestante Protestant

provecho m benefit

proveer to supply

provincia f province

provisional temporary

próximamente: próximamente en esta sala/en este cine coming soon

próximo(a) next; **próximo estreno** coming

soon

proyecto m project; plan

prueba f trial; proof; test

público(a) public; **para todos los públicos** U film

puchero m stew

pudín m pudding

pudrir to rot

pueblo m people; village

puente m bridge; **el puente de peaje** toll bridge

puerro m leek; **los puerros en ensalada** boiled leeks in vinaigrette

puerta f door; gate; **por favor, cierren la puerta** please close the door; **la puerta de embarque** boarding gate

puerto m port; harbour; mountain pass; **el puerto deportivo** marina

pues since; so

puesto m stall; job; **el puesto de flores** flower stall; **el puesto de socorro** first-aid post

pulga f flea

pulgada f inch

pulgar m thumb

pulmón m lung

pulmonía f pneumonia

pulpo m octopus; **el pulpo a la gallega** octopus with peppers and paprika

pulsar to push; **no pulse el botón más que por indicación de la operadora** do not push the button until instructed to do so by the operator

pulsera f bracelet

pulso m pulse

pulverizador m spray

punta f point; tip

puntapié m kick

puntiagudo(a) sharp;

pointed

punto m dot; point; **hacer punto** to knit; **el punto muerto** neutral

puntual punctual

puntualidad f: **se ruega puntualidad** please be punctual

punzada f stitch

puñetazo m punch

puño m shirt cuff; fist

puré m purée; **el puré de patatas** mashed potatoes; **el puré de guisantes** thick cream of pea soup; **el puré de verduras** creamed vegetables

puro m cigar

puro(a) pure

Q

que than; **qué** what, which; **¿qué?** what?; **¿qué tal?** how are you?

quedar to remain

queja f complaint

quejarse to grumble; **quejarse de** to complain about

quemado(a) burned; **quemado por el sol** sunburnt

quemadura f burn; **la quemadura del sol** sunburn

quemar to burn

quemarse to burn oneself

querer to love; to want

querido(a) m/f darling

queroseno m paraffin

quesería f cheese and wine shop

queso m cheese; **el queso de bola** a round, mild cheese like Edam; **el queso de Burgos** cream

cheese; **el queso de cabra** goat's milk cheese; **el queso de Cabrales** very strong blue cheese; **el queso fresco** curd cheese; **el queso manchego** hard sheep's milk cheese; **el queso con membrillo** cheese with quince jelly eaten as a dessert; **el queso de nata** cream cheese; **el queso de oveja** sheep's milk cheese; **el queso del país** local cheese
quien who; **¿quién?** who?
quilate m carat
quincallería f ironmonger's
quince fifteen
quiniela f football pools
quinientos(as) five hundred
quinto(a) fifth
quiosco m kiosk; **el quiosco de periódicos** newsstand
quisquilla f shrimp
quita-esmalte m nail polish remover
quitamanchas m stain remover
quitar to remove; **quitarse la ropa** to take off one's clothes
quizás perhaps

R

rábano m radish
rabia f rabies
rabino m rabbi
rabo m: **rabo de buey** oxtail
R.A.C.E. see real
ración f portion; **las raciones** snacks
radiador m radiator
radio f radio; **por la**

radio on the radio; **Radio Nacional de España (RNE)** Spanish National Radio
radio-casete m radio cassette
radiografía f X-ray; **hacer una radiografía** to X-ray
ragout m meat and vegetable stew; **el ragout de cordero** lamb stew
raíz f root
raja f split
rallador m grater
rama f branch
ramo m bunch of flowers
rana f frog
rape m angler fish; **el rape a la malagueña** angler fish baked in a sauce of almonds, tomatoes, parsley and onions
rápido m express train; heel bar
rápido(a) quick; fast
raqueta f racket; bat
raramente seldom
rascacielos m skyscraper
rascar to scratch
rastro m flea market
rata f rat
ratero m pickpocket
rato m (short) time
ratón m mouse
ravioles mpl ravioli
raya f stripe; parting
rayo m beam; ray
razón f reason
real royal; **Real Automóvil Club de España (R.A.C.E.)** Royal Spanish Automobile Club
rebaja f reduction; **rebajas** sales
rebozado(a) cooked in batter
recado m errand; message
recalentarse to overheat

recambio m spare; refill
recepción f reception; reception desk
recepcionista m/f receptionist
receta f recipe; prescription; **con receta médica** a prescription is necessary
recibir to receive
recibo m receipt
recién recently; **recién pintado** wet paint; **recién casados** just married
reciente recent
recipiente m container
reclamación f claim; complaint; **reclamaciones en el acto** any complaints must be made immediately
reclamar to claim
recoger to pick up; **se recoge la basura** rubbish is collected; **recoja aquí su tíquet** get your ticket here
recogida f collection
recomendado(a): no recomendada a menores de 13 años not recommended for under-13s
recompensa f reward
reconocer to recognize
recorrer to tour; to travel
recorrido m journey; route; **de largo recorrido** long-distance; **el recorrido en vacío** journey to pick-up point; **el recorrido turístico** tourist route
recortarse: recortarse el pelo to get one's hair trimmed
recreo m leisure; break
recto(a) straight
recuerdo m souvenir;

recuerdos greetings
recuperable returnable
recuperar to get back
recuperarse to recover
recursos *mpl* resources
red *f* net; **Red Nacional de los Ferrocarriles Españoles (RENFE)** Spanish railway network
redactar to draw up; to write
redecilla *f* luggage rack
redondo(a) round
reducción *f* reduction
reducido(a) low; limited
reembolso *m* refund; **contra reembolso** cash on delivery
reemplazo *m* replacement
reestreno *m* second run
referencia *f* reference
reflejo *m* reflection; rinse
refresco *m* refreshment; cold drink
refrigeración *f* air-conditioning
refrigerado(a) air-conditioned
refugio *m* shelter; island (*traffic*); central reservation
regalar to give
regaliz *m* licorice
regalo *m* gift; present
regata *f* regatta
regazo *m* lap
régimen *m* diet; **estar a régimen** to be on a diet
región *f* district; area; region
registro *m* register
regla *f* rule
regresar to return
regreso *m* return
regular regular; not bad
reina *f* queen
Reino Unido *m* United Kingdom
reír to laugh
rejilla *f* luggage rack

relación *f* account; report
relajarse to relax
relámpago *m* lightning
religión *f* religion
rellenar to fill in; to stuff; **rellene este cupón** fill in this form
relleno(a) stuffed
reloj *m* clock; watch; **el reloj de pulsera** wristwatch; **el reloj despertador** alarm clock
relojería *f* watchmaker's; jeweller's
remar to row
remedio *m* remedy
remitente *m* sender
remitir to send
remo *m* oar
remolacha *f* beetroot; **la remolacha en ensalada** beetroot in vinaigrette
remolcador *m* tug
remolque *m* tow rope; trailer
RENFE *see* red
renta *f* income
rentable profitable
reorganización *f* reorganization
reparación *f* repair; **reparación del calzado** shoes repaired; **reparación de neumáticos** tyres repaired
reparar to repair; to mend
repartir to deliver; to divide
reparto *m* delivery
repente: de repente suddenly
repentino(a) sudden
repetir to repeat
repollo *m* cabbage; **el repollo al natural** plain boiled white cabbage; **el repollo con manzanas** boiled white cabbage

with apples
reportaje *m* report
reposacabezas *m* headrest
reposición *f* revival
repostería *f* pastries
república *f* republic
repuesto *m* replacement; **la pieza de repuesto** spare part
repujado(a) embossed
requesón *m* cottage cheese
requisito *m* requirement; qualification
resaca *f* hangover
resbaladizo(a) slippery
resbalar to slip; to slide
rescatar to rescue
rescate *m* rescue
reserva *f* reserve; reservation; **la reserva en grupo** block booking; **en reserva** in stock
reservado(a) reserved
reservar to reserve; **se reserva el derecho de admisión** the management reserves the right to refuse admission
resfriado *m* cold
resfriarse to catch cold
residencia *f* residence; residential hotel; hostel
resistente hard-wearing
resolver to solve
resorte *m* spring (*coil*)
respaldo *m* chair back
respeto *m* respect
respiración *f* breathing
respirar to breathe
responder to answer; to reply; **no se responde de robos** the management accepts no liability for theft
responsabilidad *f* responsibility
respuesta *f* answer; reply
restar to deduct; to subtract; to be left

restaurante *m* restaurant; **el restaurante vegetariano** vegetarian restaurant

resto *m* the rest; **los restos** remains; **restos de serie** remnants

resultado *m* result

resultar to turn out

resumen *m* summary

retales *mpl* remnants

retener to keep

retirar to withdraw

retirarse: ¡no se retire! hold on!

retornable returnable

retrasar to delay; to put off

retrasarse to lose (*clock, watch*); **el tren se ha retrasado** the train has been delayed

retraso *m* delay; **sin retraso** on schedule

retrete *m* lavatory

retroceder to turn back

retrovisor *m* rear-view mirror

reumatismo *m* rheumatism

reunión *f* meeting; conference

reunirse to meet; to get together

revelar to show; to develop

reventar to burst

reventón *m* puncture

revés *m* reverse; **al revés** upside down; **volver algo del revés** to turn something inside out

revisar to check

revisión *f* service (*for car*); inspection

revisor *m* conductor; ticket inspector

revista *f* magazine; revue; **la revista infantil** comic; **la revista de variedades** variety show

rey *m* king

rezar to pray

Ribeiro *m* fresh young wine from the Orense region

ribera *f* bank

rico(a) good, tasty (*food*); rich; wealthy

riesgo *m* risk

rifa *f* raffle

rígido(a) stiff

rímel *m* mascara

rincón *m* corner; spot

riñón *m* kidney; **los riñones al jerez** kidneys in sherry sauce; **los riñones salteados** sautéed kidneys served with tomato and wine sauce

río *m* river

Rioja *m* excellent red and white table wine

riqueza *f* wealth

risa *f* laugh; laughter

rizado(a) curly

RNE see **radio**

robar to steal; to rob

robo *m* robbery

roca *f* rock

roce *m* graze

rodaballo *m* turbot

rodaja *f* slice

rodaje *m* set of wheels; shooting (*of film*)

rodilla *f* knee

rogar to ask

rojo(a) red

rollo *m* roll

romana: a la romana fried in batter or breadcrumbs

románico(a) romanesque

romántico(a) romantic

romería *f* pilgrimage

romero *m* rosemary

romper to smash; to break

ron *m* rum

roncar to snore

roñoso(a) mean, stingy

ropa *f* clothes; **la ropa blanca** bedding; **la ropa de cama** bedding; **la ropa de deporte** sportswear; **la ropa interior** underwear; **la ropa para lavar** washing

rosa rose; pink

rosado *m* rosé

rosbif *m* roast beef

rosca *f* doughnut

rosquilla *f* doughnut

rótula *f* kneecap

rotulador *m* felt-tip pen

rozar to scrape; to graze

rubí *m* ruby

rubio(a) fair; blond(e)

rueda *f* wheel; **la rueda trasera** rear wheel; **la rueda de repuesto/ recambio** spare wheel

ruega: se ruega no fumar no smoking please; **se ruega paguen en el acto** please pay as soon as you are served; **se ruega puntualidad** please be punctual; **se ruega silencio** silence please; **se ruega no tocar** please do not touch

ruido *m* noise; row

ruidoso(a) noisy

ruinas *fpl* ruins

ruleta *f* roulette

rumbo *m* direction; **con rumbo** bound for

ruta *f* route; **la ruta turística** scenic route

S

S.A. see **sociedad**

sábado *m* Saturday

sábana *f* sheet

sabañón *m* chilblain

saber to know

sabor m taste; flavour
sabroso(a) tasty
sacacorchos m corkscrew
sacapuntas m pencil sharpener
sacar to take out; **sacarse una muela** to have a tooth taken out
sacarina f saccharin
sacerdote m priest
saco m sack; **el saco de dormir** sleeping bag
sagrado(a) holy
sal f salt; **sin sal** unsalted
sala f hall; ward; **la sala de baile** dance hall; **la sala de embarque** departure lounge; **la sala de espera** airport lounge; waiting room; **la sala de fiestas** dance hall; **la sala de televisión** TV lounge
salado(a) savoury; salty
salario m wage; wages
salchicha f sausage
salchichón m salami sausage
saldo m balance; **saldos** sale
salero m salt cellar
salida f exit; departure; socket; **salida de emergencia** emergency exit; **salida de camiones** beware of lorries; **salida nacional** departure – domestic flights; **salida de vehículos** danger – vehicles exiting; **salidas vuelos regulares** departures – scheduled flights
salir to to outside; to come out; to go out
salmón m salmon
salmonete m red mullet
salón m lounge (in hotel); **el salón de belleza** beauty parlour; **el salón**

de juegos amusement arcade; **el salón de té** tearoom; **el salón de peluquería** hairdresser's
salpicadero m dashboard
salpicón m: **el salpicón de mariscos** prawn and lobster salad
salsa f gravy; sauce; dressing; **la salsa bearnesa** thick sauce made with butter, egg yolks, shallots, vinegar and herbs; **la salsa bechamel** white sauce; **la salsa tártara** tartar sauce; **la salsa de tomate** tomato sauce; **la salsa verde** parsley, garlic and onion sauce; **la salsa vinagreta** vinaigrette sauce
saltar to jump; to blow (fuse)
salteado(a) sauté, sautéed
salto m jump
salud f health; **¡salud!** cheers!
saludar to greet; **le saluda atentamente** yours sincerely
salvaje wild
salvavidas m lifebelt
salvia f sage
san m saint
sanatorio m clinic; nursing home
sandalia f sandal
sandía f watermelon
sanfaina f sautéed aubergines, red pepper and onions
sangrar to bleed
sangre f blood
sangría f iced drink of red wine, brandy, lemonade and fruit
sangüi m sandwich
sano(a) healthy
santo(a) m/f saint

sarampión m measles
sardina f sardine; **la sardina arenque** pilchard; **las sardinas a la marinera** sardines cooked with vegetables, garlic and peppers; **las sardinas en pimientilla** sardines cooked with peppers; **las sardinas rebozadas** sardines in batter
sarpullido m rash
sartén f frying pan
sastre m tailor
sastrería f tailor's
satisfacer to satisfy
sazón f season; **en sazón** in season
se him-/her-/itself; themselves; yourself; oneself
secado a mano m blow-dry
secador de pelo m hair-drier
secar to dry; **secar por centrifugado** to spin(-dry)
sección f department (in store)
seco(a) dry; dried (fruit, beans)
secretario(a) m/f secretary
secreto(a) secret
sector sanitario m First Aid
secuestrador m hijacker
secuestrar to kidnap; to hijack
secuestro aéreo m hijack
secundario(a) secondary; subordinate; minor
sed f thirst; **tener sed** to be thirsty
seda f silk
sediento(a) thirsty
seguido(a) continuous; **en seguida** straight away;

todo seguido straight on
seguir to continue; to follow
según according to
segundo(a) second; **de segunda clase** second-class; **de segunda mano** secondhand
seguridad *f* security; reliability; safety
seguro *m* insurance; **el seguro del coche** car insurance; **el seguro contra tercera persona** third party insurance; **el seguro contra todo riesgo** comprehensive insurance; **el seguro contra incendio** fire insurance
seguro(a) safe
seis six
sello *m* stamp; **poner un sello** to stamp
semáforo *m* traffic lights; **saltarse un semáforo en rojo** to go through a red light
semana *f* week; **la semana pasada** last week; **Semana Santa** Holy Week; Easter
semanal weekly
semanario *m* weekly paper
semejante alike
semifinal *f* semifinal
semilla *f* seed
sencillo(a) simple; plain
sendero *m* footpath
seno *m* breast
sentar to sit
sentarse to sit down
sentido *m* sense
sentimiento *m* feeling
sentir to feel
seña *f* sign; **las señas** address
señal *f* sign; signal; **la señal de comunicando** busy/engaged signal; **la**

señal de socorro Mayday; **la señal de tráfico** road sign
señalar to point out
señor *m* gentleman; **Señor (Sr.)** Mr; sir
señora *f* lady; **Señora (Sra.)** Mrs; Ms; Madam
señorita *f* Miss; **Señorita (Srta.) Smith** Miss Smith
septentrional northern
se(p)tiembre *m* September
séptimo(a) seventh
sequía *f* drought
ser to be
sereno(a) calm; clear
serie *f* series
serio(a) serious
serpiente *f* snake
servicio *m* service; service charge; **servicio incluido** service included; **el área de servicios** service area; **el servicio de autobuses** bus service; **el servicio automático** direct-dialled calls; **el servicio de entrega** delivery service; **servicio discrecional** request stop; **el servicio doméstico** home help; **el servicio de extranjero** foreign department; **el servicio de grúa** towing service; **el servicio de habitaciones** room service; **el servicio de lavandería** laundry service; **el servicio manual** calls through the operator; **el servicio de mesa** extra portions; **el servicio oficial** authorised dealers – repairs; **el servicio de reparto** delivery service; **los servicios de urgencia** emergency services

servicios *mpl* public conveniences
servilleta *f* serviette; napkin
servir to serve
sesada *f* brains
sesenta sixty
sesión *f* performance; **la sesión continua** continuous performances; **la sesión matinal** morning performance; **la sesión de noche** late night performance; **sesión numerada** seats bookable in advance; **la sesión de tarde** evening performance; **la sesión vermut** mid-evening performance
sesos *mpl* brains; **los sesos a la mallorquina** brains served with an onion, vinegar and egg sauce; **los sesos a la romana** brains fried in batter
seta *f* mushroom
setenta seventy
seto *m* hedge
sexo *m* sex
sexto(a) sixth
sí yes
si whether; if
sidra *f* cider
siempre always
sien *m* temple (*of head*)
siéntase: siéntese por favor please take a seat
siento: lo siento I'm very sorry
sierra *f* mountain range
siesta *f* siesta; nap
siete seven
siga follow; **siga adelante** carry on; **siga derecho** keep straight ahead; **siga las instrucciones al dorso** follow the instructions overleaf
sigla *f* symbol; acronym

siglo m century
significado m meaning
significar to mean
signo m sign
sigue: sigue Usted en zona de obras you are still in an area of roadworks
siguiente following; next
silenciador m silencer
silencio m silence; ¡silencio! be quiet!
silencioso(a) silent
silla f chair; **la silla alta para niño** highchair; **la silla plegable** folding chair; **la silla de ruedas** wheelchair; **la silla tijera** deckchair
sillita de ruedas f pushchair
sillón m chair; armchair
simpático(a) nice
simple simple
sin without; **sin embargo** however; **sin falta** without fail
sinagoga f synagogue
sino but
si no otherwise
sintético(a) synthetic
síntoma m symptom
sinvergüenza m/f rascal
siquiera even; **ni siquiera** not even
sírvase: sírvase Ud mismo please serve yourself; **sírvase frío** serve chilled; **sírvase a temperature ambiente** serve at room temperature
sirve: no sirve it's no good
sistema m system; **el sistema de refrigeración** cooling system
sitio m place; space; position
situación f situation

situado(a) located; situated
slip m pants; briefs
smoking m dinner jacket
sobrar to be left
sobre[1] on; upon
sobre[2] m envelope; **el sobre de té** teabag
sobrecarga f surcharge
sobrecargo m purser
sobredosis f overdose
sobremarcha f overdrive
sobretodo m overcoat
sobrina f niece
sobrino m nephew
sociedad f society; **Sociedad Anónima (S.A.)** Ltd., plc
socio m member; partner; **no socios** non-members
socorrista m lifeguard
socorro: ¡socorro! help!
sofocante close; stuffy
soga f rope
soja f soya
sol m sun; sunshine; **tomar el sol** to sunbathe
solamente only
solapa f flap
solar sun
soldado m soldier
soleado(a) sunny
solicitar to apply for
solicitud f application
sólo only
solo(a) alone; lonely
solomillo m sirloin; **el solomillo a la broche** spit-roasted sirloin; **el solomillo de cerdo al jerez** ham-stuffed pork fillet roasted with sherry and onion; **el solomillo de jabugo** sirloin of pork; **el solomillo mechado** beef sirloin wrapped in bacon rashers and baked in the oven
soltar to let go; to untie
soltero(a) single

solucionar to solve
sombra f shade; shadow; **la sombra de ojos** eye shadow
sombreador m eye shadow
sombrero m hat; sun hat
sombrilla f sunshade; parasol
somnífero m sleeping pill
sonar to ring
sonido m sound
sonreír to smile
sonrisa f smile; grin
soñar to dream
sopa f soup; **la sopa de ajo** garlic soup; **la sopa de cebolla** onion soup; **la sopa de cebolla gratinada** onion soup with cheese topping browned in the oven; **la sopa al cuarto de hora** fish soup with hard-boiled eggs, peas, bacon, garlic and onions; **la sopa de fideos** chicken noodle soup; **la sopa de pescado** fish soup; **la sopa de picadillo** chicken soup with chopped ham and egg and noodles; **la sopa sevillana** smooth, creamy fish and mayonnaise soup with olives; **la sopa de verduras** vegetable soup
soplar to blow
soportar to bear; to stand
sorbete m water ice; ice drink; sorbet
sordo(a) deaf
sorprendido(a) surprised
sorpresa f surprise
sorteo m raffle
sostén m bra
sótano m basement; cellar
soy I am
Sr. see **señor**

Sra. see **señora**
S.R.C. R.S.V.P.
Srta. see **señorita**
stárter *m* starting motor
su his; her; their; its; **su madre** his/her mother
suave mild; gentle; smooth
súbdito *m*: **súbdito británico** British subject
subida *f* climb
subir to rise; to increase; to climb; **subir a** to get on
submarinismo *m* scuba diving
subterráneo(a) underground
subtítulo *m* subtitle
suburbio *m* suburb
suceder to occur
suciedad *f* dirt
sucio(a) dirty
sucursal *f* branch
sudar to sweat
sudeste *m* southeast
sudoeste *m* southwest
sudor *m* sweat
suegra *f* mother-in-law
suegro *m* father-in-law
suela *f* sole
sueldo *m* salary; pay
suelo *m* soil; ground; floor
suelto(a) loose; **el suelto** loose change
sueño *m* sleep; dream; **tengo sueño** I'm sleepy
suero *m* serum
suerte *f* luck; **¡buena suerte!** good luck!; **mala suerte** bad luck
suéter *m* sweater
suficiente enough
suflé *m* soufflé
sufrir to suffer
sugerencia *f* suggestion
sujetador *m* bra
suma *f* total
sumamente extremely
sumar to add (up)

sumergible waterproof
suministrar to supply
suministro *m* supply
supercarburante *m* high-grade fuel
superficie *f* surface; top
superior superior; higher
supermercado *m* supermarket
superpetrolero *m* supertanker
suplente *m* substitute
suponer to suppose
supositorio *m* suppository
supuesto: por supuesto of course
sur *m* south
surf *m* surfing; **el surf a vela** windsurfing
surtido(a) assorted; **el surtido** variety
surtidor de gasolina *m* petrol pump
sus his; her; its; their; **sus hermanas** his sisters
suspender to put off; to call off
suspensión *f* suspension
susto *m* fright; scare
suyo(a) his; her; their; your; **el/la suyo(a)** his; hers; theirs; yours

T

tabaco *m* tobacco; **el tabaco negro** dark tobacco; **el tabaco de pipa** pipe tobacco; **el tabaco rubio** Virginia tobacco; **tabacos** tobacconist's
taberna *f* reasonably priced restaurant
tabique *m* partition
tabla *f* board; list; **la tabla de surf** surf board; **la tabla de quesos**

cheeseboard
tablao flamenco *m* Flamenco show
tablero *m* dashboard
tablilla *f* splint
tablón *m* board; **el tablón de anuncios** notice board
taburete *m* stool
tacaño(a) mean
taco *m* heel; **tacos de jamón/queso** diced ham/cheese
tacón *m* heel
tajo redondo *m* well-done roast beef
tal such; **tal libro** such a book
taladro *m* drill
talco *m* talc(um powder)
T.A.L.G.O. *m* Intercity train
talla *f* size; **tallas sueltas** odd sizes left
tallarines *mpl* noodles
taller *m* workshop; **taller de reparaciones** garage; **el taller mecánico** garage
talón *m* heel; counterfoil; stub; **el talón de equipajes** baggage check; **el talón bancario** cheque
talonario *m* cheque book
tamaño *m* size
también as well; also; too
tambor *m* drum
tampoco neither
tampones *mpl* tampons
tan so
tanque *m* tank
tanto(a) so much; such a lot of; **tantos(as)** so many
tapa *f* lid; top; **se ponen tapas** shoes heeled; **las tapas** appetizers
tapar to cover
tapicería *f* upholstery

tapón m stopper; plug; bottle top

taquilla f box office; ticket office; booking office

taquímetro m speedometer

tarde late; **la tarde** evening; afternoon; **de la tarde** p.m.

tarifa f tariff; rate; **la tarifa de cambio** exchange rate; **las tarifas postales** postal charges

tarjeta f card; **la tarjeta del banco** banker's card; **la tarjeta de crédito** credit card; **la tarjeta de cumpleaños** birthday card; **la tarjeta de embarque** boarding pass; **la tarjeta de Navidad** Christmas card; **la tarjeta postal** postcard; **la tarjeta verde** green card

tarrina f: **la tarrina de la casa** homemade pâté

tarro m jar; pot

tarta f cake; tart; **la tarta de almendras** almond tart; **la tarta helada** cake containing ice cream; **la tarta de manzana** apple pie; **la tarta de nueces** walnut tart; **la tarta de queso** cheesecake

tasa f rate; valuation

tasca f bar; economical restaurant

taxi m taxi

taxista m taxi driver

taza f cup; **la taza de picadillo** chicken soup with chopped meat and ham; **la taza de té** teacup

té m tea; **el té con limón** lemon tea

te you; yourself

teatro m theatre; **ir al teatro** to go to the theatre

techo m ceiling; roof; **el techo doble** fly sheet

tecla f key

técnico(a) technical; **el técnico** technician

teja f roof tile

tejado m roof

tejer to knit

tejidos mpl textiles

tela f material; fabric

tele f TV

telebanco m cashpoint

teleférico m cablecar

telefonear to call; to phone

Telefónica f Spanish Telephones

telefonista m/f switchboard operator; telephonist

teléfono m phone; telephone

telegrama m wire; telegram

teleobjetivo m telephoto lens

telescopio m telescope

telesilla m ski lift; chair-lift

televisión f television; **Televisión Española (TVE)** Spanish Television

televisor m television set

temperatura f temperature; **la temperatura ambiente** room temperature

tempestad f storm

tempestuoso(a) stormy

templo m temple; church

temporada f season; **la temporada de veraneo** the holiday season; **la temporada alta** high season; **fuera de temporada** off-season

temprano(a) early; **más temprano** earlier

tenaz stubborn

tendero m grocer

tendido m row of seats

tenedor m fork

tener to have; to hold; **tengo hambre** I am hungry; **tener que** to have to

tengo I have

tenis m tennis

tensión f tension; blood pressure

tenso(a) tense

tentempié m snack

teñir to dye

tercer, tercero(a) third

tercera f third gear

terciopelo m velvet

terminal f terminal; **la terminal internacional** international terminal; **la terminal nacional** domestic flights terminal

terminar to end; to finish

término m term; end; **el término municipal de Sevilla** Seville district

termómetro m thermometer

termos m vacuum flask

ternera f veal; **la ternera fiambre** veal pâté; **la ternera al jugo** veal casserole in white wine; **la ternera a la provenzal** casseroled veal, cooked with onions, garlic and herbs; **la ternera simple** veal steak

terraza f terrace

terremoto m earthquake

terreno m land

terrón m lump of sugar

tesoro m treasure

testigo m witness

testimonio m evidence

tetera f teapot

texto m: **el texto del telegrama** message here

tez f complexion

ti you

tía f aunt(ie)

tibio(a) warm

tiempo m time; weather; **a tiempo** on time

tienda f store; shop; **la tienda de campaña** tent; **la tienda de deportes** sports shop; **la tienda libre de impuestos** duty-free shop; **la tienda de repuestos** car parts shop

tiene he/she has; you have

tienes you have

tierno(a) tender

tierra f earth; land

tiesto m pot

tijeras fpl scissors; pair of scissors

tila f lime-flower tea

timbre m doorbell; official stamp; **el timbre de alarma** communication cord

tímido(a) shy

timón m rudder

tímpano m eardrum

tinta f ink

tinte m dye

tinto(a) red

tintorería f dry-cleaner's

tío m uncle; bloke

tiovivo m merry-go-round

típico(a) typical

tiple f soprano

tipo m sort; type; fellow; **el tipo de cambio** rate of exchange

tíquet m ticket

tirador m handle

tirantes mpl braces

tirar to throw; to throw away; to pull; **para tirar** disposable; **tire** pull

tiritas fpl elastoplast

tiro m shot; shooting; throw

títere m puppet

titular m headline

título m university degree; title

toalla f towel

toallitas fpl: **las toallitas limpiadoras para bebés** baby wipes

tobillo m ankle

tobogán m slide

tocadiscos m record-player

tocador m dressing table; powder room

tocar to touch; to ring the (door-)bell; to handle; to play; **tocar el claxon** to sound one's horn

tocinito m: **los tocinitos con nata** caramel cream with whipped cream

tocino m bacon; **el tocino de cielo** rich caramel cream

todavía yet; still

todo(a) all; **todo** everything; **todo el mundo** everybody; everyone; **todo incluido** all inclusive

toldo m awning

toma f tap; socket; lead

tomar to take; **¿quiere tomar algo?** would you like a drink?; **tomar el sol** to sunbathe; **tomar una copa** to have a drink

tomate m tomato

tomillo m thyme

tomo m volume

tonel m barrel

tonelada f ton

tónica f tonic water

tono m tone; **el tono de marcar** dial(ling) tone

tonterías fpl nonsense

tonto(a) stupid

toquen: no toquen please do not touch

torcedura f sprain

torcer to twist; to bend; **torcer a la izquierda** to turn left

torcerse to strain; **torcerse el tobillo** to sprain one's ankle

torero m bullfighter

tormenta f thunderstorm; **la tormenta de nieve** blizzard

tornasol m sunflower

tornillo m screw

torno m dentist's drill

tornos mpl turnstiles

toro m bull

torpe clumsy; dumb

torre f tower; **la torre de control** control tower

torrijas fpl slices of bread dipped in milk and beaten egg and fried

torta f cake

tortilla f omelette; **la tortilla española** Spanish omelette made with potato, onion, garlic, tomato, peppers and seasoning; **la tortilla francesa** plain omelette; **la tortilla de legumbres** vegetable omelette; **la tortilla a la paisana** sausage and vegetable omelette; **la tortilla de patatas** potato and onion omelette; **la tortilla al rón** sweet rum omelette; **la tortilla Sacromonte** omelette of brains fried in breadcrumbs, with potatoes, peas and peppers; **la tortilla soufflé** sweet omelette soufflé

tos f cough; **la tos ferina** whooping cough

toser to cough

tostada f toast
tostador m toaster
total total; **en total** in all
tournedós m thick slice of beef fillet; **tournedós Rossini** beef fillet with foie gras and truffles, in a sherry sauce
trabajar to work
trabajo m work; job
tracción f: **la tracción delantera** front-wheel drive; **la tracción trasera** rear-wheel drive
traducción f translation; **se hacen traducciones** translations done
traducir to translate
traer to fetch; to bring
tráfico m traffic
tragaperras m slot machine
tragar to swallow
trago m a drink
traje m suit; outfit; **el traje de baño** bathing suit; **el traje de esquí** ski outfit; **el traje de etiqueta** evening dress (*man's*); **el traje de noche** evening dress (*woman's*); **se hacen trajes a medida** suits made to measure
trámite m procedure; formality
trampolín m diving board
tranquilizante m tranquillizer
tranquilo(a) quiet; calm; peaceful
transatlántico m liner
transbordador m car-ferry
transbordo m transfer; **hay que hacer transbordo en Madrid** you have to change trains in Madrid
transeunte m/f passer-by

transferencia f transfer(ral); **hacer una transferencia** to transfer some money
transferir to transfer
tránsito m traffic; **en tránsito** in transit
transmisión f transmission; **la transmisión automática** automatic transmission
transmisor m transmitter
transpirar to perspire
transportar to carry; to transport
transporte m transport; **transporte escolar** school bus; **transportes** transport company; removers
tranvía m tram(car); short-distance train
trapo m rag
tras after; behind
trasero(a) rear
trasladar to transfer; to move
tratamiento m treatment; course of treatment
tratar to treat; **tratar/ trátese con cuidado** handle with care
través: a través de through; across
travesero m bolster
travesía f crossing; **Travesía Libertad** Avenue "Libertad"
trece thirteen
treinta thirty
tren m train; **el tren directo** through train; **el tren de largo recorrido** intercity train; **el tren de mercancías** freight train; **el tren ómnibus** stopping train
tres three
triángulo m triangle; **el triángulo de avería** warning triangle
tribuna f stand
tribunal m law court
trigo m wheat
trimestre m term
trineo m sleigh; sledge
trípode m tripod
tripulación f crew
triste sad
trompeta f trumpet
tronco m trunk
tropezar to slip; to trip
trópicos mpl tropics
trozo m bit; piece
trucha f trout; **la trucha a la navarra** trout baked with ham; **las truchas a la molinera** trout cooked in butter and served with lemon
trucos mpl pool
trueno m thunder
trufa f truffle
tu your
tú you; **tú mismo(a)** you yourself
tubería f pipes; piping
tubo m pipe; tube; **el tubo de desagüe** drainpipe; **el tubo de escape** exhaust pipe; **el tubo de respiración** snorkel
tuerca f nut
tulipán m tulip
tumba f tomb
tumbona f deckchair
tumor m growth
túnel m tunnel; **túneles en 2 km** tunnels two kilometres ahead
turismo m tourism; sightseeing
turista m/f tourist; **la clase turista** tourist class
turístico(a) tourist
turno m turn; **por torno** in turn
turquesa turquoise
turrón m nougat
tus your (*plural*)

tuve I had
tuviste you had
tuvo he/she/it had
tuyo(a) yours; **el/la tuyo(a)** yours
TVE see **televisión**

U

Ud(s) see **Usted**
úlcera f ulcer
últimamente lately
último(a) last
ultramar: de ultramar overseas
ultramarinos m grocery shop
un(a) a; an
undécimo(a) eleventh
ungüento m ointment
único(a) unique; single
unidad f unit; **Unidad de Vigilancia Intensiva (U.V.I.)** intensive care unit
unir to join; to unite
universidad f university
universo m universe
uno(a) one: oneself
unos(as) some
untar to spread
uña f nail (human)
urbanización f housing estate
urbano(a) city
urge it is urgent; **urge vender** for quick sale
urgencias fpl casualty department; **urgencias infantil** children's casualty ward
urgente urgent; express
urinarios mpl toilets
usar to use
uso m use; custom; **uso externo/tópico** for external use only
Usted you; **Usted mismo(a)** you yourself;

Ustedes you (plural form); **Ustedes mismos** you yourselves
útil useful
utilizar to use; **utilice monedas de ... pesetas** use ... peseta coins
uva f grape; **la uva moscatel** muscatel grape; **la uva pasa** raisin
U.V.I. see **unidad**

V

va he/she/it goes; you go
vaca f cow
vacaciones fpl holiday; **de vacaciones** on holiday
vaciado m plaster (for limb)
vaciar to empty
vacilar to hesitate
vacío(a) empty
vacuna f vaccine
vacunación f vaccination
vado m: **vado permanente** no parking at any time
vagón m railway carriage; **el vagón de fumadores** smoker
vagón-restaurante m restaurant car
vainilla f vanilla
vajilla f crockery
Valdepeñas m light red or white wine
vale m token; voucher
valer to be worth; **vale** O.K.; **vale la pena** it's worth it
válido(a) valid; **válido hasta ...** valid until ...
valiente brave
valija f suitcase
valla f fence
valle m valley
valor m value

válvulva f valve
vapor m steam; steamer (ship); **al vapor** steamed
vaporizador m spray
vaquero m cowboy
vaqueros mpl jeans
variante f bypass
varicela f chickenpox
variedad f variety
varilla graduada f dipstick
varios(as) several
vas you go
vasco(a) Basque
vaselina f vaseline; petroleum jelly
vaso m glass
vatio m watt
veces fpl times; **¿cuántas veces?** how many times?
vecindad f neighbourhood
vecino(a) m/f neighbour
vegetariano(a) vegetarian
vehículo m vehicle; **el vehículo en carga** loading vehicle; **el vehículo largo** long vehicle; **vehículos pesados** heavy lorries crossing
veinte twenty
veintiuno twenty-one
vejiga f bladder
vela f candle; sail; sailing; **hacer vela** to go yachting; to sail
velero m sail(ing) boat
velocidad f speed; **segunda/tercera velocidad** 2nd/3rd gear; **cuarta/primera velocidad** top/bottom gear; **a gran velocidad** at high speed; **velocidad controlada por radar** speed checks in operation; **velocidad limitada** speed limit
velocímetro m

speedometer
velódromo *m* cycle track
veloz fast
vena *f* vein
vencer to defeat
vencimiento *m* expiry date
venda *f* bandage
vendaval *m* gale
vendedor *m* vendor; **el vendedor de periódicos** newsagent
vender to sell; **se vende/véndese** for sale
vendimia *f* grape harvest
veneno *m* poison
venenoso(a) poisonous
venir to come
venta *f* sale; country inn; **en venta** for sale; **venta anticipada de localidades** tickets on sale in advance; **la venta de billetes** ticket office; **venta de localidades con 5 días de antelación** tickets on sale five days before performance; **venta al por mayor** wholesaler's; **venta al por menor/al detalle** retailer's; **venta de parcelas** plots for sale; **venta de pisos** flats for sale; **venta de sellos** stamps sold here
ventaja *m* advantage
ventana *f* window
ventanilla *f* window (*in car, train*); serving hatch
ventilador *m* fan; ventilator
ventoso(a) windy
ver to see; to watch
veraneante *m/f* holidaymaker
verano *m* summer
verbena *f* street party
verdad *f* truth; **de verdad** true; **¿verdad?** don't you? etc; didn't he?

etc; do you? etc; did he? etc
verdadero(a) true; genuine
verde green; unripe
verdulero(a) *m/f* greengrocer
verduras *fpl* vegetables; **las verduras estofadas** vegetable stew with broad beans, onions, green beans, peas, lettuce and garlic
vergüenza *f* shame
verificar to check
verja *f* railings
vermut *m* vermouth
verruga *f* wart
versión *f*: **la versión integra** uncut version; **la versión original con subtítulos** original version with subtitles
verter to pour; **prohibido verter basuras/escombros** no dumping
vesícula *f* blister
vestíbulo *m* hall; lobby
vestido *m* dress
vestirse to dress oneself
veterinario *m* vet(erinary surgeon)
vez *f* time; **una vez más** once more; **en vez de** instead of
vía *f* track; rails; platform; **la vía de acceso** slip-road; **por vía oral/bucal** orally
viajar to travel; **viajar en avión** to fly; **viajar en primera clase** to travel first class
viaje *m* journey; trip; **el viaje de ida y vuelta** round trip; **el viaje de negocios** business trip; **el viaje organizado** package holiday
viajero *m* traveller

víbora *f* viper; adder
vichyssoise *f* cold soup made from leeks, potatoes, onions and cream
víctima *f* victim
vida *f* life
vidrio *m* glass
vieira *f* scallop
viejo(a) old
viento *m* wind; **hace mucho viento** it's very windy; **sin viento** calm; **viento lateral** crosswinds
vientre *m* belly
viernes *m* Friday; **viernes santo** Good Friday
viga *f* beam (*of wood*)
vigilante *m* lifeguard
vigilar to guard
vinagre *m* vinegar
vinagreta *f* salad dressing; vinaigrette sauce
vino *m* wine; **el vino blanco** white wine; **el vino de la casa** house wine; **el vino clarete** light red wine; **el vino común** ordinary wine; **el vino dulce** sweet wine; **el vino espumoso** sparkling wine; **el vino de mesa** table wine; **el vino del país** local wine; **el vino rosado** rosé wine; **el vino seco** dry wine; **el vino tinto** red wine
viña *f* vineyard
violento(a) rough
violín *m* violin
violoncelo *m* cello
viraje *m* turn; swerve; **el viraje en U** U-turn
virar to tack (*sailing*)
viruela *f* smallpox
visado *m* visa
visibilidad *f* visibility
visita *f* visit; visitor; **la**

visita con guía guided tour
visitar to visit; **visite piso piloto** visit our show flat
visor *m* viewfinder
víspera *f* eve
vista *f* view; eyesight
vitrina *f* shop window
viuda *f* widow
viudo *m* widower
víveres *mpl* groceries
vivienda *f* housing
vivir to live
vivo(a) live; alive, bright
vodka *f* vodka
volante *m* steering wheel
volar to fly
volcán *m* volcano
volován *m* vol-au-vent
voltaje *m* voltage
voltio *m* volt
volumen *m* volume (*sound, capacity*)
voluntad *f* will; intention
volver to come back; to go back; to return; **volver en sí** to revive; **volver algo** to turn something round
vomitar to be sick
vomitorio *m* exit (*stadium*)
vosotros(as) you (*plural*)
voy I go
voz *f* voice; **en voz alta** aloud
vuelco *m* spill; **dar un vuelco** to overturn
vuelo *m* flight; **el vuelo**

charter charter flight; **el vuelo nocturno** night flight; **el vuelo regular** scheduled flight
vuelta *f* turn; return; change; **dar vueltas** to twist (*road*); **dar una vuelta** to take a walk
vuestro(a) your; **el/la vuestro(a)** yours

WYZ

wáter *m* lavatory; toilet
whisky *m* whisky
y and
ya already
yate *m* yacht; **el yate de motor** cabin cruiser
yema *f* egg yolk; egg dessert with brandy; **las yemas de coco** coconut sweets eaten as a dessert
yerno *m* son-in-law
yeso *m* plaster (*for wall*)
yo I
yodo *m* iodine
yogur *m* yoghurt; **el yogur natural** plain yoghurt
yugular jugular
zambullirse to dive
zanahoria *f* carrot
zancudo *m* mosquito
zapata *f* brake shoe
zapatería *f* shoeshop
zapatero *m* shoemaker; cobbler; shoe repairs

zapatilla *f* slipper; **la zapatilla de tenis** tennis shoe; **zapatillas de deporte** trainers
zapato *m* shoe; **los zapatos de medio tacón** low-heeled shoes; **los zapatos de tacón** high-heeled shoes
zarzamora *f* blackberry
zarzuela¹ *f* Spanish light opera
zarzuela² *f*: **la zarzuela de mariscos** seafood casserole; **la zarzuela de pescado** fish in a spicy sauce; **la zarzuela de pescado a la levantina** casserole of assorted fish and seafood with paprika and saffron
zona *f* zone; **la zona azul/de estacionamiento limitado y vigilado** controlled parking area; **la zona recreativa** recreation area; **la zona reservada para peatones** pedestrian precinct; **la zona restringada** restricted area; **las zonas de tarificación** charge bands
zorro *m* fox
zumo *m* juice; **el zumo de limón** lemon juice; **el zumo de naranja** orange juice
zurcir to darn
zurdo(a) left-handed

COLLINS

for your PC

Collins Electronic Dictionaries
are now available for use with
your personal computer.

For details write to:
Collins Dictionaries: Dept. RDH
PO Box, Glasgow G4 0NB